WORK, OIL AND WELFARE

Knut Halvorsen   Steinar Stjernø

WORK, OIL AND WELFARE

The welfare state in Norway

UNIVERSITETSFORLAGET

© Universitetsforlaget 2008

ISBN 978-82-15-01243-8

All rights reserved. No part of this publication may be reproduced, stored in a retrieval system, or transmitted in any form or by any means, electronic, mechanical or photocopying, recording, or otherwise, without the prior permission of Universitetsforlaget. Enquiries should be sent to the Rights Department, Universitetsforlaget, Oslo, at the address below.

www.universitetsforlaget.no

Universitetsforlaget AS
P.O. Box 508 Sentrum
NO-0105 Oslo
Norway

Coverdesign: NORMANN/SANDVIK DESIGN
Design: Rusaanes Bokproduksjon AS
Typeset: Adobe Garamond 11/13
Printed: AIT Trykk Otta AS

Geographisches Institut
der Universität Kiel
ausgesonderte Dublette

Inv.-Nr. 09/A4 1204

Preface

Thanks to the oil in the North Sea, Norway is one of the richest countries in the world. At the same time, Norway – in common with the other Nordic countries – is characterized by a strong work ethic.

Work, Welfare and Oil. The Welfare State in Norway discusses how Norway tackles this combination. It describes the development of the Norwegian welfare state and constituent policies on employment and family, pensions and benefits, health and social services and the voluntary sector. A final chapter discusses the likely implications of globalization, immigration, demographical change and shifts in ideological climate for the welfare state. Aimed at primarily students and scholars, but not forgetting the wider interested public, the book offers a short, evidence-based introduction to the Norwegian welfare state and social policy. Comparisons with other western, industrialized countries, set the different areas of Norwegian social policy in relief.

We would like to take this opportunity to express our gratitude to Ann-Helen Bay, Berit Bringedal, Ådne Cappelen, Anne Lise Ellingsæter, Aksel Hatland, Håkon Lorentzen, Ivar Lødemel, Rolf Rønning and Einar Øverbye for useful comments and suggestions for improving the manuscript. We are particularly indebted to Nanna Kildal, who read the whole manuscript; her comments inspired us to reflect more profoundly on the particularities of the Norwegian welfare state.

April 22 2008

Knut Halvorsen *Steinar Stjernø*

Contents

Preface 5

Chapter 1   From poverty to a welfare state 9

Chapter 2   Economy, oil and well-being 25

Chapter 3   Work, work, work! 41

Chapter 4   Families: At work? 58

Chapter 5   Security in old age: Protecting the frail and elderly 74

Chapter 6   Health for all! The Health care system: medical treatment and sickness benefits 88

Chapter 7   The ineradicable poverty 105

Chapter 8   Civil society: Trust and participation 120

Chapter 9   The municipal social service state 132

Chapter 10   Prospects and challenges 144

List of boxes, figures and tables 163

References 165

Index 177

Chapter 1
From poverty to a welfare state

Norway, along with its Nordic neighbours enjoys in a rare combination an extensive welfare state, a relatively egalitarian income distribution, and a competitive economy with strong growth – on a par with the US. Here, however, growth is coupled with inequality, poverty and a weakly developed welfare system. Norway is constantly welcoming visitors from China, South Africa and many other countries who want to study the structure and functioning of the welfare state.

In literature and research the welfare state in Norway is categorized as a social democratic welfare regime and member of the family of the Scandinavian welfare state (Esping-Andersen 1990), which are known to be among the most developed welfare states in the world. Conceptually, *welfare regime* refers to a country's idiosyncratic policy mix of labour market, family, public pensions and cash transfer system. The social democratic welfare regime is characterized by:

- A historic obligation on the part of the state to full employment to be achieved through active labour market policies.
- A universal system of relatively generous social benefits related to unemployment, sickness, disability, old age, etc.
- An extensive family policy which favours gender equality.
- A basic minimum pension for all citizens and income-related supplementary pensions based on years of employment and income.
- Extensive public health and social services, whereas the voluntary sector only to a small extent deliver health and social services.
- Welfare funded in principle by tax revenue.

This welfare state differs from the two other main families of welfare state regimes which exist in Europe – the conservative welfare regimes which are found in Germany and other countries on the continent, and the liberal welfare regime which is found in the UK and Ireland. This book describes the specific characteristics of the Norwegian welfare state – compared both to other welfare regimes and to the other Nordic countries. This introductory chapter delineates how the welfare state developed. What were the historical contexts for the most important welfare reforms? Who were the main actors? Succeeding chapters delve into the different parts of the welfare regime and the aspects that were mentioned above.

The first social policy reforms

All welfare states represent different 'delivery systems', that is, the balance provisions and mode of delivery vary. Welfare is provided by individuals and families, labour market, public services, and voluntary sector. The industrialization of Europe, particularly in the latter part of the nineteenth century, required a different welfare balance, however.

In many European countries, governments viewed with growing concern the social consequences of industrialization. Whereas people in agrarian societies subsisted in non-monetary or barter economies, industrialization forced people to sell their manpower and work in dangerous and stressing conditions. As the labour *market* became increasingly important for maintaining a family, the need for protective measures against the hazards of life, accidents at work, sickness and provision in old age and unemployment, was recognized with increasing urgency. Doing something about the miserable working and living conditions of the workers became the leading social issue of the day, known in Norway as 'the worker question'.

Germany was considered the birthplace of the welfare state in Europe. The authoritarian chancellor Bismarck was worried by the radicalization of the industrial working class. Realizing that repression could only be part of the answer, he hoped that a public social insurance system would curb socialist agitation and create a sense of loyalty between the state and workers. During the 1890s he introduced health insurance, accident insurance, disability pension and old age pension. The German pension system was built on an 'insurance principle': social security arrangements were a kind of insurance against the hazards of life. Workers and employers paid a proportion of the wage into a fund to finance the pensions. However, the German system was restricted to the industrial working class: other groups such as peasants were left out, although white collar groups set up their own social insurance system after a time. The result was a fragmented and socially differentiated social security system (Stjernø, 1995; Kuhnle 2001).

The German reforms were witnessed with interest also in Norway (Kuhnle 1978). However, contrary to Germany at that time, Norway had had a democratic constitution since 1814, and a parliamentary system of government, whereby governments need the assent of Parliament to rule, since 1884. There was no aristocracy, and Norway's small upper class was not very rich compared to the upper classes of other countries, and lacked the capacity for making large investments. The class structure was more egalitarian than Germany's or the UK's – or Sweden's and Denmark's as well. The 1537 Lutheran Reformation of Norway subjected the Church to the state. And as the Church lost most of its land and wealth to the state in the process, it was unable to establish a prominent role in charitable work. Thus, charities and voluntary organizations could not be an alternative to public responsibility for social welfare. On the other hand, Lutheranism is supposed to have strengthened two key aspects of modern welfare ideology in Norway – the work ethic and equality. While work as the fulfilment of God's will is consonant with an ideological emphasis on full employment, the idea of a priesthood of all believers contributed to an egalitarian ideology (Christiansen and Markkola, 2006).

From the mid-nineteenth century, a range of voluntary organizations was established. These often grew out of broad-based social movements in civil society (see chapter 8) each with the purpose of addressing a particular welfare issue. They included, for instance, the Red Cross, followed by the Norwegian Women's Health Organization (1906), National Council for Norwegian Women (1904), National Association for Public Health (1910). As there was no wealthy bourgeoisie to fund this voluntary sector, it did not conceive of itself as an alternative to public involvement in health and social welfare. On the contrary, it advocated more government involvement, and in the twentieth century became a more or less integrated aspect of public welfare policy. Thus, because of the absence of a rich and beneficent bourgeoisie, the subordination of the Church and the voluntary sector's viability as an alternative to state welfare, the state became more or less by default the main engine of modernization, developing an infrastructure for welfare provision.

Peasants who owned their own land constituted the majority of the population and were increasingly a class to be reckoned with, particularly after the introduction of municipal democracy in 1837. A liberal party (Venstre) and a conservative party (Høyre) had been founded in 1884, followed three years later by the Labour Party (Arbeiderpartiet). While the first two were successful in general elections, Labour remained without a member of Parliament – the Storting – until 1903. The early success of peasants as a political force both in local and national chambers of government made them more positive to the state than the peasant classes in many other European countries (Kangas og Palme, 2005). Besides, the relatively strong position of democratic government in Norway was important to the development of a more universal and integrated social security system than was the case in, for instance, Germany.

The 1860 education reform, which introduced a single curriculum in the nation's schools, was a milestone in the democratic modernisation of Norwegian society. From that year, a series of reforms established an integrated educational system for children from all classes and segments of the population. In 1889, the Liberal Party, in power since 1884, introduced the *elementary school bill*. The elementary school was called the *people's school,* a name aimed at highlighting its democratic, integrative and formative purpose – it should 'unite social classes' while promoting a 'sense of equality and community'

(Slagstad, 1998). A similar way of thinking underlay social democratic educational reforms in the twentieth century as well. The educational reforms were both an expression of and helped strengthen the relatively – in a European perspective – egalitarian class structure. Egalitarianism, the weak bourgeoisie, and the predominant role of the state were key characteristics of nineteenth century Norway, and the same characteristics should come to be influential in the development of a welfare state.

The poor law of 1845, the first of its kind, placed responsibility for the poor with local councils; aid was to be financed through local taxation. It was revised in 1863 with the intention to distinguish more clearly between 'unworthy' and 'worthy' needy. The able-bodied should provide for themselves, whereas aid for the physically and mentally ill and for orphans was unconditional. However, it soon became evident that the poor relief system was not an adequate response to the social problems. In 1870, around 20 per cent of the population of the largest cities was being helped by the poor law authorities (Seip, 1983). A new debate brought new ways of thinking and new concepts into focus. The authorities had wide margins of *discretion* and could invoke *means-testing* as key characteristics of poor relief; in practice, only those without means or property were therefore entitled to assistance. Now the idea of *social insurance* was launched. The idea was that wage earners and/or employers should pay in a certain amount to a central scheme to guard against loss of livelihood. It didn't take long before taxation was mooted as an alternative way of financing welfare payments.

The Liberal Party was increasingly perturbed by the working and living conditions of many workers and the growing political agitation of labour activists. It was clear to the government that neither families nor the Church or voluntary organizations could adequately address the social problems that accompanied industrialization. In 1885, the government therefore appointed a 'worker commission' to report on compensation for workplace accidents, sickness benefits and old age pension. In 1894, Parliament passed an industrial accidents act and in 1909 a sickness insurance act (Seip, 1981). Old age pensions became the subject of prolonged political debate and were not introduced until 1936. From 1910 to 1920 a series of reforms aimed at improving working conditions in manufacturing and protect workers and others at the workplace was implemented. The Liberal Party – often supported by the Conservatives – argued for the German insurance model of funding social welfare payments (see above) (Seip, 1981), whereas the Labour Party argued that social benefits should be financed through taxes.

The controversy gained momentum from different conceptions about the responsibility of the individual versus the state. The insurance principle was said to encourage workers to see a clearer relationship between their contributions and ensuing social benefits, whereas tax financing made this relationship unclear (Hatland, 1992). Besides, tax financiation would have a more redistributive effect, as the rich would have to contribute more.

These early social reforms, which took place before the Labour Party came into power, were often introduced with cross-party consensus. Controversies were normally not concerned with the social reforms in themselves, but the mode of financing and managing them. One instance where consensus was lacking concerned a bill on the rights of illegitimate children. It was eventually passed into law in 1915, entitling these children to bear the name of and inherit their father. Unmarried mothers were entitled to economic support. The Church and the Conservative Party feared it would harm the family, but the majority of the Storting regarded the reform as a question of the equal treatment of all the children and argued that men should be made responsible for their behaviour. At the time, these reforms were radical in an international perspective.

The first decades of the twentieth century were marked by a rapid transformation of Norwegian society. Unlike Sweden, for instance, Norway had no strong industrial and financial upper class, and foreign investors consequently played a more significant role in the development of large scale industry (Stråth, 2001). Hydroelectric plants were built to capture waterfall energy, producing cheap electricity for metallurgical and chemical industries. The government intervened several times against tendencies towards monopolization and to protect national interests against foreigners. Of particular importance were the 'concession laws' which made it difficult for foreigners to buy waterfalls, mines and other natural resources. Natural resources should be under national control.

Rapid industrialization created a larger and more militant working class. Organised workers called for better living conditions and for social reforms to be enacted. The Labour Party's increased electoral support grew apace in the first decades of the twentieth century. The trade union movement (LO) worked successfully with the Labour Party to organize and mobilize the working class, and a number of strikes to improve wages and working conditions followed. A communist party was founded in 1923 but it never represented a substantial threat to the Labour Party in the competition for the working class vote.

In the 1920s unemployment rose to a high level – from 2.3 per cent in 1920 to 25 per cent of all unionized workers in 1925. In the construction industry, 35 per cent were out of work by 1927. Successive non-socialist governments were unable to create new jobs or reduce unemployment. The Labour Party had become influential and acquired political positions in many municipalities. It used this power to enact welfare reforms at the local level – municipal old age pension, single parent benefits, dental care for school children, nursing homes for elderly, etc. To some, the reforms could stand as models for national legislation, particularly the tax financed old age pension introduced by the Labour Party in the capital of Oslo (Hatland, 1992).

Under and after the Great Depression, which hit Norway in 1928, the Labour Party replaced revolutionary rhetoric with pragmatism, reformism and a stronger emphasis on concrete measures against unemployment. The fascist road to power in Germany and the need for concrete measures to increase employment led to a compromise with the Farmers' party in 1935 and the establishment of a Labour government.

The same year, the Trades Union Congress (LO) and employers' organization signed an industrial relations agreement. It laid down procedures for collective bargaining, industrial disputes, strikes and lockouts. It was a historical compromise and watershed in the development of labour market policy. The Trades Union Congress accepted in reality the ownership rights of employers, and the employers recognized the rights of trade unions to have a say, negotiate wage settlements and make their opinions known on a range of other issues in the workplace. This marked the beginning of a long truce in industrial relations. As mentioned already, the same year also marked the beginning of a long period of social democratic government and social democratic dominance in Norwegian politics – interrupted only by the German occupation 1940–45.

The old age pension of 1936

When the Labour Party came into power in 1935, the world's economy was recovering. The Labour Party had won the election by promising 'jobs for the whole nation' and was soon initiating social reforms. Public spending grew. Public works were started to create jobs. In 1938, unemployment benefits for industrial workers were introduced.

The road to an old age pension came to be long and complicated. The Labour Party had been arguing for a tax-funded old age pension since 1888, in contrast to the Liberal Party's preference for a social insurance plan (Seip 1981). During World War I, several local councils had adopted old age pension schemes which were funded from the rates. In 1923, a majority of Labour and Conservative Storting members approved a law that introduced a means-tested old age pension plan to be paid for by taxes. The Liberal Party and Farmers' Party had voted for a social insurance scheme. However, the new old age pension plan never actually materialized because of the 1924 recession and increasing unemployment (Hatland, 1992).

In 1936 the Labour Government set out a pension bill for what were called at the time 'the blind, the deaf and the disabled'. It also launched a revised old age pension bill. The government thought that a universal scheme would be too costly, and proposed instead a means-tested system. The insurance principle would encourage the individual worker to see a clearer relationship between his own contributions and the social benefits paid by the state, whereas a system funded by taxes would make this relationship unclear. On the other hand, the insurance principle would exclude people out of work or unable to find employment, and many years of contributions would be needed to develop a well-functioning system. Then again, a scheme paid for by taxes would be easier to get up and running. And, as mentioned, tax financing would have a more redistributive effect, .

The government agreed to a compromise with the Liberal Party about financing, with some money coming from taxes and the rest from employee contributions (Seip, 1981). It meant in reality that the insurance principle had been abandoned and that the old age pension would now be considered a public responsibility. However, most parties were unhappy with the 1936 design. Benefits were low, means-testing excluded many citizens and the financing meant that those who contributed most received little in return (Seip, 1981; Hatland, 1992). But it was founded on an idea of solidarity and pointed towards the social security system with broad coverage that evolved after World War II.

After World War II: A welfare state for all

When Germany attacked Norway in 1940, the king and government fled to London where they remained – as an exile government – until the war ended in 1945. The Germans installed Vidkun Quisling, the leader of a small fascist party, at the helm of a puppet government. The German occupation was not as brutal as in many countries, as the Germans considered Norwegians Arians and Norwegian resistance was mainly civil resistance, the spreading of illegal newspapers, and sabotage. However, many Norwegians – particularly the Jews, political leaders and members of the illegal resistance movement – were sent to concentration camps in Germany, and others were held in prison camps in Norway. Many fled to Sweden and the UK to escape German persecution. During the war, the widespread feeling of community between people of different political persuasions facilitated cross-party collaboration and understanding, fuelling consensus on social policy reforms as well.

In 1942, William Beveridge presented a plan for the construction of a welfare state in the UK. Among his recommendations were child benefits for every family with children and a public health system for all citizens. The Quisling government had introduced universal child benefits during the war. When Norwegian politicians returned from the UK, they were familiar with the ideas of Beveridge. In 1945 the political parties rallied behind a 'Joint Programme' (Fellesprogrammet), where they promised to abolish the poor relief system and integrate and coordinate social benefits with a wide-ranging social security system with coverage for sickness, disability and old age. There was now a general consensus among the political parties on the way forward for social policy. What they did not agree upon was the speed of the reforms and whether social benefits should be means-tested or universal – that is, an entitlement enjoyed by all citizens irrespective of income.

The Labour Party won the 1945 election and retained its majority until

1961. In 1949, it presented a more detailed reform programme – 'The Future of Norway'. Several reform programmes were announced in rapid succession. Unemployment benefits had been introduced in 1938; now followed child benefits (1946), sickness benefits (1956), old age pension (1957) and disability pension (1960), covering all major eventualities. The new benefits were for all social and income classes, and means testing was out. In this respect, they were 'universal'. However, eligibility to most of them depended on the recipient having a history of gainful employment. Only child benefits and the basic old age pension were truly universal. The parties in the political centre (the Farmers' Party and the Liberal Party) and to the right (The Conservative Party) were often more in favour of universality than the Labour Party. The Labour Party was first and foremost concerned with the interests of the wage-earner and the cost of social reforms. But in the view of the Farmers' Party, Liberal Party and Conservatives, since groups other than wage earners contributed to these tax-financed benefits, everybody should be entitled to them (Baldwin, 1990). Thus, universalism was not primarily borne of a social democratic ideology, but of a compromise on risk-sharing between the political representatives of different social classes (Baldwin, 1990; Hatland, 1992).

The social democratic order: 'Full employment' and regional policy

In the 1930s, the Labour Party had adopted the electoral slogan *Jobs for the whole nation!*

The period from the early 1950s to the late 1970s has been called 'the social democratic order' (Furre, 1991). It came also to be known as the era of 'full employment'. Industries were established, and the state stimulated industrial growth with cheap hydropower, allocating seed money for heavy industry and providing the requisite infrastructure. Employment in manufacturing increased, and workers who were willing to move from the country to the cities could easily find work. However, it was full employment for the male half of the population; most women were still housewives.

During this period, particularly in the 1960s, industry and commerce were restructured and rationalized. Mergers and bankruptcies depleted the countryside of manufacturing and commercial firms, concentrating them in towns and cities, leaving many rural districts, especially in the north of the country, to face depopulation. However, this process was not as radical as in Sweden or Finland. There had been strong opposition to the brutal politics of centralization since the late '40s (Knudsen, 2002). This opposition was strong in all political parties. The Labour Party had many voters in rural districts and in northern Norway, and depended on them too for its majority in the Storting – contrary to what was the case in Sweden where there was more large scale industry and where social democratic voters were more concentrated in the cities. The electoral system favoured voters in thinly populated counties, particularly in the north. Consequently, sustaining the geographical population distribution was more important in Norway than Sweden. Labour market policy, social policy, regional and agricultural policy were integrated to this end. Whereas in Sweden, labour market policy encouraged workers to move from rural districts and the north to cities in the south, Norwegian labour market policy entailed a mixture of regional policy, credit policy, traditional Keynesian stabilization policy, public construction work, building roads, etc.

The result was that Norway was not urbanized to the same extent as the other Nordic countries. The strong expansion of health and social services in the late 1960s and 1970s was channelled through the municipalities and contributed further to slow urbanization and migration from the north to the south. Today, regional policy is still a cornerstone of Norwegian politics: The government takes money from high income municipalities and passes it on to low income municipalities; tax relief is used to incentivize people to stay in the north; higher education and hospitals were decentralized to stem migration from the periphery. This regional policy did not stop centralization, but it did make urbanization a less dramatic process than in neighbouring countries. But it has been costly, at the expense of investments in roads and railways in urban areas.

The long period of social democratic government, rising standards of living and expansion of social security improved relations between central government and workers, as had happened earlier among peasants (about trust, see chapter 8). As in other Nordic welfare states, this trust distinguishes citizens from citizens in most other European countries.

From World War II to the 1960s, the political system in Norway was characterised by a quasi bipartite constellation. There was a large social democratic party (the Labour Party) with around 50 per cent of the vote, and there were the four 'non-socialist' parties the Conservatives, Liberals, Centre Party, and Christian People's Party. Before the 1961 election, a left wing socialist party (SV) was established. It won two parliamentary seats and held the balance between the two blocs. The Labour Party had lost its absolute majority, foreshadowing the end of the strong social democratic reign in Norwegian politics. The non-socialist bloc won the 1965 election and formed a coalition government.

Table 1.1 Social reforms in Norway 1840–2005

1845	The first poor law
1894	Accident insurance for workers; Law on labour protection
1906	State contribution to unemployment benefits
1908	Accident insurance for fishermen
1909	Sickness benefits for manual workers
1911	Accident insurance for sailors
1915	Laws on protection of children's interests; working day restricted to 10 hours
1919	Working day restricted to 8 hours
1935	Sickness insurance for fishermen
1936	Disability pension for blind and handicapped; means tested old age pension
1938	Unemployment benefits for industrial workers
1946	Child benefits from the second child; state bank for housing
1948	Old age pension for sailors
1949	Unemployment benefits for agricultural workers
1950	Old age pension for government employees
1951	Old age pension for lumbermen
1953	Sickness benefits for all wage earners
1956	Paid maternity leave
1957	Old age pension for all
1958	Single mother allowance
1959	Income related unemployment benefits for all wage earners
1960	Extended disability pension and paid rehabilitation
1964	The Social Assistance Act; widow's pension
1966	Income related old age pension on top of the basic pension
1974	Law on day care for children
1977	Work environment protection Act
1978	Improvement of sickness benefits to the level of own wage
1991	The Social Services Act
1998	Cash support to families that do not have a place for their children in day care

Table 1.2 Main political parties, electoral support (per cent) and main electoral groups

Name	Founded	Electoral support 1961	Electoral support 2005	Main electoral groups	Chairman 2006 -
The Labour Party (Arbeiderpartiet)	1887	46.8	32.8	Workers, middle class	Jens Stoltenberg
Socialist Left Party (Sosialistisk Venstreparti – SV)	1961	2.4	8.7	Middle class, public sector, women	Kristin Halvorsen
The Centre Party (Senterpartiet – Sp)	1920	9.4	6.5	Farmers, the periphery	Aslaug Haga
Christian People's Party (Kristelig folkeparti – KrF)	1933	9.6	6.8	Housewives, elderly,	Dagfinn Høibråten
The Liberal Party (Venstre – V)	1884	8.8	5.9	Middle class	Lars Sponheim
The Conservative Party (Høyre – H)	1884	20.0	14.1	Business, upper and middle class, private sector	Erna Solberg
The Progress Party (Fremskrittspartiet - FrP)	1973	-	22.1	Workers, men, petty bourgeoisie	Siv Jensen

When a new middle class developed – partly as a result of the expansion of the welfare state – in the 1960s, the Labour Party was able to compete with Venstre (the Liberal Party) and Høyre (the Conservative Party) for their votes. This rivalry engendered wider political consensus, in the area of welfare policy as well.

In the early twentieth century, some voluntary organizations had established social institutions and hospitals. The post-WWII social democratic government gradually shoe-horned them into the national health system in another health and social sector expansion phase. Thus, the voluntary sector did not achieve such a prominent role as in the UK and on the Continent.

A new milestone in the development of the welfare state was the 1967 Act on supplementary and income-related old age pension scheme. The new old age pension consisted of two elements – a basic pension to which all citizens irrespective of work experience and income were entitled, and an income-related element calculated on the basis of earnings and years in employment (see chapter 5). Later, unemployment benefits and sickness benefits were included in this system, which was financed by contributions from employers and employees amounting to a certain percentage of the wage – and subsidized by general tax revenues. This system was modelled partly on the social insurance approach common in Continental Europe, but in reality was tied to taxation in the government budgets and generally viewed more as a tax than as a social insurance contribution. The new scheme was inspired by the supplementary pension system created by Swedish social democrats after a bitter conflict with the non-socialist parties in 1959. It did not provoke such intense divisions in Norway, and was approved by an almost unanimous parliament.

Table 1.3 Parties in government 1945–2005. The party of the Prime Minister in bold

Period	Parties in government		Type of government
1945–1961	The Labour Party	Social democratic	Majority
1961–1963	The Labour Party	Social democratic	Minority
1963–1963	**H**, KrF, Sp, V	Conservative, Christian, Agrarian, Liberal	Minority
1963–1965	The Labour Party	Social democratic	Minority
1965–1971	H, KrF, **Sp**, V	Conservative, Christian, Agrarian, Liberal	Majority
1972–1973	**KrF**, Sp, V	Christian, Agrarian, Liberal	Minority
1972–1981	The Labour Party	Social democratic	Minority
1981–1983	H	Conservative	Minority
1983–1986	**H**, KrF, Sp	Conservative, Christian, Agrarian	Minority
1986–1997	The Labour Party	Social democratic	Minority
1997–2000	**KrF**, Sp, V	Christian, Agrarian, Liberal	Minority
2000–2001	The Labour Party	Social democratic	Minority
2001–2005	H, **KrF**	Conservative, Christian, Liberal	Minority
2005–	**The Labour Party**, SV, Sp	Red – green (Social democratic, Socialist, Agrarian)	Majority

It was designed as an answer to certain questions about the role of the state and justice. Should the state do more than provide basic security to ward off poverty in old age, that is, should pensions be pegged to the standard of living people were accustomed to as wage earners? Should people with a history of gainful employment be entitled to higher pensions than those without? Or should everybody receive the same public pension, so that those who want to secure their standard of living could do that through private savings or a private pension plan? In Norway, there was consensus that all citizens should be included in a national pension scheme. In other countries different answers were found to these questions.

In 1973, a right wing populist and anti-tax party – the Progress Party (FrP) – was established. In a few years it campaigned on an anti-immigration ticket and won new groups of voters. FrP toned down its concern with taxes in favour of social welfare and health politics, alongside a preoccupation with immigration and ethnic minorities. It declares itself today as a liberalist party. FrP's electoral basis is in the working class and business. It competes with the Labour Party for the working class vote and with the Conservatives for the business vote (Svåsand and Wörlund, 2005).

The development of social services

A characteristic of the Norwegian welfare state is the level of commitment to children, the disabled and the elderly. Historically, these services grew out of the of local councils' responsibility for the poor and incapacitated. As mentioned, the Lutheran reformation had long ago reduced the ability of the Church to be a provider of social services for the needy, and the voluntary organizations did not possess the capacity to solve the social problems. Norway developed social services for the elderly later than Sweden and Denmark, and later still for children. Poor houses were replaced by old age homes from the 1880s to the 1920s. The late 1960s saw the beginning of a wider commitment to care for senior citizens. The number of inmates in retirement homes increased, and more people enjoyed domiciliary care in their homes. Service employee figures rose too (chapter 9). The expansion of day care for children had to wait until the 1970s (chapter 4 and 9) when Gro Harlem Brundtland became a member of a labour government and later Prime Minister – the first female Prime Minister in Norway (1981, 1986 – 1996).

Increasing labour market participation

From the early 1970s, an increasing proportion of the adult population sought a livelihood from gainful employment. This was an effect of at least three key factors. First, the surge of women into higher education after the student revolt was accompanied by a change of attitudes and gender ideology. Second, new technologies in the household lessened time required for cleaning and cooking, allowing women to combine housework with a paid job. Third, many women found employment in the public sector, leading to further expansion of the social services and more vacancies for women. Increased female employment put an increasing burden on the social services in the care of the elderly and children, and the new social services created increased opportunity for employment for women. Whereas the rate of employment in Norway was close to that of many other industrialized countries in the early 1970s, it exceeded the OECD average in the years to come. This was mainly due to the influx of women. The expansion of the welfare state was what Esping-Andersen (1990) terms an 'employment machine' for women. However, from a gender perspective, the labour market came to be more segmented than in other European countries (see chapter 3).

Oil revenue – a social safety net

The oil embargo instituted by the Arab nations in 1973 caused an economic setback in the world economy. In industrialized nations, unemployment reached unprecedented levels in the post-war period. High inflation in the US due to the Vietnam War aggravated the situation. Most governments in Western Europe attempted to curb the growth in public spending, and this meant cuts in social benefits. In Norway, the labour government was looking forward to increasing oil revenue thanks to the discovery of oil in the North Sea. It maintained an anti-cyclical Keynesian economic policy, letting budget deficits grow in the hope of an upswing in the economy. However, by 1978 the Labour government found it impossible to continue in this vein, and initiated a series of cuts in social spending in the years ahead. However, the cuts were mainly adjustments and not of a radical character.

In 1978, the electoral victory of Margaret Thatcher in the UK indicated growing popularity of neo-liberal ideology, with its emphasis on the free development of the market and personal responsibility and scepticism to the state and public responsibility. The Labour Party lost the 1981 election, ceding power to a Conservative government. The new government wanted to curb spending growth in the National Insurance Scheme and implemented cuts in social benefits. However, compared to what took place in most other Europeans nations in that period – particularly in the UK – the cuts in Norway were relatively modest and had no effect on the structure of the welfare state. Indeed, social spending continued to grow also under non-socialist governments (see chapter 2).

The late 1980s and early 1990s brought an almost total collapse of the financial sector and increasing unemployment. The financial sector had been deregulated in the 1980s, and many people had taken up mortgages at relatively cheap rates, which were now becoming increasingly difficult to manage. The government had to refinance some of the leading banks and become key stakeholder. However, whereas Sweden faced the most serious economic crisis since the 1930s, leading to heavy cuts in social benefits and services, Norway again avoided radical interventions in social benefits and services (Kautto, 2002; Kangas and Palme, 2005). The Labour Party and a coalition of the parties in the political centre alternated in government (cf. table 1.3). These governments were concerned by the rising cost of the National Insurance Scheme, and suggested several actions. One was a ceiling on child benefit, another was to tighten eligibility to disability pensions, single mother allowance and employment benefits. On the other hand, due to the growing oil revenue, social services kept growing, with day care for children expanding particularly fast. In 1998, a non-socialist coalition government introduced *cash for care* for parents whose children were not in day care institutions financed by the government (see chapter 4). A heated debate arose between the government on the one hand and the Labour Party and the Socialist Left Party on the other. The non-socialist government wanted parents to enjoy freedom of choice, i.e. between institutional and other forms of day care. The centre-left opposition were worried in case the benefit slowed the emancipation of women in the labour market. They wanted the resources spent on providing day care for all children.

Besides the cash for care benefit, social policy issues in the last decade have revolved around day care facilities, poverty and the reform of the old age pension. In 2004, the political parties – except the Socialist Left Party and the Progress Party (see above and chapter 10) – reached a compromise on a reform of the old age pension to reduce costs and create incentives for people to delay retirement (see chapter 5). The 2005 election resulted in a 'red–green' government of the Labour Party, Socialist Left Party (SV) and Centre Party (Sp). The government has pledged to stop the privatization of the economy and social services and make institutional day care universal. Also this government has promised to eradicate poverty.

The following chapters

The Norwegian welfare state grew out of specific historical conditions. Some researchers pinpoint the relative homogeneity in terms of ethnicity, language and religion (Baldwin, 1997) and argue that this made easier the development of a welfare state which covered all citizens. Others refer to the relatively egalitarian class structure, which facilitated a social alliance between the workers and the rural periphery and a political alliance between the Labour and the political centre during social democracy's heyday (Esping-Andersen, 1985; Baldwin, 1990). Although Norway was more homogeneous in terms of ethnicity and religion and had a more egalitarian class structure than most other European nations, homogeneity was a socially constructed idea of use in the nation building process, says the Norwegian anthropologist Marianne Gullestad (2001).The historian Anders Bjørnson (1990) argues that the *working class* was heterogeneous and socially fragmented in terms of geography, culture, skills, etc, and that solidarity and unity were products of the labour movement's own struggle and organizational work. Another historian – Peter Baldwin (1990) – draws the attention to influence of the farmers and the parties of the political centre and argue that their interests were crucial in the development of the universal character of the Scandinavian welfare state.

We return to this in the final chapter. Here suffice to say that the Norwegian welfare state redefined the relative weight of the delivery systems mentioned at the beginning of this chapter – the market, the individual and the family; the state, and the voluntary sector. Gainful employment became increasingly necessary. The state acquired a key role in providing welfare, more than in most non-Nordic countries. Much of the care of children and the elderly is now within the province of state welfare, but the voluntary sector still plays but a minor role.

But there has been more political consensus here than in most other European nations. Compared to other countries, there have been only modest cuts in some cash benefits, whereas social services have expanded continuously. There are many reasons for this. There was a continuous social democratic majority government from the 1930s to the 1960s (only interrupted by World War II), and since that time social democratic centre-right governments have alternated, where most often moderate parties in the political centre have been influential. The election system is based on proportional representation, which favours the parties of the political centre and has contributed to stability also in social policy. The political parties of the right have not been advocates of strong cuts in social security and social welfare (see chapter 10), and in general the expansion of the welfare state has not caused much political strife. Finally, the discovery of oil in Norwegian waters in the 1960s ushered in a period of unprecedented wealth (see chapter 2), so there was never any need to cut welfare spending or rationalize the social security system.

In the following chapters we examine the welfare state in more detail. The labour market is discussed in chapter 3, after a description of Norway's economy and financing of the welfare state in chapter 2. Chapter 4 discusses the role and responsibility of the family and the nexus between the labour market and the family, while chapter 5 describes the role of the state in organizing a public pension system for the frail and elderly. Chapter 6 depicts health issues – health indicators, economic transfers to the sick and medical services. Chapter 7 is about the role of social assistance and the struggle against poverty, while chapter 9 portrays the role of municipalities in delivering social and health services at the local level.

Finally, chapter 10 sums up, discusses the character of the Norwegian welfare state and its prospects and challenges in the decades to come – financial, demographical, ideological and political.

Chapter 2
Economy, oil and well-being

Industrialization came later to Norway than Sweden and much of Western Europe, but Norway had a plentiful supply of natural resources such as minerals, timber, fish stocks, whales in the Antarctica. Norway had a world-class merchant fleet, which helped fuel economic growth. By 1905, hydroelectric power was stimulating a fast growing manufacturing sector. Between 1930 and 1970, Norway grew less dependent on natural resources. By the 1970s, oil and, some years later, gas from the North Sea made Norway one of the wealthiest countries in the world (measured as GDP per capita, see table 2.1).

Prosperity, the expansion of the labour market and welfare state were closely connected of course. This chapter looks at the economy of a modern and advanced welfare state. Which economic factors and policies facilitated the emergence of a welfare state in a relatively undeveloped country lacking in social security systems and social services? How has it affected quality of life? Is there more or less social inequality? What economic challenges can be identified for the Norwegian welfare state?

An open and mixed economy

As a small country with a small internal market, Norway is dependent on exporting raw materials and products to other countries and import consumer goods. The Norwegian economy is part of the world economy and while Norway has been an advocate of free trade it is affected by global trends. The agricultural sector is an exception, as it is protected against foreign competition.

In 1954 Norway, Finland, Iceland, Sweden and Denmark formed a common Nordic labour market. In 1960 Norway joined EFTA – a free trade agreement between the EEC and seven non-EEC members. The Norwegian people voted to stay out of the European Union in plebiscites in 1972 and '94, though Norway did sign an agreement with the European Union, EEA (European Economic Area) where it accepted the 'four freedoms', free movement of (trade of) goods and services, of capital and people. This contributed further to the openness of the economy, although protectionism continued when it comes to agriculture.

Norway's main trading partners are the Nordic countries, particularly Sweden, EU countries, especially Great Britain, Germany and France, and the US. Oil and gas represented more than 50 per cent of total export. Norway exports marine produce (wild and farmed fish), metals (aluminium, iron and steel), paper and pulp.

After World War II, the Labour Party realized that improving public welfare, equality and creating opportunities for all required economic growth. Rebuilding society, especially the northern regions after the German occupation and increasing living standards were key objectives of public policy. 'Full employment' was both a means and a goal. The Labour government advocated a mixed economy with a strong state component to fight recessions and unemployment. Keynesian principles of deficit spending were adopted to shore up consumption and investments. The government invested, for instance, in public housing. The Labour Party wanted social policy to be 'productive' – to stimulate rather than slowing growth. Universal education became a social policy goal, but it was also meant to create prosperity. Thus, a deliberate political agenda facilitated strong economic growth.

Under the long period of social democratic governments after World War II, the state became strongly involved in establishing metallurgic industries to which it supplied cheap electricity. State ownership was central to the Norwegian economy. The state owns today 71 per cent of the shares in the country's biggest oil company, Statoil-Hydro, and 34 per cent of Norway's biggest private bank, DNB-Nor. It is a dominant shareholder in the largest telephone company (Telenor), civic aviation company (SAS) and aluminium works (Norsk Hydro). Rail and postal services are almost fully owned by the state. Most hydroelectric power plants are owned by the state or local councils. Taken together, the state owns about 55 per cent of the Norwegian manufacturing sector.[1] Nevertheless, foreign investment in Norway is higher than all the state's shares in Norwegian companies put together.[2]

The Labour Party, often through compromises and alliances with the parties of the political centre, established several institutions to cushion the impact of the market on public welfare. These regulating institutions are in force in agriculture, fisheries and hydroelectric power generation. State banks with cheap loans stimulated investment in manufacturing, legislation tempered the labour market and welfare state. Norway is a mixed economy where a strong state is integrated with the private sector of the economy (Mjøset, 2003). It is classified as a coordinated production regime, where 'firms typically engage in more strategic interaction with trade unions and other actors' (Hall and Gingerich, 2004, 8 after Esser, 2005), in contrast to

---

1 According to Finansnæringens Hovedorganisasjon, reported in *Aftenposten* 23.5.07).
2 Estimated to be around NOK 500 billion, *Aftenposten* 7.7.07.

liberal market economies where coordination problems are 'solved primarily by competitive markets' (ibid.).

The solidaristic legacy of full employment had not yet been eroded by the market efficiency demanded by economic globalisation and the European single market. It was possible 'to design policies that can resolve the presumed trade-offs between equality and efficiency' (Palme, 2005:2). In order to stabilise the economy during the 1991–92 recession the then Labour government launched what it called a 'solidarity alternative'. It was a combination of moderate wage growth and expansionist finance policy.

The tripartite arrangement of state, trade unions and employers is intact to a large extent: The state for example can intervene during wage negotiations to head off strikes or keep wage increases below a certain level in order to avoid weakening Norway's competitiveness in the global market. Another example is the 2002 IA Agreement (and renewed for another five year period in 2006), about inclusion in the labour market. The aim is to reduce absenteeism from work, create more jobs for disabled people into jobs and increase the actual age of retirement (which at present on average is about 60 years, although the formal pension age is 67 years in most professions) (see chapter 3).

Industry and services

As in other industrially advanced countries, the last 50 years saw fewer and fewer people working in the primary sector, stagnation in the secondary and a strong increase in the service sector (and especially in public services) (see table 2.1). A characteristic feature in Norway is the predominance of small firms: 86 per cent have fewer than 20 employees and 98 per cent fewer than 100 (Hammer and Øverbye, 2006).

Table 2.1 Production and employment by sector in Norway 1960 —2005/6

	Production % of GDP		**Employment % of total**	
Sector	1960	2005	1960	2006
Agriculture, fishing and forestry	9	1	20	3
Manufacturing, electricity, mining, oil and construction	35	36	37	20
Services and public sector administration + correction terms	56	63	43	77

Sources: Statistics Norway: Historical Statistics 1968, Statistics Norway 2006. This is Norway. What the figures say. Oslo.

The most dramatic structural change was in agriculture: From 1949 to 2005 the number of farms fell from 213 000 to 53 200. Whereas farming was the sole source of income for 20 per cent of all employed and self-employed in 1949, this is the case for only 0.5 per cent.[3] However, the agricultural sector is upheld by subsidies and protection against import from other countries. An OECD report ranks the protection of farmers as number three among OECD countries after only Iceland and Korea (OECD, 2007).

Traditional manufacturing industries have shed countless jobs, but this was compensated by higher employment in the petroleum sector and related activities. Restructuring of industries was possible because a generous welfare state could afford high unemployment benefits, disability benefits and early retirement schemes for those who have been made redundant. It became, moreover, difficult to maintain an egalitarian (compressed) wage structure and reduce inequality (see below). Public employment constitutes a large part of employment in the tertiary sector – 41 per cent, and represents 30 per cent of total employment.[4] Compared to other European countries (EU-15) Norway stands out with a particularly high secondary sector, for which it can thank its huge oil production (see below).[5] Around 100 000 persons, or 5 per cent of total workforce, are directly or indirectly working in the oil sector.[6]

Industrialization spawned massive urbanization. By 2007, 78.3 lived in towns and cities, with fewer and fewer choosing live in the country. In-migration as well as migration flows go to densely populated areas, and especially to the (four) big cities. In addition there is a large excess of births in urban settlements.[7]

Economic development

The transformation described above took Norway in less than 80 years from a position as a rather poor country to one of the most affluent in the world (see table 2.2). From 1922 to 1976 GDP per capita increased tenfold (2006 prices).[8] In 1970 Norway was the nineteenth richest country in the world; in 2005 only Luxembourg was ranked higher.

---

3 Statistics Norway. 2006. This is Norway. What the figures say. Oslo.
4 Ibid.
5 Eurostat. 2007. Europe in figures. Eurostat Yearbook 2006-2007. Luxembourg: Eurostat.
6 SNF-Bergen cited in *Aftenposten* 28.10.2007.
7 Statistics Norway: Population Statistics 1 January 2007.
8 Statistics Norway: Historical statistics; Statistics Norway. 2006. Økonomisk utsyn, Økonomiske analyser 1/2006, Oslo.

Table 2.2 Gross Domestic Product per capita (PPP US$ 1) in selected countries 2005

	Norway	Sweden	Denmark	Germany	France 2)	Italy	United Kingdom	US
GDP per capita	47 206	32 111	34 137 2)	27 100 2)	26 920	26 430	32 860	41 789

Source: OECD 2006.
1) GDP measured by Purchasing Power Parity converts national prices to common international and comparable prices.
2) Figures for 2002.

Average GDP per capita increased by 3 per cent 1970–2000, that is, twice as much in half the time of growth 1870–1940. GDP per capita (adjusted for purchasing power) is higher than the United States, and well above the other European states (see table 2.1). In the same period (1970–2000) average working time fell by 25 per cent. Due to the large number of part-time working women and fewer weekly hours, annual average working hours was 1370 in Norway, as compared to around 1600 in the United States.[9] This means that labour productivity and total productivity are high, mainly explained by the high educational level of the working-age population – 23 per cent of the adult population were highly educated in 2002.

Yet, because of the high price of goods and services, purchasing power and actual individual consumption are lower than in several other European countries such as Germany, the Netherlands, Switzerland and UK (Svennebye, 2005). This is a result of a deliberate policy of heavy taxation on goods such as alcohol, tobacco, gasoline and the high labour costs. High food prices due to the protected agriculture sector play a role as well. More GDP goes to *public consumption* such as health and education in the EU-15 countries on average, though well below Sweden and Denmark (Alstadsæter et al., 2005).

As percentage of GDP, imports accounted for 29.5, and exports 43.6 per cent. This translates into a trade surplus of Euro 38.5 billion in 2005.[10] Norway has enjoyed a trade surplus since 1970, with the exception of 1986–88. Norway's foreign debt (Euro 350 million first quarter of 2007) is hugely offset by loans to foreign countries through investments of the Pension Fund.

Despite a costly welfare state, Norway's global competitiveness is line with the other Nordic countries, high. In 2006, it was ranked as number 12 among 125 countries, but Finland, Sweden and Denmark are ranked in second to fourth place, according to the Global Competitiveness Report 2006–2007 (World Economic Forum, 2006). Neither does a huge public sector

---

9 St.meld. nr. 8 2004-2005 *Perspektivmeldingen.*
10 Statistics Norway. 2006. *Økonomisk utsyn, Økonomiske analyser* 1/2006, Oslo.

represent an impediment to economic growth. A study of the last 200 years shows that Sweden's economic growth was the equal of the United States (Lindert, 2005). One explanation is that high-trust countries, such as the Nordic welfare states, have lower transaction costs, which is good for the economy (Tingaard Svendsen and Haase Svendsen, 2006).

Oil dependency

In 2004 Norway was the seventh biggest oil producer in the world; the economy is therefore highly sensitive to crude oil prices. Since 1960 oil prices have varied strongly, but have peaked in recent years.[11] To manage the huge state revenues from the oil sector the government set up a petroleum fund. Today it incorporates two funds, the *Government Pension Fund-Global* (NOK 1776 billion) and *Government Pension Fund-Norway*, previously known as the National Insurance Scheme Fund (worth NOK 184 billion in 2005). These funds – taken together – were of the same magnitude as total GDP in 2005 (NOK 1717 billion). By the end of 2007 the fund was NOK 2,094 billion, and is expected to reach NOK 2467 billion by 2009, 106.5 per cent of GDP.[12] This fund is the third largest pension fund in the world. It is a sort of nest egg for the old age pensions of future generations – present obligations are estimated to be around NOK 3874 billion (485 billion euros).[13]

Total tax revenues and other oil-related income were NOK 374 billion (47 billion euros) in 2007 and represented around 36 per cent of total tax revenues. Without income from the petroleum sector the state budget for 2008 would have had a deficit of NOK 36.4 billion (almost five billion euros).[14]

The huge production and export of oil and gas may to some extent shield Norway against setbacks in the world economy, and Norway was not hit as hard as other countries by the two oil price shocks in 1973 and 1979. But Norway is not totally unaffected by global recessions such as the one in 1991–1994. Yet, the production of oil from the North Sea has had a strong effect on aggregate demand both directly and through higher public expenditures thanks to heavy taxation of the oil industries. Falling exports of other products were cushioned by higher domestic consumption. As a result unemployment levels are lower than in other European countries (see chapter 3). On the other hand, oil money increases the value of the Norwegian currency (NOK), which creates problems for other export industries and contributes to de-industrialization (Øverbye et al., 2006).

---

11 St.meld. nr. 1 2006-2007 *Nasjonalbudsjettet 2006*.
12 St.meld. nr. 1 2007-2008 *Nasjonalbudsjettet 2008*.
13 St.meld. nr. 2 2006-2007 Revidert nasjonalbudsjett 2007.
14 (www.regjeringen.no/en/defp/fin/Press-Center/Press-releases 2007/Statens inntekter, 11.10.2007.

The Pension Fund protects the welfare state against retrenchment in times of economic setbacks. In 2006, the oil revenue which was pumped into the government amounted to a sum that equalled spending on sickness benefits, parental leave, and the total public costs of the hospital sector. However, the fund is not without limits. The aim of both previous governments and the red–green government which came into power in 2005 is to not spend more than the return from the Pension Fund, which is stipulated at 4 cent of value of the fund. Keeping inflation at this level would otherwise be hard to achieve, harming the competitiveness of the export industries as a consequence.

The Pension Fund invests its money abroad in shares and bonds. It is not allowed to invest in ethically questionable activities such as arms production or where child labour is involved. A global recession would reduce the value of the fund. Opponents to this way of saving the oil revenue want at least some of the fund to be invested in infrastructure, such as roads and railways, in Norway. This, however, would put a premium on labour, cause wages and inflation to rise, which would destroy the export industry.

According to prognoses, exploitable reservoirs of oil will be empty some years after 2030, and natural gas around 2080. It would probably be wise to use some of the income from oil and gas to develop new productive activities that can take over after the oil era. The 'paradox of plenty' is that a country becomes accustomed to spending money on imported goods, while ignoring the importance of modernising its productive sector in a globalized economy.

Taxation

A central feature of the Norwegian economy is the important role of the public sector, financed through heavy taxation. Tax revenues as percentage of GDP were in 2005 45 per cent. Of total revenues, taxes on income and production came out more or less neck and neck – respectively 36 and 37 per cent. Social security and pension premiums accounted for 24.5 per cent. It is difficult to compare with other countries because the tax structures and social security systems differ. The sharply taxed huge income generated by the oil sector also sustains the high GDP level (Alstadsæter et al., 2005). However, taxation of private persons in Norway is lower than in the other Nordic countries, with the exception of Iceland. It is about the same as Belgium, France, Italy and Austria, whereas taxation levels below 25 per cent are found in Korea, Japan, US and Mexico. The level of taxes *after* deduction of transfers and subsidies to private persons, was 27.5 per cent of GDP in 2004.[15] Only Sweden and Denmark had higher levels than Norway in a selected

---

15 Statistics Norway 2004. *General government, key figures income and expenditures 2004.* Oslo.

group of OECD countries (ibid.). The taxation level of companies is 28 per cent, which about the same level as the OECD average.[16]

Total tax rates for wage earners, including direct taxes, value added tax and other consumption taxes, are higher than other countries'.[17] For wage earners, maximum marginal tax rate is 47.8 per cent, but income tax on ordinary incomes is 28 per cent for both private persons and companies. Direct taxation levels[18] are lower for wage earners than the EU average (EU 15). Value added tax (VAT) is 25 per cent, but 14 per cent on most food items. Besides, there are extra taxes on alcohol beverages, tobacco, chocolate and sugar, cars and gasoline.

Finally, there are municipal taxes and user fees. Municipal activities are financed mainly by taxes, government transfers and municipal fees. The main income source is the general income tax, most of which goes to municipalities. Besides, municipalities are entitled to claim property (land) tax within certain limits. Government transfers consist of a block grant plus earmarked transfers for specific tasks. Municipal fees are charges on municipal services such as water supplies, sanitation and child day care (see chapter 9 for details).

Before taxes are calculated various deductions are made, including for example paid interest as well as private pension premiums up to a certain limit. Whereas most OECD countries have skipped general property tax in order to attract foreign capital, with Sweden being the latest, property is still taxed in Norway.[19] The tax system has lost some of its progressive character in recent decades, but retains a so called 'top tax' ranging between 9 and 12 per cent for higher incomes. This means that some of the tax burden has been transferred from high income to low income brackets (Thoresen, 2005).

In 2007, 45 per cent of total government revenues were transfers to the private sector (mostly households), with the rest going to public investments and consumption (public services) and to the pension fund.[20] Such transfers represented 17 per cent of GDP in 2004, which is below the average of selected OECD countries (Alstadsæter et al. 2005) (see chapter 9 on municipal taxes).

The welfare state in the economy

The welfare state plays an important role in the Norwegian economy. The *state* redistributes income, creates employment, constitutes a social safety net, offers education and various health and social services. In many respects the

---

16 *Dagens Næringsliv* 20.4.2007.
17 OECD cited in *Aftenposten* 30.3.2006.
18 Income tax plus employers' premium minus child allowances as percentage of wages
19 *Aftenposten* 29.3.07.
20 St.prp. nr. 1 2007–2008. *Statsbudsjettet 2007*.

welfare state and public sector make up for deficiencies in the market. However, it is *productive* and does not run contrary to the logic of the market. According to Global Entrepreneurship Monitor Norway is ranked higher than almost all other European countries, and is almost at the US level, when it comes to entrepreneurship (Bosma and Harding, 2007). The model of social protection combines universal benefits with earnings-related benefits. It stimulates labour market participation and increases tax contributions by widening the tax base. Tax-financing reduces the cost of labour more than the insurance method preferred by Continental welfare states with resources allocated according to need under a framework which not only is compatible with but also stimulates economic growth. The welfare state impacts on economic development as well as on people's behaviour and attitudes. It contributes first and foremost to a reduced social distance between people by creating equal opportunities through free schooling and redistribution of income.

Figure 2.1

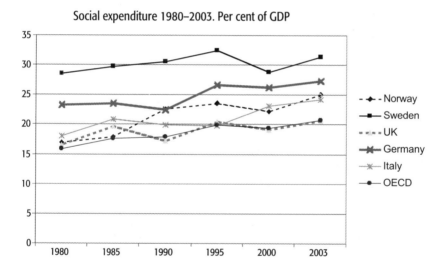

Source: OECD Social expenditure database. SOCX 1980–2003. OECD 2007. www.oecd.org/else/social/expenditure. Accessed at May 29 2007.

Figure 2.1 puts Norway among the big spenders in terms of social expenditure. In 2003, Norway spent 25.1 per cent of its GDP on cash benefits and public social services, whereas the OECD average was 15.9 per cent. Of social expenditures cash benefits represented in 2005 59 per cent and services 41 per cent. Compared to other industrialized countries, public transfers are higher.[21] In 2005 58 per cent of social expenditures were financed by public

---

21   NOSOSCO 2007, 203.

authorities through taxes, 26 per cent by employers and 14 per cent the insured (through contributions and special taxes.[22]

In addition, public subsidies comprise *tax relief* for private and occupational welfare arrangements and schemes, especially pensions. *The fiscal welfare*, which is invisible in state budgets – represents a huge income loss, such as non-taxable child benefits (see figure 2.3) and especially tax deductions for pensioners.[23] In several other OECD countries tax relief is granted on social grounds instead of direct cash benefits.

We should not deduce from these figures that Norway is a less generous welfare state than other European countries.[24] First, the Gross National Product is higher in Norway than there. Second, social expenditures are also a reflection of social problems. The low unemployment level in Norway compared to most other countries results in lower social expenditures, such as unemployment benefits and social assistance benefits (Hatland, 2005). Besides, such comparisons (figure 2.2) based on gross expenditures exaggerate the costs of social benefits, because 'benefits are taxable and social services expenditures are made up of wages to employees in the social service sector, which are also subject to taxation' (Palme, 2005:3). The difference between *gross* and *net* social expenditure as percentage of GDP is around 5 percentage points.[25]

Most cash benefits are under the umbrella of the National Social Security Scheme. These benefits constitute 25 per cent of the total state budget in 2008. Most of the expenses, such as old age pension, disability pension and sickness benefits, are financed by premiums (NOK 196 billion (24.5 billion euros), the rest is paid by the state. In comparison, Pension fund surplus is estimated to increase by NOK 344 billion (43 billion euros) in 2008. [26]

By the end of 2003, 43 per cent of the population above 18 years had a pension, social security or social assistance as their main income. As demonstrated in figure 2.3, there are also many tax-free transfers, the most important being the family allowance (especially child allowance given to all children up to the age of 18). A great majority of elderly receives free or subsidised services at home or in health or care institutions. Most children between one and five years are in subsidised kindergartens (see chapter 9).

---

22 NOSOSCO 2007, 300.
23 St.meld. nr. 1 for 2006-2007 *Statsbudsjettet for 2006*.
24 In fact, in a ranking from 1995 of overall welfare regime generosity among OECD countries, Norway was ranked second after Sweden (Esser 2005).
25 NOSOSCO 2007, 210.
26 St.meld. nr. 1 2007–2008 *Nasjonalbudsjettet for 2008*.

Figure 2.2 Tax free transfers 2003

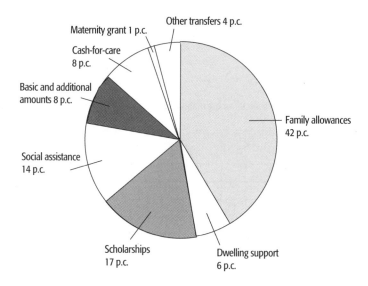

Source: Statistics Norway 2004© Income statistics for persons and families 2003.

More than half of the transfers included in figure 2.2 are for families with children. The largest benefit is family allowance which constituted 42 per cent, whereas cash-for-care for families with young children constituted eight per cent[27] (see chapter 4). Around 10 per cent of all cash benefits are tax exempt, slightly above the wider Nordic level.[28] This in contrast to several other OECD countries where cash benefits are generally either not taxed at all or only moderately.

Levels of living

UNDP's annual *Human Development Report* includes a human development index based on life expectancy at birth, adult literacy rate (per cent aged 15 and above), combined gross enrolment ratio for primary, secondary and tertiary schools and GDP per capita. In the last years, Norway has topped the list on what admittedly is a rather crude measure of human development, followed by Sweden, Australia, Canada and the Netherlands,[29] see table 2.2.

In 2006 life expectancy (see figure 2.3) for a newborn girl was 82.7 years

---

27 Statistics Norway. 2003. *Income statistics for persons and families 2003*. Oslo.
28 NOSOSCO 2007, 211.
29 UNDP Human Development Report 2004.

and 78.1 years for a newborn boy (ranked no. 13[30] – see also chapter 6). There has been a consistent increase in life expectancy since 1930, apart from the WW II years. The gap between male and female longevity has narrowed over the last 15 years.

Figure 2.3

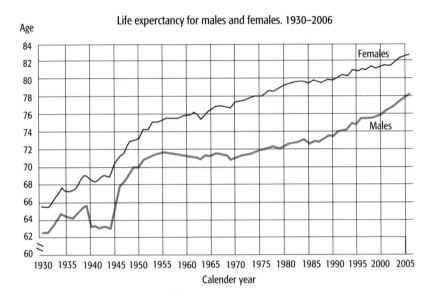

2007 © Statistics Norway.

The high GDP per capita results in high living standards in terms of housing, cars, electrical appliances, travel, clothing, leisure etc. Around 80 per cent live in their own homes (detached or semi-detached houses). The average person occupies 50 m^2 living space. In 2004 only 7 per cent of households were 'crowded'.[31] Housing expenditures represent a high per cent of a household's income. Around 20 per cent of all households own a holiday home, and many more have access to one or more.[32]

Norway is one of the most egalitarian countries in the world when it comes to income. According to the *UNDP Human Development Report* (2004) the 10 per cent richest had about six times the disposable income (or consumption) of the 10 per cent poorest. Another measure of income (in)equality, the Gini coefficient, was .0.26, which places the country at number seven in the world (see also table 2.3). Yet income inequality has increased in the last two decades.

---

30   UNDP Human Development Report 2003.
31   Defined as more persons than number of rooms in a household.
32   Statistics Norway. 2006. *This is Norway. What the figures say.* Oslo.

In 2006, 5.8 per cent of all households had a disposable income per consumption unit (OECD scale) of less than 50 per cent of the median income (poverty threshold)[33] (see chapter 7). In 1990 the 10 per cent highest income households had 19 per cent of total disposable household income after tax per consumption unit. By 2006 it was 20.6 per cent. In comparison, the 10 per cent lowest household income bracket had only 4.1 per cent of total household income.[34] Nevertheless, income distribution among the lowest 90 per cent of income groups has remained practically unchanged since 1990 (Christensen et al., 2007). The Gini coefficient, which measures inequality, increased from 0.22 in 1990 to .25 in 2006 (Epland, 2004; Pedersen et al., 2007 Statistics Norway, 2008a).

A main factor in explaining increased inequality is that salaries of directors of private companies have increased much faster than workers' pay. From 1999 to 2005, the average top-management salary doubled (in the biggest, private companies), while full-time manufacturing workers saw a pay rise of only 29 per cent (Randøy and Skalpe, 2007). We can measure the wage gap by comparing the 10 per cent with lowest wages with the 10 per cent with the highest. In 2005 Norway had the narrowest wage gap of 20 OECD countries with a ratio of 2.3, though it widened faster in Norway after 1995 than in most other OECD countries.[35] Another reason is that the economic boom has created higher dividends, which mainly have benefitted households in the highest wage and salary brackets. The 10 per cent with the highest income increased their per cent of total income from capital from 1993 to 2004 from 71 to 94 per cent (Christensen et al., 2007). Yet, the income differences are much greater when calculated before transfers and taxation, and this demonstrates that the welfare state still redistributes income.

The wealth gap, however, is even wider: The 10 per cent of the wealthiest households owned 66 per cent of total financial assets in 1998.[36]

The sex wage gap has gradually narrowed. The average female wage was 6 per cent lower than for men in the same profession and business with the same work experience, length of education, education type, working hours (Barth et al. 2005). As for sex related development, Norway is first on the Human Development Report index (see table 2.3.)

---

33 Statistics Norway. 2007: *Inntektsstatistikk for husholdninger 2006*, www.ssb.no.emner/05/01/iffor. 27.3.2008).
34 Ibid.
35 *Aftenposten* 21.6.07.
36 Statistics Norway. 2000. *Fordeling av brutto finanskapital for hushold etter desiler 1996–1998*. Oslo.

Table 2.3 Life expectancy, Gini index, Gender-related development index, happiness, loneliness and subjective general health in selected countries (2002)

	Norway	Sweden	Denmark	Germany	France	United Kingdom	USA
Life Expectancy	78.9	80.0	76.6	78.2	78.9	78.1	77.0
Gini-index a)	0.26	0.25	0.25	0.28	0.33	0.36	0.41
Gender related development index (rank)	1	2	13	19	15	9	9
Happiness 1)	7.93	7.89	8.33	7.01	7.15	7.42	
Loneliness 2)	21	26	16	29	38	31	
Subjective General health 3)	75	74	77	62	62	71	

a) year 2000
1) How happy are you. Average scores on a scale from 0 to 10 (European Social Survey 2004/2005).
2) How often felt lonely past week, percentage answering some/most or all or almost all of the time (European Social Survey 2004/2005).
3) Percentage answering very good/good (European Social Survey 2004/2005)
Source, Otherwise: UNDP: Human Development Report 2004.

OECD country survey data reveal only a weak relationship between happiness, life satisfaction and GDP per capita. Other factors affect one's sense of well-being, such as hours at work and time off. But even if we include these factors, Norway is still on top, and way ahead of United States. According to an OECD paper, other factors affecting people's well-being should be included, such as equity, employment opportunity, health, social cohesion (social relationships and participation in community life, (Boarini et al., 2006; Fleurbaey and Gaulier, 2007).

In general, people in Norway regard themselves as happy, but as table 2.3 shows, the average Dane is happier, after the average Swiss, who's happiest of all (result not presented in table 2.3). It goes to show that the Human Development Index presented earlier in this chapter does not tell the whole story about people's sense of well-being. Only every fifth person feels lonely (see table 2.3). The proportion of socially isolated people is very low, despite the fact that more and more people are living alone. The average persons living alone enjoys worse living conditions than the rest of population, is more likely to be marginalized in the labour market, have poorer mental health and an unhealthier life style (Mørk, 2006).

Norway is also on top when it comes to general trust among people (European Social Survey 2004/05, see chapter 8). The homicide rate is low and decreasing. The same for suicides and persons killed in traffic accidents. But crime is increasing, especially theft and robbery.

Norway is in the top 10 on happiness, satisfaction with life or subjective well-being. But despite greater affluence, several countries do better than Norway (apart from Denmark and Switzerland, for example Iceland, Ireland, Finland according to European Social Survey 2004/2005). It seems that after a certain level of economic growth, more growth does not result in higher happiness or satisfaction with life (Barstad and Hellevik, 2004; Layard, 2005). One reason could be that income disparity causes a wider range of life-styles which in turn widens the social and cultural distance between people (Risa, 2006).

Challenges

This chapter has drawn a rather idyllic picture of the Norwegian economy. However, there are challenges. First, Norway is highly dependent on the production and income from the oil. A sharp fall in oil prices would make a significant dent in government takings, gross domestic product and export. Second, as oil prices are calculated in US dollars, a collapse of the value of the dollar could have serious repercussion on the Norwegian economy and the welfare state. Third, the strong dominance of the oil sector and dependency on oil are to the detriment of other sectors in the economy. The question is if Norway will be remain land of plenty after the 'oil era'. Until now it has been possible to save most of the government's income from the petroleum sector, but if the government spends significantly more, we may not be able to finance public sector expansion. We would have to rein in the public sector, and cut down on consumption, with high unemployment as a result (Storsletten, 2006).

Norway also relies on manufactured goods imported from abroad. So far, imports have been financed mainly by huge exports of petroleum products and high oil prices. After the 'oil era', the trade balance will probably begin to occupy negative territory. Strong restructuring of the economy will be necessary to retain international competitiveness. In addition, Norway will have to handle ecological problems on a widening front, and climatic change from global emissions of carbon dioxide.

However, so far Norway has demonstrated high global competitiveness, and the welfare state has contributed to this. Market driven adjustments in politics and the economy have also been of importance (Dølvik, 2007). A generous social security net gives people the safety they need to tolerate necessary structural changes in the economy (Hutton, 2007). The 'productive' social policy is an incentive for women to seek higher qualifications, increasing productive work in the formal sector of the economy. Welfare state arrangements have made it easier to reconcile work and family life than in most other European countries (see chapters 3 and 4).

Despite economic affluence, some modern problems are increasing, such as drug (and gambling) addiction, alcohol problems and overweight/obesity as well as problems related to divorce and family break-ups (50 per cent of all children are born out of wedlock by cohabiting parents, see chapter 4). Increasing numbers of seniors will affect the cost of public pensions and health and social services (see chapter 5). Besides, the tendency for people to retire earlier reduces tax revenues and increases social expenditure (see chapter 10).

Chapter 3
Work, work, work!

Norway and the other Scandinavian countries are often called 'labourers' societies (Arendt, 1958) or 'employment regimes of the Scandinavian type' because paid work and full employment are cornerstones of public policy in general and the welfare state in particular. The aim is 'maximizing the productive potential of citizenry' (Esping-Andersen 1999). By the 1930s politicians were already aware of the need for social policy had to be 'productive' and conducive to economic growth (Debes, 1939 according to Slagstad, 1998). The welfare state of the Scandinavian type maximises job offers by high public employment and demand-side policy,[37] an active labour market policy which aims to vocationally rehabilitate the disabled but at the same time letting the workforce enjoy paid sick and parental leave.[38]

The labour movement and the social democratic parties and governments have been strong supporters both of the work ethic and ideology of full employment. The duty of political authorities to create opportunities for employment was inscribed in Norway's Constitution in 1954. Despite generous unemployment benefits with respect to level of compensation and contribution period (eligibility criteria), employment commitment is high in Norway as in the other Scandinavian countries (Svallfors et al. 2001; Hult and Svallfors 2002; Esser 2005). This is not least due to the fact Scandinavian welfare regimes and their regulated and coordinated market economies provide agreeable working conditions (ibid.).

The Norwegian welfare state is also based on a commitment to ideals of equality, social justice, social security, solidarity and social integration. The work ethic is strong, and full employment remains a central means to redistribute wealth, reduce inequality, poverty and dependency, enhance self-reliance and secure integration into the mainstream society. Non-disabled persons not only have a right to work, but a social duty to do so: to create economic growth, and by paying taxes, contribute to the financing of a large public sector and decent economic support for those outside the labour

---

37 Policy that aims to stimulate employers to increase their demand for labour.
38 These three processes are defined as commodification, which means that people have to sell their labour power (a commodity) in order to survive, recommodification and decommodification respectively (see Esping-Andersen, 1990).

force. After World War II, self-reliance was mainly required of able-bodied men. Women were supported by their husbands. Today, all able-bodied people are supposed to be self-reliant. The central aim is 'everybody at work'.

This obligation is reflected in the fact that the unemployed have to register at a job centre, take steps to find a job and be willing to accept suitable jobs. Failure in any of these areas leads to forfeiture of the right to economic support, such as social assistance or unemployment benefit. While the right to work and society's obligation to secure 'work for all' have been stressed, today the duties of the individual to find paid work tend to overshadow the duties of the state to find work for him. It is called the 'work approach' or 'policy of activation'. This means, for example, that the unemployed must be prepared to move and/or to take whatever the job centre feels is a 'suitable' job. People have to be less 'picky' to reduce the gap between qualifications required and qualifications on offer (St.meld. nr. 9 2006–2007).

Legal regulations and bargaining system

The Norwegian labour market is regulated by the Working Environment Act, by legislation promoting workplace democracy, and by collective agreements between business and labour (trade unions). A centralized system of bargaining combines with negotiations at company level to set wages, hours and conditions under the parameters determined in the central bargaining process. Norwegian settlements were more centralized than any other OECD area country in the 1990s. In practice, striking for higher wages in Norway is cut short by compulsory arbitration and mediation. If the partners fail to agree, the National Wage Board, composed of representatives for employers, employees and the state (Industrial Dispute Court), can set the wage increase (*tvungen lønnsnemnd*). During this process it is illegal to strike.

Centralized collective bargaining has resulted in low unemployment compared to other OECD countries because increases in wages have been determined with an eye to the consequences for international competitiveness. Thus, the national setting of wages is export-led and wage restraint is obtained when unemployment is low and trade unions can normally achieve substantial increases in wages. Another consequence of the centralized bargaining system is that highly educated people are paid less than in most other Western countries, which is a competitive advantage for Norway.

These labour market institutions were shaped in the immediate pre- and post-war era, and facilitated by broad class compromises and a spirit of national reconciliation (see chapter 1). Coordination of wages has long been closely coordinated with economic policies, and the government, business and labour have given priority to the competitiveness of exposed sectors (Dølvik et al. 1996). Despite these institutional arrangements, the Norwegian labour market is considered flexible,[39] though not as flexible as Denmark's in terms of job protection and large job mobility. And a compressed wage structure results in limited wage flexibility.

Since 1954 there has been a common Nordic labour market, which allows people from one Nordic country to work in another without needing a special work permit. This entitlement was extended in 1994 to all EU countries. Citizens of Eastern European countries that joined the European Union in May 2004 need a work permit for a transitional period. Non-EU specialists that are urgently needed in industries can also get a work permit. There are quotas for guest farm labourers needed for the harvesting season. Around 100,000 persons from EU countries are now working in Norway.[40]

In order to prevent so-called social dumping, an agreement which came into force January 1 2007 provides for a *minimum* hourly wage of Euro 16.50 (NOK 132.25) for skilled workers from EU countries (Tariffnemnda) (Forskrift om almenngjøring av tariffavtale for byggeplasser i Norge).

Employment and unemployment

The 1970s saw unprecedented expansion in the public sector and oil industry, with rapid growth in jobs as a result. It facilitated the entry of women into the labour market. The unemployment rate was almost negligible until the mid 1970s, but accelerated from 1988 to 1993. According to Norwegian standards, unemployment rates were unacceptably high in these years. Along with increasing unemployment, employment levels and labour force participation rates fell. At the same time the number of disability pensioners rose rapidly, as did the student population. Since then unemployment has fallen in line with the upturn in the world economy.

The labour market trends can be measured in many ways. The most important indicators are labour force participation rates (full-time and part-time) for various categories, public versus private sector employment, (gross and net) unemployment rates and indicators of redundancy (early retirement) from the labour market. Also temporary employment and temporal withdrawal from the labour market in terms of sickness leave are relevant measures of the health of the labour market. Even the total volume of working hours and working hours per employed and per capita are relevant measures.

In 2006 around 50 per cent of the adult population was gainfully employed, of which almost half were female (47 per cent). The number of employed is 70 per cent higher than in 1946, while the population increase during the same period (1946–2006) was 50 percent. The increase in employment represents, however, only 9 per cent of the increase in total work-

---

39 Flexibility refers to employment protection, wage structures and working hours (Goul Andersen et al. 2002).
40 St.prp. nr. 1 for 2007-2008 *Nasjonalbudsjettet for 2008*.

ing hours, mainly as a result of working hour reforms from a 48 hour week in 1946 to a 37.5 hour week today, longer vacations (2 weeks in 1946, five weeks in 2002), and more women and students working part time.[41]

The workforce of employed plus registered unemployed aged 16–74 was 72.4 per cent of total population in 2005 (table 3.1), while the proportion of employed was 69.1 per cent. Male employment was 72.5 per cent and female employment 65.6 per cent. Lowest participation was in the youngest age group, 16–24, with 52.9 per cent, mainly due to the high proportion of young people in further education. In 2001 only Switzerland and Iceland had higher labour force participation in the *15–64 age bracket* than Norway. The average for EU (15) countries was at the same time 69.2 per cent, compared to Norway's 80.3 per cent. Female labour force participation rate is also high compared to other European countries (figure 3.2), but more women are working part-time, especially in comparison with the other Nordic countries.[42] In 2004, 30 per cent of all working women had part-time jobs defined as working less than 30 hours per week on average, and 43 per cent if one defines part-time as less than 36 hours per week. Whereas women in the age group 20–66 years spent 2.14 hours on work in 1971 per weekday (Monday to Friday), this had increased to 3.54 hours by 2000. In the same period women's time used on houshold work was reduced from 6.42 to 4.01 hours (Vaage, 2002). Norwegian women spend less time on household work than women in other countries according to International Social Survey Programme comparing 34 countries, but considerabley more than Norwegian men (Knudsen and Wærness, 2008).

Table 3.1 Labour force participation and unemployment 1985–2006 (percentages)

	1985	1990	1995	2000	2005	2006
Labour force participation rate [1)]	68.8	69.2	74.2	73.4	72.4	72.7
Unemployment rates [2)]	2.6	5.2	4.9	3.4	4.6	3.5
Average duration of unemployment [3)]	21.6 [5)]	26.0 [5)]	25.0 [5)]	15.0	21.7	20.0 [5)]
Proportion of long-term unemployed [4)]	18.0	40.0	40.0	16.0	26.0	33.0
Average working hours per week	36.2	36.0	35.6	35.1	34.9	34.6

1) Persons who work at least one hour per week, 16–74 years. Average figures.
2) According to labour force surveys. Registered unemployment is somewhat lower.
3) Weeks.
4) Six months or more during the calendar year.
5) Own calculations based on statistics published by NAV (www.nav.nobinary/1073747598/file).
Source: Statistics Norway: Labour market statistics, respective years.

---

41 Statistics Norway, 2007 www.ssb.no/magasinet/analyse/art-2007-03-02-01.html.
42 NOU 2004:29 Kan flere jobbe mer?

Whereas labour force participation in Norway was close to that of many other industrialized countries in the early 1970s, it passed the OECD average from then on (see figures 3.1 and 3.2).

Figur 3.1 Labour force participation rate 1973–2004

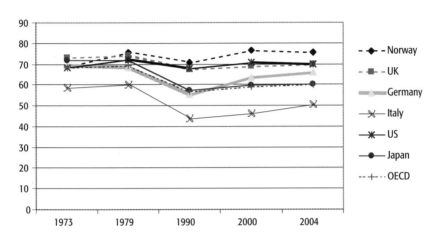

Source: OECD Employment Outlook 1993 and 2005.

This was mainly due to the increased participation of women. The expansion of the welfare state was what Esping-Andersen (1990) called 'an employment machine' for women. Of total employment, 18 per cent worked in health and social services in 2005. 82 per cent of these were women.[43]

Whereas the female participation rate in Norway in 1973 was 50.1 per cent and below that of the UK and the US, it reached 76.5 per cent in 2000 – well above that of the UK with 68.9 per cent and that of the US with 70.7 per cent. In 2006, only Iceland, Sweden and Denmark had a higher female participation rate. Although there is much part time work among women, it bears witness to the importance of labour market participation to women as well.

As mentioned, Norway has higher labour force participation than most other countries, especially the older age groups (see table 3.2). This is due to the pension age, which for most occupations is 67, but can be extended to 70.

---

43 Statistics Norway: Statistikkbanken, table 03 257.

Figur 3.2 Female labour force participation rato 1973–2004

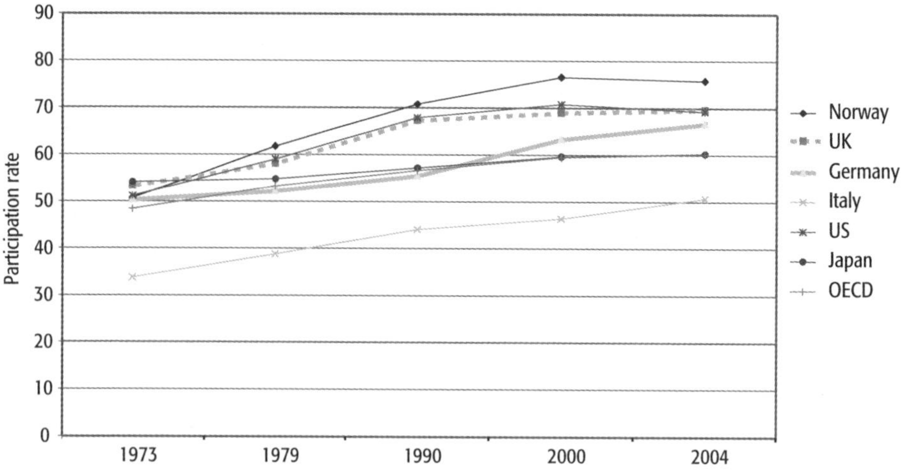

Source: OECD Employment Outlook 1993 and 2005.

Table 3.2 Employment rates 55–64 years for selected OECD countries (2005) (percentages)

	Norway	Sweden	Denmark	France	Germany	USA	UK
Men	73	72	67	44	54	67	66
Women	62	67	53	38	38	55	48

(Source: OECD, St.meld. nr. 2 2006–2007 Nasjonalbudsjettet for 2006.

At the same time unemployment rates have been lower than in most other countries (table 3.3) apart from the young non-student population, with high jobless rates. Nevertheless, there has been a dramatic increase in the number of people on disability pension/rehabilitation allowance, mainly due to a more demanding workplace and redundancies both in the private and public sector (Røed and Fevang, 2006; St.meld. nr. 9 for 2006–2007). In 2006 10.9 per cent of the population, or 333,500 persons aged 18–67, were on disability pension (see chapter 5).

The yearly fluctuations in unemployment figures and persons in governmental labour market programmes correlate with the health of the economy. Labour market surveys tend to operate with higher unemployed figures. The proportion of long-term unemployed is small (see table 3.1), because structural unemployment has been handled through early retirement, redundancy packages and disability pension schemes.

Table 3.3 Unemployment levels in selected countries (2005) per cent

Norway	Sweden	Denmark	Germany	United Kingdom	United States	EU-15	OECD
4.6	6.3	5.0	9.5	4.6	5.1	7.9	6.6

Source: Aetat Arbeidsdirektoratet: Årsstatistikk om arbeidsmarkedet 2005.

There is hidden unemployment among disability pensioners and people retiring early insofar as many as 30 per cent in the age group 25–54 years would have preferred to work, at least part time, rather than being on pensions.[44] The same is the case of the 17 per cent of part-time employees who would have preferred a full-time job, in 2006.[45] One is also concerned for the large numbers of people in part-time or temporary jobs, which represent 10 per cent of all jobs. This could be the downside of high job security, making employers reluctant to hire people on a permanent basis. There are also categories of people on the margins of the labour market alternating between short-term jobs and spells of unemployment. Nevertheless, only 3 per cent of Norwegian wage earners believed that they were in danger of losing their job, as against 24 per cent in United Kingdom and United States (Survey conducted by *Right Management Consultants*).[46]

Discrimination makes it difficult for some immigrants to enter the labour market, resulting in much lower labour force participation rates and higher unemployment rates among immigrants and refugees. Yet, since 1996 labour force participation rates have increased among all ethnic miniority groups (Statistics Norway, 2008b). Some immigrant ethnic groups fare better than others on labour force participation rates, with lowest participation rate among Somalis. A consequence of this is that 30 per cent of all participants in labour market programmes were immigrants.[47]

Persons aged 16–24 were more likely to be unemployed, 12.5 per cent for men and 11.5 per cent for women in 2005. Unemployment rates are highest among persons with low education and/or of immigrant background. For the latter category it was 8.2 per cent.[48] There are small regional disparities in

---

44 St.meld. nr. 9 2006-2007, *Arbeid, velferd og inkludering*, p.153.
45 Statistics Norway, 2007. Økonomisk utsyn, Økonomiske analyser 1/2007, Oslo: Statistics Norway.
46 *Aftenposten* 21.5.05.
47 Statistics Norway: Registrert arbeidsledighet blant innvandrere, 1. kvartal 2006.
48 Ibid.

unemployment, although registered unemployment is somewhat higher in the northern counties. Over a twelve-month period 15.5 per cent of the population aged 16–66 had been registered as job-seekers. Some people are out of work more or less permanently. The incidence of long-term unemployment is an indicator of structural unemployment. Only 12 per cent of registered unemployed had been unemployed for one year or more.[49] Twelve or more months without work counts as long-term unemployment according to EU conventions. 0.2 per cent of the labour force was in this category in Norway in 2000, compared to 3.9 in EU-15 (Andersen and Jensen, 2002). In 2005 Norway had the lowest long-term unemployment rate in Europe.[50] The government is concerned not so much about unemployment, but lack of manpower in many sectors of the economy. There are more vacancies than there are people to fill them, and there are also problems finding people with the right qualifications in the right places.

In 2002 workers became entitled to five weeks of paid holidays (six weeks for workers 60+). Standard weekly working hours fell from 45 hours in 1960 to 37.5 hours today, which includes a half hour lunch break in many professions. Estimated average working hours per *capita* (15–64) was in 2001 1057 hours, as compared for example to Sweden 1207 hours on average per year[51] (Andersen and Jensen 2002). Since 1962, the total volume has not changed much, even though as mentioned 700 000 more people – mostly women working part-time – have entered the labour force. In 2001 annual *de facto* working hours *per employed* were 1364, which is significantly lower than other western capitalist countries. More people are doing the same amount of work. The number of women with *housework* as their main activity fell sharply.[52] But unpaid housework still accounts for more working hours than paid work,[53] totalling 40 per cent of GDP in 1990 according to one estimate.[54]

Involuntary part-time work and temporary work are quite salient as a form of hidden unemployment. Official unemployment figures do not include various forms of hidden unemployment or under-employment. In 2001, 100,000 partly employed wanted to work more hours (Andersen and Jensen, 2002). It has nevertheless to be mentioned that *long* part-time work defined as more than 15 hours a week gives full social rights entitlements. Only a few employees are outsiders with low pay, little protection and in 'non-standard' jobs (casual short-term contracts), apart from persons of school age (Halvorsen, 2002).

Workers from the new EU countries (which joined May 1 2004) such as

---

49 Aetat Arbeidsdirektoratet. 2004. *Årsstatistikk om arbeidsmarkedet 2004*. Oslo.
50 Eurostat 2006.
51 Statistics Norway. 2006 Labour Statistics.
52 St.prp. nr. 1 for 2007-2008 Arbeids- ogi inkluderingsdepartementets budsjett for 2008.
53 Statistics Norway: Tidsnyttingsundersøkelsen 2000.
54 St.meld. nr. 4 1996-97 *Langtidsprogrammet 1998-2001 Fakta og analyser*.

Poland are entitled to a work permit if they have got a job offer before entering the country. In some instances, the building trade often fails to pay such workers the mandatory minimum wage that is set in order to avoid social dumping, and must work under conditions that violate working time regulations.

There are worrying wage disparities between men and women, especially between those with children. They represent 15 percent of the age group 20–45 with a full-time job. 40 per cent of the wage difference in the private sector and 20 per cent in the public sector is caused by higher female absenteeism for maternal and parental leave (Hardoy and Schøne, 2007). This should be an argument for increasing of the daddy quota (see chapter 6) substantially, giving male household members greater responsibility for care.

Labour market policy

Industrialized countries rely basically on two strategies to reduce unemployment. First, countries where economic liberalism has prevailed, like US and UK, reduce taxes and increase flexibility. They remove unfair dismissal and temporary employment safeguards, keep unemployment benefits low, and attempt to quell the influence of trade unions on wage setting and workplace environment. The result is more people in work, relatively high economic growth, but increasing wage disparities with even the employed falling below the poverty line – particularly in the US. The other main strategy is found in the Nordic welfare states. Here, taxation is high but worker protection better. Social benefits are more generous, making it less risky to take temporary work. There are extensive labour market programmes, and trade unions have a say in a centralized bargaining system. Also this has resulted in a low unemployment, strong competitiveness and economic growth, and poverty is almost non-existent among the employed. However, thanks to centralized wage bargaining, the wage structure is compressed and more people of working age are on disability or sickness benefits, etc.

Stimulating the demand for labour was the labour market policy watchword in the late '40s and '50s. The government stimulated the macro economy by activating financial and monetary policy mechanisms. In a globalised economy the room for such measures has become much more restricted. Efforts to save doomed businesses have proved futile. More has therefore been done to encourage people outside the labour market to take paid work, while improving the balance between supply and demand in terms of qualifications and locations. Several mechanisms are involved in stimulating the supply side including labour market training, employment in public sector, wage subsidies, sheltered employment etc., and offering disabled people vocational rehabilitation such as training or education. The unemployed are also obliged to take part in job-clubs, where they learn to apply for a job and present themselves at job interviews. In short, an active labour market policy plays on three strings at the same time, make the unemployed fit for work, prevent exclusion from the labour market, and take a targeted approach to the least qualified (St.meld. nr. 2 2005–2006:59–60).

Making the workforce more mobile and flexible will ease necessary structural changes in an increasingly globalized economy. Plant downsizing and organisational change have in the short run resulted in more people on unemployment benefits, sickness benefits and disability pension (Røed et al, 2005; Rege et al., 2005). Without a social security net, these structural changes would have been difficult to implement. Labour unions regard this as a competitive advantage for the Nordic welfare model in a globalized economy, although persons who are exposed to downsizing pay a high price in terms of higher risks of an early death, disability, mental health problems or divorce.[55]

An active policy for restructuring Norwegian industries to meet increased global competition is essential to full employment. In an instance of such restructuring, the government is privatising public companies and making public sector services more market oriented. For the time being, labour market policies have responded to high labour demand and growing labour shortages by focusing on filling vacancies. Mobility requirements are to be strictly enforced to counteract bottleneck problems in the labour market. In reality it turns out that entitlement to unemployment benefits is not waived because a beneficiary does not want to move residence in order to take a vacancy (Andreassen, 2003).

A wage subsidy mechanism is supposed to encourage employers to hire unemployed persons, or persons with special needs. And to reduce unemployment an entrepreneur grant programme was launched, open to anyone planning to establish a new business, but with an emphasis on the unemployed, female entrepreneurs and people from economically disadvantaged areas. Grants are provided for business planning purposes and as seed money.

An important factor in meeting the labour market needs for skilled labour is basic and higher education. The government used the education system to fight youth unemployment in the 1990s. More than 40 per cent of youngsters aged 20–24 were primarily occupied with gaining an education in 2005. And to encourage women to take paid work, the mechanisms included day care centres for children, after school childcare, and rights to leave of absence for pregnant women and for men and women with small children (see chapter 4). *The Working Environment Act* provides against unfair dismissal during pregnancy and leave of absence. Up to a point, childcare expenses are tax deductible. All this has allowed women to combine raising a family with paid work. A male breadwinner family model has been substituted by a 'one-and-a-half-earner family' model. There is still a long way to go before we can talk

---

55 According to an interview with researcher Mari Rege in *Dagbladet* 27.12.2007.

about an 'adult worker family model', where it is assumed that all adult workers are in the labour market (Lewis, 2001:163).

The government allocated 2.7 per cent of total social expenditures to combating unemployment in 2002, as compared to for example 8.6 per cent for Denmark.[56] Also compared to other European countries, the figures for Norway are low.[57] On the other hand, rehabilitation cost 32.5 percent of total spending, against 5 per cent on average for EU (15) countries in 2004.[58] Norway spent about the same amount on active and 'passive' (cash transfers) benefits in 2003.[59]

It is difficult to measure the societal impact of labour market programmes and vocational rehabilitation because of possible selection effects, so-called creaming. Evidence studies suggest the likelihood of limited positive effects mainly due to lock-in effects and substitution effects.[60] Positive effects are greatest during an upturn of the economy. However, programme participants like them because they get the chance to meet others in the same situation and they increase work motivation. Vocational rehabilitation has not reduced the inflow into disability schemes. In recent years, due to a decline in unemployment, labour market measures have gradually been de-escalated. An exception to this is programmes that aim at integrating vocationally disabled into the labour market.

Recent reforms

In 2000, business, labour and government signed what is known as the IA Agreement (Inclusive Working Life Agreement) where they committed themselves to reducing sick leave, getting more disabled people into the labour market and encouraging older people to work longer (increase the de facto pension age). By October 2004, companies that had signed up to the agreement employed 57 per cent of the workforce. They are called IA companies (Midtsundstad, 2005). The aim is to induce a greater sense of social responsibility in companies in both private and public sector. Subsidies help companies make the necessary modifications for a disabled person. IA com-

---

56 NOSOSCO. 2003. *Social Protection in the Nordic Countries.* Copenhagen: Nordic Statistical Committee.
57 Eurostat, 2004: European Social Statistics, *Labour market policy, Expenditure and participants,* 2006 edition (Data 2004), Eurostat.
58 Ibid.
59 ESS 2006:3 *Svensk aktiveringspolitik i nordisk perspektiv.* Stockholm: Finansdepartementet. p.19.
60 Lock-in effects refer to the risk that participants reduce their labour search activity when being on a labour market programme of long duration. Substitution effects refer to the fact even if a person in programme succeeds through participation in getting a job, another unemployed outside the programme is unsuccessful.

panies are supported by 'Worklife' centres set up in each county. An evaluation of the IA Agreement's first five years found a potential reduction in absenteeism, but that was all (St.meld. nr. 2 for 2005–2006).

In 2006, a major policy reform merged the labour market social security authorities into a single organisation called NAV (Norwegian Public Labour and Welfare Service). By 2010, a NAV service should be up and running in every municipality, sharing premises with municipal social assistance offices. This joint front-line service in every municipality will coordinate cash benefits, rehabilitation and work-related business. The basic philosophy is activation. Norway and the other Nordics have pursued active labour market policies for years (ALP), especially in times with high unemployment. With the introduction of NAV, activation has taken the new form of workfare programmes. In contrast to ALPs, which were organized centrally, workfare is managed by local authorities. And while participation used to be voluntary and rights based, it is now compulsory and needs based. Eligibility to cash benefits such as the recently introduced needs-tested qualification support hinges on one's activation performance. The authorities set therefore as a condition for enjoying one's rights to benefits a satisfactory activation record. This means in practice that one has to qualify, take further education and/or be prepared to take any job available. Cash benefits are allocated for shorter intervals at a time, and activation requirements must be met in a shorter timeframe as well. Both instance the stronger emphasis on activation. The people most affected by the new rules are the unemployed, persons on sick leave, single mothers on transitional allowance and persons on social assistance. In the event of a poor activation record, support can be reduced or withdrawn.

Immigrants have a right and duty to complete an introductory programme lasting one to three years. Participation automatically entitles the person to introduction support (*introduksjonsstønad*) (Hammer and Øverbye 2006).

Protection of unemployed and vocationally disabled

Norway's historically strong Protestant work ethic will often condition the enjoyment of social rights on past earnings, an approach which undermines the principle of universalism; 'production oriented universalism' would be an appropriate name (Edling 2006). The activation policy ('the work approach') has informed social policy making with increasing vigour of late. Instead of 'passive' income support, the present centre-left government is echoing former centre-right governments in requiring recipients of 'passive' support to be active in labour market programmes. The most recent suggestion is to require people to sign a welfare contract if they want income support – called *qualification support* – from the reorganised welfare service, NAV. This support is not needs-tested and amounts to 1625 Euro per month.

To partially compensate for loss of income from unemployment, people over 18 are entitled to *daily cash benefits while unemployed*. It is statuary social security scheme for wage earners. Eligibility hangs on registration with a local job centre, a capacity to work, consistent job seeking activity, readiness to take *any* type of part- or full-time work or join labour market scheme for which he or she is physically and mentally capable (*work test*). An unemployed person who does not fully meet the availability requirements due to circumstances such as age, health or work of caring nature may nevertheless be entitled to unemployment benefits. However, from 2006, the unemployed are not obliged to take work if the wage is lower than the unemployment benefit or they expresses a wish to be self-employed.

Unemployment benefits

Unemployment benefits have a dual function. They should provide recipients with the means to a decent standard of living, but at the same time act as an incentive to look for work more effectively and accept flexible hiring and firing procedures. The latter mechanism is supposed to increase the efficiency of the labour market. Benefits must stay below a threshold to avoid creating a disincentive to seek a new job.[61] Over-generosity could make the unemployed less eager to look for a new job or likely to refuse offers on grounds of pay, location or working conditions. The outcome could be longer unemployment periods. High levels of compensation could also undermine the standing of the unemployment benefit schemes in the eyes of the public (Halvorsen 2005). People may suspect that unemployed can get a job if they really wanted to, and that they rather prefer to live on benefits.

People who have had a paid job are eligible to unemployment benefits if their income was above a certain limit (1.5 times the Basic amount, see chapter 5) in the preceding calendar year (*contribution* period), or at least three times the Basic amount in the three preceding calendar years. Entitled to unemployment benefit only kicks after at least a 50 per cent reduction in working hours. Persons who have given notice voluntarily, refused to take a suitable job, refused to participate in labour market measures or failed to attend the employment office when summoned, may face a prolonged waiting period or temporary suspension of benefits.

The calculation of daily cash benefits is based on income from work, unemployment and other benefits during sickness, maternity or adoption. The highest benefit basis is six times the Basic amount. The benefit rate per day is 0.24 per cent of the calculation basis and is paid five days a week. There are four (reduced to three in 2008) waiting days before unemployment benefits

---

61 Yet, a comparative study suggests that generous benefits generate *stronger* commitment to take paid work (Esser 2005).

are paid. An income basis of Euro 25,000 gives a daily unemployment benefit of Euro 60. This gives normally an annual compensation (net *replacement rate*) of 62.4 per cent of the calculation basis. The higher the calculation basis, the lower the compensation. People on unemployment benefit are entitled to an extra payout known as the holiday supplement (feriepenger). In additon Euro 2 per day is granted for each dependent child under the age of 18.

The benefit *duration period* varies depending on past earnings. Earnings amounting to at least twice the Basic Amount works out as 104 weeks, while less than twice the amount equals 52 weeks.

When a person has exhausted his right to unemployment benefits he can draw a so-called 'waiting benefit' (ventestønad). It is mainly meant for labour market programme participants.[62]

Regardless of these benefits, the unemployed will frequently have financial problems, which, along with loss of self-respect, cause psychological distress (Halvorsen 2004). Somewhat higher levels of compensation could reduce distress, increase job seeking efficiency and a better match between jobseekers and employers.

There has been a marked fall in the number of unemployed claiming unemployment benefit, from 63 per cent in 2004 to 48 per cent in 2006.[63] This is the result of stricter eligibility criteria such as contribution period i.e. minimum length of participation in paid work in a given time span. It indicates that the unemployed are increasingly likely to be newcomers to the labour market and ineligible for unemployment benefit.

Compared to other countries, the Norwegian unemployment benefit scheme is not particularly generous when it comes to criteria of eligibility (especially the contribution period), levels of compensation and duration of benefits (see table 3.4). Self-employed (under the age of 64), youths (students) and the most vulnerable are excluded from the scheme.

As in most other countries criteria in Norway require the claimant to be involuntarily unemployed, to search actively for employment, to have signed on at the jobs centre, be ready and willing to take work, and be available for the labour market. In almost all countries levels of compensation have an upper limit. Those who do not qualify for an earnings-related benefit are entitled to a flat rate and means-tested social assistance allowance. In contrast to the *compulsory* unemployment insurance scheme in Norway, the other Nordic countries (included Finland) have retained their voluntary schemes (Edling, 2006).

---

62 www.odin.no
63 www.nav.no/tables, accessed 9.10.07.

Table 3.4 Unemployment benefits in selected countries (1.1.2006)

	Norway	Sweden	Denmark	Germany	France	United Kingdom
Duration	104 weeks (52 weeks if income below twice the Basic amount)	300 days (can be prolonged up to 600 days)	4 years	Dependent on the duration of compulsory insurance coverage and the age of the beneficiary (up to 18 months for new entitlements after 1 February 2006)	Dependent on the duration of length of insurance: Minimum 7 months, maximum 42 months	Contribution-based Job-seekers' allowance: 182 days Income-based Job-seekers Allowance: Unlimited duration as long as entitlement conditions continue to be satisfied
Levels of compensation	62.4%	80% of reference earnings	Based on average earnings of preceding 12 weeks, 90% of reference earnings	67% of net earnings (60% for beneficiaries without children)	75% of former daily salary	Flat Rate benefit
Child supplement	Yes	No	No	Yes		No

Source: Mutual Information System on Social Protection in the EU Member States and the EEA (MISSOC) 2006.

Persons without minimum earnings to entitle them to unemployment benefits (or have not had paid work last three years) are typically students, persons on vocational rehabilitation, housewives and immigrants. They have to apply for social assistance with their local authorities (see chapter 7). Young, able-bodied persons on social assistance have to pass the same work test as unemployment benefit recipients. In addition, the Social Services Act allows local councils to require beneficiaries to work up to 15 hours a week, i.e. workfare (see chapter 7).

Benefits during vocational rehabilitation

A person may be entitled to benefits during vocational rehabilitation if he or she is resident in Norway and has been employed for three years immediately prior to filing a benefit claim.

Vocational rehabilitation allowance is granted to persons between 19 and 67 whose ability to obtain income from work or occupational choice are permanently reduced by at least 50 per cent due to illness, injury or incapacity. Vocational rehabilitation is granted while the person is in vocational training, during waiting periods before vocational rehabilitation or up to six months (there have been calls to halve the period in 2008) after the vocational rehabilitation or while she applies for suitable work.

Compensation usually works out at around 58 per cent of expected earnings (Røed 2006). The rehabilitation allowance is calculated on the basis of the highest income of the preceding calendar year or the average of the three calendar years before incapacitation. The maximum benefit basis is six times the Basic amount. The annual benefit rate is 66 per cent of the calculation basis. For persons on no or low pensionable income, a minimum yearly benefit 1.8 times the Basic amount is provided. A supplement of Euro 3.35 per day is granted for each dependent child under the age of 18. Maximum benefits may not exceed 90 per cent of the calculation basis.[64] The current centre-left government would like to get rid of the medical rehabilitation allowance, vocational rehabilitation allowance and time limited disability pension, replacing them with a time-limited work-related income benefit (St.meld. nr. 9 for 2006–2007).

The average number of disabled persons registered with the jobs centre and under consideration for vocational rehabilitation was 89,500 in 2006.[65] The majority were already receiving vocational rehabilitation allowance. Despite high demand for labour, there has only been a moderate decrease in the number of persons on vocational rehabilitation, a reflection of the great number of persons of working age outside the labour market (700,000), for health and/or social reasons.

Challenges

The high female labour force participation rate, combined with one of the highest fertility rates in Western Europe, testifies to the success of the Norwegian welfare state (Esping-Andersen, 1996). On the other hand, Norway's labour market is highly gendered, with female jobs concentrated in the public sector and private service sector, and/or in less well-paid professions such as nursing or pre-school teachers, whereas the majority of men work in the private sector and/or in better paid management positions. In 2003, 61 per cent of men in private sector were employed in male-dominated businesses (85 per cent or more were men) (Teigen, 2006).

Norway also faces two other challenges to employment policy and the la-

---

64 www.odin.no
65 St.prp. nr. 1 2007-2008 *Arbeids- og inkluderingsdepartementets budsjett for 2008.*

bour market – demographic trends and a huge budget surplus because of the oil fund.

An ageing working force and smaller entry-level cohorts represents a huge labour market challenge in a situation with a significant labour shortfall, especially in the public health and care sector. Non-employed people of working age will need to be enticed to join the labour market to meet this increased demand. Increased immigration will be necessary too. Given the very low unemployment figures, excessive wage increases are likely, some economists fear, to fuel inflation and harm competitiveness particularly for export-oriented companies, create unemployment and destroy important sectors of the industrial base. A necessary overhaul of the economy means redundancies and early retirement of older workers. These people will have to be transferred and equipped to do jobs in other industries, and often in a different part of the country. Should older workers remain in the labour force until the age of 67 (OECD, 2006)? That's the challenge. The draft pension reform (see chapter 5) must be seen in relation to this challenge, not least because it recommends incentives to get people to work past normal retirement age, a policy most of the political parties are in favour of.

There is also a potential labour reserve among female part-timers. Flexible working hours and equal parenthood policies could help tap into this potential. Finally, the NAV reform and the IA Agreement are expected to cut the number of persons claiming disability pensions and sickness benefits. One right-wing party (Fremskrittspartiet) is already voicing opposition to immigration hikes – though they condone guest workers on short-term contracts. The present centre-left government is also worried about the low percentage of first-generation immigrants in the labour force, namely 57.5 per cent as compared with 69.4 per cent in the whole population.[66] Only higher fertility rates – which are unlikely – can solve the long-term problem of ageing population and shortage of labour.

The fortunate economic situation that was described in chapter 2 represents another challenge. Many Norwegians fail to understand why the government refuses to spend more on people's everyday problems – like waiting lists for treatment, child and elderly care, traffic congestion, etc. However, this can't be done without creating more jobs – particularly in the public sector – which would increase the need for manpower. If many more jobs were created, it could sap the industrial sector for manpower and harm the industrial base of Norway. Besides, it would probably tighten the economy, prompting over-generous wage settlements, damaging the international competitiveness of export-oriented sector.

---

66 www.ssb.no/innvrgesys/main html)

Chapter 4
Families: At work?

The family is one of the most important social welfare institutions. It is where primary socialization takes place, income redistributed and the needy cared for – in Scandinavia that means children in particular. It is a place for the maintenance and the reproduction of labour. The role of the family is significantly different in different parts of the world and in different welfare regimes in Europe as well, but all modern welfare states have some kind of family policy, however different in substance and scope.

In this chapter we shall discuss family structure and family policy in Norway. First, we describe the historic evolution of modern family policy before looking at the family structure and family policy in a comparative perspective. We round off with a discussion of some of the pertinent challenges.

The development of family policy

Family policy can have several different objectives:
- Reduce poverty and improve living conditions for young families
- Improve living conditions for children
- Facilitate higher fertility and reproduction of the population
- Afford preferential treatment to a certain kind of living arrangement, union and family
- Make it easier for women with children to work outside the home
- Create more equality between men and women in care and domestic work
- Childcare and schooling in preparation for participation in tomorrow's knowledge economy.

Today, modern family policy provides for two different kinds of support to families – cash transfers and social services. Welfare regimes and political parties will balance these objectives and the means to achieve them differently. In the early phases of family policy in Scandinavia, young families were supported economically as an important way of reducing poverty and creating greater equality in living conditions between families. Today, helping women reconcile paid employment with the demands of motherhood and encouraging men to shoulder more of the practical care of children are the leading policy aims, increasing the role of the social services and mechanisms like maternal and parental leave.

The first modern legislation on the family was the 1892 Act which required both parents to support their children and the father to contribute a maternity grant. As mentioned in chapter 1, in 1915 new – and for the time – radical laws gave illegitimate children the same right as legitimate to inherit the father and bear his name.

The first real universal benefits in Norwegian social policy were the child benefits that were introduced in 1946. Now, every family was entitled to monthly cash support from the second child. In 1970 this was extended to the first child as well. In the succeeding years, cash transfers through child benefits were seen as an integral part of tax policy.

In the mid-1960s, motherhood started to change. A growing number of mothers started working outside the home, mostly part time. As in other countries, the student revolt of the late 1960s and early 1970s hastened changes in gender relations and family ideology. Female participation in the labour market increased, while the 1980s saw women enter full-time jobs in numbers (Ellingsæter and Gulbrandsen, 2007). Family setups with a male breadwinner and female housekeeper were gradually replaced by a dual earner family with both in employment, although the women tended still to work part time.

In the same period, first-time mothers became older; women did not give birth to as many children as before and the rate of divorce increased – partly because new contraceptives and free abortion made family planning easier. The rate of marriage decreased, and many young people preferred living together without being married. These changes took place earlier in Scandinavia than in other European countries, although Norway lagged somewhat behind Sweden and Denmark (Noack, 2004). The proportion of women in higher education increased, and gender emancipation moved onto the political agenda. These changes in the family structure influenced the welfare state as well. In 1972, the Storting decided to establish a council on gender emancipation, and in 1978 a law on gender emancipation followed (see table 4.1).

Table 4.1 Family reforms in Norway 1892 – 2005

1892	The first laws on children	Obliged both parents to provide for their children. Obliged the father to a maternity grant to the mother
1915	Castberg's laws on children	Gave children born out of wedlock the right to inherit the father and carry his name
1919	Benefits to widows and mothers	Introduced in some municipalities (Oslo and others)
1946	Child benefits	Benefits to all families from the second child
1957	Widow pension and transitional allowance	To children of widows and single mothers on a discretionary basis
1966	Widow pension and child pension	Pension based on the husband's income. Pension to the children when their parents died
1970	Child benefits extended	Benefits to the first child as well
1971-80	Transitional allowance	Divorced and separated were included
1972	Council on emancipation	Established
1975	Law on day care	Goal: day care for all children
1978	Law on abortion	Women achieve the right to decide the first three months of pregnancy
1978	Law on emancipation	Discrimination against women forbidden
1987-93	Parental leave	Gradual extension to 42 weeks with 100 per cent compensation
1976-	Day care	Increased and continuous building of day care facilities
1993	Cohabitation	Regulating certain financial aspects of cohabitation
1993	Partnership between homosexuals	Registered partnership gives homosexuals the same legal rights and duties as a married couple
1998	Cash for care	To parents that do not use day care for one year old children (the next year extended also to two year old children)
1998	Transitional allowance	Reduced entitlements for single mothers: Maximum three years when children are under eight and obligation to seek work
2004	Price of day care	Political compromise to reduce the costs of day care
2005	Price of day care	A maximum price for place in day care introduced
2008?	Universal day care	Full coverage of day care for children 3-6?

Source: Based on Skevik (2004) and developed further by the authors.

Free abortion had been an issue since 1913, as abortions were often carried out in unhealthy and dangerous circumstances. In 1964, the Storting passed a law allowing for legal abortion. However, it also required the woman to make her case before a committee of two medical doctors, most often men, with the power to veto her application. Many women found this humiliating, and the new feminist movement of the 1970s campaigned for free abortion. As more women were elected to Parliament, a more liberal atmosphere changed the ideological climate. Despite vocal opposition from the Christian People's Party, and other conservative parties, in 1978, free abortion up until the end of the twelfth week of pregnancy was passed into law. Beyond twelve weeks, a committee would decide, and beyond eighteen weeks abortions could only take place on the most urgent grounds. The number of abortions has been stable the last 25–30 years (around 14–15 000 each year) but as the number of fertile women has increased, the *rate* of abortions has actually decreased in practice.

Towards a modern family policy

Women's march into the labour market was only slowly accompanied by policies tailored to reconcile the combined role of wage-earner and mother (Leira, 2006). In 1975, the Storting approved a law on day care. Although the number of day care places grew, it was mostly part time places for children aged five to six (Ellingsæter and Gulbrandsen, 2007). Whereas Denmark and Sweden forged ahead in extending coverage, Norway continued to lag behind. This was due to structural and political differences between Norway and her Scandinavian neighbours. Norway was and is less urbanized, and whereas Swedish social democracy was ideologically addressing the emancipation of women as early as in the 1930s, the Norwegian Labour Party was more traditional in this respect. Besides, the existence of a political party rooted in Christian pietism did much to preserve traditional gender roles and family ideology longer in Norway. So while employment and family policies were integrated in the neighbouring countries at an early date, this was not the case for Norway.

A breakthrough for a woman and family-friendly social policy came with the premiership of Gro Harlem Brundtland, at the head of a Labour government, in 1981 (see chapter 1). Her second government, from 1986, consisted of 44 per cent women, which at that time – and even now in most countries – was most unusual. The years to come witnessed an offensive in terms of women- and family friendly politics – both by the Brundtland governments and succeeding non-socialist coalition governments. A programme for establishing day care institutions was approved, and from the beginning of the 1980s maternal leave was gradually expanded from 18 to 42 weeks with 100 per cent compensation in 1993 – or alternatively 52 weeks with 80 per cent compensation. In the 1990s several reforms were implemented to give parents the opportunity to spend more time together with their children.

The real day care offensive came in the 1990s (Leira, 2006). The 1992 day care reform launched by the non-socialist coalition government (KrF, Sp, V) aimed at giving families a real choice between day care and home care. By 2007, Norway had almost caught up with her neighbours in providing daycare for children aged 3–5, but is still lagging behind for the under-threes (see chapter 9). As in Sweden, fathers were expected to take parental leave as well; the maximum time was later expanded to six weeks. The red-green government which came into power in 2005 promised full day care coverage. At the same time, it promised to reduce the price of day care. This combined goal became a moving target, as demand continued to grow. However, massive investments will probably result in full coverage very soon – and Norway will have caught up with Denmark and Sweden. Thus, the centre-left parties demonstrated that family policy should not only be about economic transfers, but about promoting female labour market participation and more gender emancipation in family life.

Counter-attack: 'Freedom of choice'

Although the day care is now uncontroversial and accepted even by KrF, family policy is still an arena of struggle. In the election campaign in 1997, KrF and the other non-socialist parties campaigned for a *cash for care* package for families with children. Not all parents want to put their infants (the under threes) into state-financed day care centre, they argued. These parents should be given money instead, a sum equivalent to the cost of a place in a day care institution. Parents should have a free choice between different forms of day care – public and private day care, one of the parents staying at home, etc. The Labour Party and SV were afraid that women in low paid work would be tempted to stay at home with the children for the sake of the money. But they would be trapped again in a traditional gender role, and lose the chance to earn pension credits. It would slow the integration of immigrant women even more. And if enough women left the workplace, the supply of labour supply would tighten, according to concerned economists. However, KrF and its partners won the 1997 election and went ahead with their cash for care reform when in government (Leira, 2002). Evaluation research some years later showed that the arguments of both sides were rather exaggerated in the event (Ellingsæter 2003). However, later research argues that the effect of cash for care is that mothers decreased their working time considerably and with almost 20 per cent in the period from 2002 to 2002 (Rønsen, 2005). The current red green government has pledged to end the cash for care benefit when day care is universally available, but will sustain it in part from 2005 to 2009.

Although everybody wants participation in the labour market to increase, the controversy over cash for care does show lack of agreement on whether the welfare state should support one particular family model – the dual earner family. The classic left–right cleavage on the degree of state involvement in civil society continues. Whereas the centre-left argues for public family policy which enables mothers to work outside the home, and fathers to shoulder more of the duties at home, the centre-right wants to give families a free choice, and allow mothers to stay at home when the children are small if that's what they want. This conflict is probably going to be permanent in family policy.

A comprehensive and generous family policy

The development we have just described means that Norway has a more comprehensive and generous family policy than most other European countries. Table 4.2 illustrates the relative priority that Norway gives to benefits and services to the family.

Table 4.2 Expenditure on families and children as percentages of GDP (2001), power purchasing parity (US$) and total social expenditure (2002)

	Norway	Sweden	Denmark	UK	Germany	France	Italy	US
Of GDP	3.2	2.9	3.8	2.2	1.9	2.8	1.0	0.4
PPP per capita	1173	1016	1108	134	487	746	249	134
Of total social expenditure	12.2	9.7	13.4	6.7	10.7	9.3	3.9	–

Sources: OECD Social Expenditure Database 1980–2001; NOSOSCO 2003.

By most indicators, Norway spends more than other countries except Denmark on families and children, and public expenditure also constitutes a larger percentage of total social expenditure relative to other nations. In Western Europe, the UK and countries in Southern Europe are the low spenders. Norway spends more than three times as much of its GDP than Italy and almost 50 per cent more than the UK on families and children. We saw in chapter 3 that the female employment rate is higher in Norway and Scandinavia than in other countries. At the same time, the fertility rate is higher in countries where women take part in the labour market.[67] Thus, the invest-

---

67 See 'Key statistics. Extending opportunities: How active social policy can benefit us all (www.oecd.org/socialmin 2005. Accessed Februar 28 2006).

ment in social benefits and services makes it easier to combine paid work and care for the children.

Demography and family structure

The family structure in Norway as in other Scandinavian countries has changed significantly the last 50 years. The average number of persons per household has decreased from 3.3 in 1960 to 2.2 in 2007. More are living alone (4.3 per cent in 1960, 17.3 per cent in 2007).[68] This is not because people don't want to be in a relationship, but because an increasing number of marriages and cohabiting unions break down (Noack and Seierstad, 2003). The rate of divorce is much higher than it was, with 20 out of every 1,000 married couples under 40 filing for divorce each year (Noack, 2004). Based on the present frequency of divorce, Statistics Norway estimates a fifty per cent dissolution rate of marriages entered into today.[69] However, many of those who divorce or leave a relationship find themselves another partner after living alone a shorter or longer period.

It is now normal for people, particularly the young, to live together without being married. Every fifth cohabiting couple is not married, and most of them might be considered a marriage.[70] Every second person aged 20–79 has personal experience of cohabitation (Noack, 2003). 40 per cent of all children are born out of wedlock. Gradually, cohabitation has come to be regarded more on par with marriage in law and in terms of social benefits.

The age of women giving birth to their first child has increased steadily from 23 in 1967 to 27.5 today. In the last 50 years, fertility has decreased in most countries in Western Europe. This was the case in the Nordic countries in the 1960s and 1970s as well, but here the tendency reversed in the mid 1980s when the fertility increased again (Lappegård, 2007).

Table 4.3 shows that the fertility today is clearly higher in Norway than in most other countries in Western Europe (except France) – particularly in Italy. An OECD analysis maintains that the reduction of the fertility rates is due to two types of change. First, higher education and increased employment among women have changed family formation. Second, values among younger women have changed and made women less supportive of the traditional role of women in the home (d'Addio and Ercole, 2005).

---

68 Statistics Norway, http://www.ssb.no/emner/02/01/20/familie/, accessed 06/09/2007.
69 http://www.ssb.no/emner/02/02/30/ekteskap/arkiv/, accessed at May 29 2007.
70 Defined as couples that have lived together more than two years, Noack, T. (2003). «Dagligdags og uutforsket.» Samfunnsspeilet 1.

Table 4.3 Fertility – births per woman in fertile age 2006

Norway	Denmark	UK	Germany	France	Italy	US	EU	China	Japan	Tanzania
1.78	1.74	1.66	1.39	1.84	1.28	2.09	1.47	1.73	1.40	4.97

Source: CIA Factbook, http://www.odci.gov/cia/publications/factbook/rankorder/2127rank.html.

Although changes in family structure are more pronounced in Norway than elsewhere in Europe, the fertility rate is also somewhat higher (see table 4.3).

Scandinavian women are more fertile than women in other European countries – except in France – probably because family policy is more extensive and views of the family more liberal. There is nothing special about having children out of wedlock, nor, logically about young non-married women giving birth. Even the female minister of oil in a centre right government with a Christian Prime Minister had a baby with a father whose name is not publicly known. The OECD analysis concludes that many countries could increase their fertility rate by introducing a more active family policy with child benefits, tax credits, reduction of the costs of having children, better day care facilities and longer parental leave. Countries such as Japan, the UK, US and Korea could increase fertility rates by 2.0 – 2.4 per cent if they lowered the cost of having children, increased the length of parental leave, developed better child care, and increased opportunity for part-time work (d'Addio, 2005).

The 'Nordic pattern of fertility' has women giving birth to the first baby later, and continuing to give birth longer, than in many other countries. At the same time, there are increasing differences between women, both in terms of when they give birth and how many children they get (Lappegård, 2007).

Some researchers maintain that the positive effects of the extensive family policy on fertility rates in Norway are somewhat exaggerated. Rønsen and Skrede (2006) explain the relatively high fertility rate largely as an effect of the gender-segregated labour market, insofar as we find higher fertility rates particularly among part time public sector nurses and teachers. Long parental leave and generous family benefits for professional women in the public sector seem to agree more with their career ambitions than private sector provisions. These women are often in part time jobs and do more of the housework than their husbands. A falling fertility rate among these well-educated groups in the public sector may indicate lack of satisfaction with the 'gender equality light' version of emancipation which still is found in Norway. A sustainable fertility pattern, these researchers argue, would not only need effective mechanisms allowing women to combine work and motherhood, but also a change of norms to strengthen gender equality.

Family benefits in perspective

Modern family policy consists of a bundle of measures aimed at supporting families and reconciling family life and employment: cash transfers, tax rebates, parental leave, day care. We shall describe cash transfers and parental leave below, but day care is discussed in chapter 9 in connection with municipal social welfare.

Child benefits, transitional allowance, and cash for care

There are two ways of improving the financial situation of families with children – cash in hand and tax deductions. Both are pegged to the number and age of children in the family. Besides, the government can subsidize services for children. Both tax deductions and direct transfers have been used by Norwegian family policy. Tax deductions will normally favour the traditional male breadwinner family and housewife model, as high earning men will benefit more, and make it relatively less advantageous for women to take low paid or part time employment. Direct cash transfers such as universal child benefit do not constitute disincentives to female employment in this respect. Universal child benefit means that families and single parents receive a monthly sum from the government irrespective of their financial situation.

In 2000, eligibility for child benefit was extended to all children aged 16 and 17 as well. However, in 1996 child benefit, particularly for multi-children families, was reduced. In 2004, these cuts equalled the cost of cash for care (see below) (Epland and Kirkeberg, 2007). In 2005, the child benefit rate was NOK 970 (122 euros) per month for each child younger than 18. Single parents receive an additional NOK 660 (83 euros) per month per child. Child benefit is not taxable.

Child benefit is higher in Norway than in most other countries in Western Europe – particularly the UK and Italy (table 4.4).

Transitional allowance makes it possible for single parents – mostly mothers – to stay at home with their children. A lone mother or father can claim benefits for three years altogether until the youngest child is eight, but longer if the person is in training, is sick or the child is sick. Income from part time work will be deducted. Child care benefit was NOK 2,850 a month for one child and 3,718 for two children (2006, not taxable). 27,000 persons, mostly women, receive transitional allowance (2005). The median time reception of transitional allowance is 14 months, but one third of the recipients take up benefits more than one period. Persons who have taken up transitional allowance have lower income and fewer assets than other single parents. When the transitional allowance expires, they often end up in part time work or low paid jobs or on other social benefits such as social assistance or disability pension. However, if a secondary or higher education is completed during the transitional allowance period, their economic prospects tend to improve significantly (Dahl, 2003).

Table 4.4 Child benefits 2005

	NOK per month per child	Age limit
Germany	1241	18–27
France	466–1194	20
Italy	Calculated on the basis of income and family members	18
UK	564–846	16–19
Sweden	817	16
Denmark	846 – 1190	18
Norway	970	18

Germany: Age limit 27 when a young person is in vocational training or in higher education, and no age limit when handicapped.
France: The amount per child increases with the number of children.
Denmark: The amount is 1190 NOK for a child 0–3 years and is reduced as the child becomes older.
Sweden (2004): Increasing supplements for the third, fourth etc child – e.g. NOK 218 for the third child.
UK (2004): 846 NOK for the first child and other children NOK 564. Age limit 19 for children in non-advanced education.
Italy (2004): Example: A family with two children will receive NOK 2018 a month if the yearly income is less than NOK 92 000 and 312 NOK a month if the income is 223 000 – NOK 245 000 a year.

In 2008, *cash for care* (cf. above) to families without children aged 1–2 in day care is 3,303 NOK a month. If the child is in day care for a few hours per day/week, the equivalent amount is deducted from the benefit, gradually falling to zero as day care increases to the maximum. As mentioned above, the introduction of cash for care was accompanied by a reduction in child benefit. In other words, the reform really redistributed cash transfers from families with children of all ages to families with children under three who weren't in day care.

In 2006, 48 per cent of parents with children under three received cash for care benefit – a clear reduction from the 75 per cent of 1999 (Ellingsæter and Gulbrandsen, 2007). This downward trend is probably due to the great popularity of public day care and continuing expansion of day care provision.

Parental leave

As with day care, a system of leave of absence makes it less difficult for parents to combine parenthood and employment. Between 1987 and 1994, maternal leave improved in several respects. When a child is born, working parents can stay aware from work for 44 weeks without loss of income – or 54 weeks at an 80 per cent income rate. There is an income ceiling, however. Nine weeks are reserved for the mother and six for the father; the rest can be freely divided between them. The 'daddy quota' is used by almost all fathers (90 per cent in 2003), though only 14 per cent of fathers stay at home with the children for more than the designated number of weeks. Norway was the first country to introduce a quota which, if not taken, is lost (see table 4.5).

Table 4.5 Entitlements to maternal and paternal leave in 2005–2006

	Weeks for the mother (before + after birth)	Weeks for the father	Optional	Sum	Compensation as a per cent of wage
Germany	6+8=14			14	Max NOK 108 per day
France	6+10			16	80 %
Italy	20				80 %
UK	18			18	90 % in 6 weeks, then 946 NOK per week
Sweden	7+	10 days	69	77	80 %
Denmark	4+14=18	2 weeks	32	52	100 %, but max. NOK 3463 per week
Norway	3+6=9	6 weeks	29	44	100 %, but of max. 325 000 NOK a year

Source: Missoc 2004 and 2005. Figures for Norway 2006. Parents can choose a leave of 54 weeks with 80 per cent compensation or a leave of 44 weeks with 100 per cent compensation.
Norway: Alternatively 52 weeks with 80 per cent compensation.
Sweden (2003): 50 days for the mother before birth and 480 days for the parents after birth. Compensation is 80 per cent of wage for 390 days and 90 days at a reduced rate.
UK: 2003.

At the same time, a 'time account' was introduced. This makes it possible to extend leave up to two years and combine maternal or paternal leave with different degrees of part time work. However, only a tiny fraction of parents uses this opportunity (2.2 per cent of mothers and 0.9 per cent of fathers in 2003) (Brandt, Bungum et. al. 2005).

The daddy quota shows the ability of public family policy to influence parental behaviour in a way regarded desirable by the government – in this case to encourage men to take more responsibility for their children and achieve a better balance between the amount of childcare provided by mothers and fathers.

Conclusion: The characteristics of family policy

Norwegian family policy has developed from being mainly concerned with cash support and universal child benefits in the years after World War II to a wide range of policy instruments: cash transfers, social services, and parental leave – in sum a family policy which as in the other Nordic countries is more extensive than in other welfare states. Today family policy seeks to improve the living conditions of children and provide for their socialization in day care and schools as an investment in the future. Family policy seeks to enable women to combine the role of the wage-earner who contributes to the wealth of the country with the role of the mother who takes care of her children. This is in contrast to the family policy of Germany and Italy. Finally, family policy promotes gender equality in the care of children.

Two distinctive characteristics set off modern family policy in Scandinavia from similar policies in Europe: First, there is an emphasis on gender emancipation and participation in the labour market. Second, the Scandinavian family enjoys a high degree of individualized rights.

In Europe, there exist three family policy models. One supports a dual earner family, the second a traditional male breadwinner family, while the third lets families or the market find their own solutions (Ellingsæter, 2006). The Scandinavian welfare state belongs to the first type. This welfare state is more 'woman-friendly' than other European welfare states (Leira, 2002). Family policy is intended to support gender emancipation. Family policy has facilitated increased female participation in the labour market while stimulating gender equality in the care of children, as we saw with the daddy quota (cf. above). Social democratic ideology has long emphasized female emancipation. Arrangements such as parental leave are in harmony with the 'work approach' because it makes it easier for both parents to return to work. It encourages housework and childcare equality as well. As the parental leave benefits of the male spouse are related to his wage, it acts as an incentive for him to stay at home while she returns to work. Although the last decades have brought an increasing emancipation between men and women in unpaid domestic work, women still bear the brunt of household chores. In 2000, women did two thirds and men one third of the work (Kitterød, 2002). Nevertheless, Norwegian women and men are more likely to share housework than couples on the Continent (Geist, 2005).

Again though, compared to Sweden and Denmark, Norwegian social policy has not always been without a certain duality. While it embraces the 'work approach', we can observe a 'family approach' as well. Cash for care, which is not related to past work (see above) aims at supporting the role of the family as a producer of care (Brandt et al., 2005). This 'dualism' or paradox derives from the constellation of parties in Norwegian politics – particularly the role of KrF. Whereas the Labour Party and parties to the left have supported mechanisms which promote gender equality and enable parents to both work and raise a family, the right have insisted on children's need for parental care (Ellingsæter, 2006), and supported cash benefit solutions rather than parental leave, for instance. These differences are set to stay for a while.

Table 4.6 compares attitudes to work, gender and family in six European countries.

Table 4.6 Reconciliation of work and family life. Attitudes in six European nations. Per cent who agree and agree strongly with different statements[71]

	Norway	Sweden	Denmark	Germany	France	UK
Both should contribute to income	72	84	77	77	74	61
Work is best for women's independence	45	63	80	80	81	55
Men's work is job, women's is household	9	8	14	21	18	19
Family life suffers when the woman is working	29	26	29	42	45	37

Source: ISSP 2002

We notice a certain ambiguity in attitudes in Norway. On the one hand, the idea that work is best for women's independence is less widely acknowledged in Norway than in the other five countries, and the same seems to be the case, although more weakly, when it comes to the idea that both spouses should contribute to income. On these two indicators, Norway differs from the other Nordic countries too. On the other hand, people in Norway, Sweden and Denmark are clearly less likely than people in Germany, France and the UK to agree with the statement that men should be the breadwinners, women the housekeepers and that family life suffers when the woman works outside the home. This ambiguity of public opinion can probably be related to the 'dualism' of Norwegian family policy.

---

71 *Norwegian Social Science Data Services* has made available these data from the *International Social Survey Programme Family and Gender Roles 2002*. The NSD has no responsibility for the analysis or the interpretation of data.

Compared to other European nations, Norwegian family policy combines a pro-active approach with a high degree of individualism. Certainly, partners have a reciprocal obligation to provide for one another, but the family has a weaker legal obligation to take care of other members than in many other nations – particularly on the continent and in Southern Europe. For instance, parents are not obliged to support their children financially after they turn 18 or leave secondary school, even if they go on to study at university. From 18 years, students can apply for a loan and grants from the Norwegian State Educational Loan Fund (a state bank). If they are not studying, they are entitled to social assistance (see chapter 7) (or unemployment benefit under certain criteria). Moreover, the social welfare agency cannot inform the person's parents that they have filed for social assistance. Young persons leave home at an earlier age in Norway than in other countries. Only 35 per cent of the 20–24 age group lives with their parents, whereas 86 per cent do in Southern Europe and 51 per cent in Central Europe. Virtually none over the age of 25, live with their parents (Hellevik, 2005).

In Norway, unlike Germany, Austria and Greece, there is no legal obligation on the family to support parents should they lose the ability to take care of themselves. The introduction of a universal old age pension in 1936 handed responsibility for the financial well being of the elderly to the state, and the moral obligation to support old parents financially became weaker. When one's aged parents fall ill or are disabled and no longer able to take care of themselves, local authorities provide assistance in the home (home helps and home support of different kinds) and at a certain point of time take the old person into a nursing home (see chapter 9).

This legal individualism does not mean that parents don't help their grown-up children or that they in turn don't help their parents when the need arises. Many children receive parental help during their studies. 50 per cent of 18–21-year-olds receive some parental support; the percentage falls with increasing age, of course. 29 per cent of persons aged 26–29 received financial support from their parents in the last year (Hellevik, 2005). Besides, it is not uncommon for parents to help their offspring buy a place to live. About 70 per cent of young persons have received such support (Andersen and Gulbrandsen, 2006). At the same time, most people help their parents out in different ways, especially in old age, sickness and disability – looking after them, running errands, providing transport, making repairs and generally keeping them happy. And grandparents are increasingly helping their children and grandchildren in practical and economic ways.

Table 4.7 Unpaid help to a relation outside the household (own children not included). Type of help includes care, housework and household repairs. In per cent

	Once a week or more	Less often than once a week, but at least once a year	Never
Norway	19	59	22
Denmark	13	44	43
Sweden	16	47	37
Netherlands	17	35	48
Germany	18	42	40
UK	22	27	51
France	16	34	50
Spain	9	24	67

Source: ESS 2004.

As table 4.7 indicates, Norwegians are more likely to help relations outside the household than citizens of other European countries. Only 22 per cent say that they never do this, half the percentage of these other countries; 19 per cent say that they give help once a week or more often – which is second only to the British.

The substitution theory – that public services crowd out family assistance – was challenged by the *family support theory*, according to which formal services actually strengthen family care by sharing care burdens. Very often care responsibilities are shared between families and the welfare state. *The task-specific model* sees the two parties as providing different kind of support (Kröger, 2005). The volume of family care has remained stable in periods of welfare state expansion as well as in periods of welfare state contraction (Lingsom, 1997). The family acts as a buffer by coping with some of the deficiencies in formal care services (Wærness, 1990). Nevertheless, compared to England, Germany, Spain and Israel, Norway has the highest number of elderly totally dependent on the welfare state for help. But the number of older people cared for by their family is higher in Norway than in Spain and Israel and very close to the levels of Germany and England (Daatland and Herlofson, 2004).

Thus, individualism must not be misinterpreted as egoism and narcissism. A comparative analysis of the relationship between the family and the welfare state found no important differences between Norway and Catholic-conservative welfare states such as Germany and Spain in terms of intergenerational family solidarity (Daatland and Lowenstein, 2005). The public social services for the elderly do not crowd out help from the family, but help families cope with the problems and challenges of daily life. But it has changed relations between family members of different generations (see chapter 9). In Norway, the elderly are supported by the family and welfare state, whereas the family dominates in Germany, Spain and the UK. This gives the elderly more autonomy and establishes a different combination of independence and responsibility from what is found in conservative and liberal welfare regimes – a situation that is preferred by the elderly as well.

Chapter 5
Security in old age: Protecting the frail and elderly

Social benefits to the elderly and disabled constitute the cornerstone of a welfare state. Persons who are no longer able to work due to their age are no longer reliant on the support of their children to cope financially. Thanks to the disability pension, people with a reduced capacity for work can also enjoy a decent albeit a modest standard of living. This chapter describes the principles of old age pension and disability pension/rehabilitation allowance under the National Social Insurance Scheme. Who is entitled and how much do they get? What are the challenges to the present old age pension system, and what can explain the sudden rise in the number of people of working age drawing disability benefits?

Historical background

The earliest old age pension schemes were introduced in some municipalities at the end of nineteenth century. A nationwide old age pension scheme passed through parliament in 1923, but was not implemented until 1936. This was a modest and means-tested scheme. Means-testing of old age pensioners was abolished in 1957. Before the old age pension existed, old people lived on their assets and savings and/or were supported by their families. Persons without families depended on charity, the church, and (from 1741) on public poor relief in the parish (later in the municipalities). As mentioned in chapter 1, social security for loss of earnings due to accidents, sickness, unemployment or old age was being discussed by 1885. A commission set up by parliament suggested several schemes. A work injury benefit scheme for manufacturing workers was established in 1894, and a sickness benefit scheme for low paid workers in 1907 (implemented in 1911).

Before World War II, parliament debated regularly the practicalities of providing an old age pension scheme. One issue was whether it should be a public or private undertaking. Another related to financing: should it be based on the principle of 'pay-as-you-go' or should it be funded? A third was whether a public old age pension should provide more than basic security or income maintenance. These questions are still with us. Unlike the German old age pension scheme, where only those in paid work are included, the Norwegian scheme is universal in principle for all persons above the age of 67. This means that women have inalienable pensions rights as *citizens*, not as wives or mothers (Petersen and Åmark 2006). Disability pension was introduced in 1961 along with rehabilitation allowance (see chapter 3). These benefits were included in the National Insurance Scheme in 1967.

The present system

All residents of Norway or people working in Norway or on permanent or movable installations on the Norwegian continental shelf, are *compulsorily* covered under the National Insurance Scheme. Compulsorily insured are also certain categories of Norwegian citizens working abroad.[72] Compulsory means that they have to contribute by paying premiums when in paid work, but get in return pensions or benefits when and if required.

Persons covered under the National Insurance Scheme are entitled to old age, survivor's and disability pensions, benefits to single parents (see chapter 4), cash benefits in case of sickness (chapter 6), maternity, adoption (see chapter 4), unemployment (see chapter 3), and medical benefits in case of sickness and maternity (see chapter 6). Funeral grants and attendance benefit in case of disablement and are also part of the scheme, but are not further outlined here. Employers are compelled to buy *occupational injury insurance* in private insurance companies.

Many benefits under the National Insurance Scheme have a floor. Parliament sets the floor each year in response to general income level fluctuations, and in consultation with the business, labour and organisations of the disabled and old age pensioners (Øverbye et al. 2006). The floor was 8352 euros as of May 1 2007.[73]

The national social insurance scheme for the *working-age* population is based on four main principles: compensation for loss of income; earnings testing; individuality; and rehabilitation. The principle of *earnings testing* means that the actual amount of money paid out under all or most social benefits depends on the ability of the claimant to earn an income. The level of compensation (after taxation) shall never exceed 100 per cent of previous net income. The scheme is meant to support the 'work approach' (see chapters 3 and 7). The principle of *individuality* means that most benefits are designed for individuals rather than households or families.[74] Finally, the scheme is based on the principle of *rehabilitation*. The purpose is to 'help people help themselves' to become self-reliant again where feasible.

---

72 www.odin.no
73 Ibid.

Most benefits are universal, all legal residents are eligible in principle, though most of them are earnings-related. The level of compensation is calculated on the basis of past income, often however not above an upper ceiling. The result is that those outside the labour market such as immigrants are not fully covered and have to rely on family or means-tested social assistance for economic support. Besides, earnings must have been lost fully or partly due to illness, disability, unemployment, loss of supporter or old age. Alternatively, one can become eligible for some benefits if the costs of managing the disability etc. exceed a certain level.

Old age pension

The old age pension system consists of two elements. First, every resident is entitled to a relatively generous minimum pension irrespective of his/her employment history. Second, there is an earnings-related pension that is calculated on the basis of previous income and the number of years in employment – up to a certain point or ceiling. A ceiling means that the compensation level is reduced gradually for persons with earnings above average earnings. The aim of the old age pension system is first to prevent poverty, second, to maintain the standard of living into old age for those who have been employed, and third, to reduce income differences among old people. A public old age pension scheme represents compulsory savings, so a need for private savings is reduced. It is regarded as a 'pay as you go' scheme, since current employees make regular contributions which are paid out to those entitled to a pension, and relies thus on a contract between generations.

The pension age is 67, but people are entitled to stay in their job and earn pension points (see later) until age of 70. If a person earns more than twice the Basic amount (8352 euros in 2007) between the ages of 67 (increased to 68 in 2008) and 70, the pension is reduced by 40 per cent of the excess income. After 70 there are no reductions in pensions. Due to the possibility to retire early on a 'Negotiated Early Retirement Pension Scheme' (AFP), or disability pension, the average expected pension age in 2004 was about 60 years, which nevertheless is among the highest in Europe. In many OECD countries the official age of retirement is much higher than the effective age of retirement, and the latter has decreased substantially since 1970. Number of years that workers can expect to spend in retirement has increased (OECD 2006, 32). About two thirds of new old age pensioners in 2004 had been on early retirement or disability pension before that date.[75] All public employees and around 30 per

---

74 There are exceptions to this principle. The minimum pension is higher for a single person than for a person living with another person on a minimum pension or a supplementary pension.
75 St.prp. nr. 1 2005-2006 Arbeids- og sosialdepartementet budsjett 2006.

cent of private employees were entitled to occupational pensions alongside public pension. In addition, 19 per cent of the working population has bought an individual private pension (Solem and Øverbye, 2004). From 2006 all employees in private sector are entitled to a mandatory occupational (supplementary) pension scheme wholly financed by the employers.

Calculation of old age pension

Old age pension consists of a basic pension, a supplementary pension and/or a special supplement, and income-tested supplements for children and spouse.

Persons aged 16–66 who have been members of the National Insurance Scheme for a minimum of three years are entitled to a basic pension. The basic pension is independent of previous income and contributions paid. A full basic pension requires a membership period of at least 40 years.

A person is entitled to a *supplementary* pension if his/her annual income exceeded the average Basic amount in any year for three years after 1966. Full credit (pension points) is given for incomes up to six times the Basic amount. Further, one third of income between six and 12 times the Basic amount is credited as income for these years. Income exceeding 12 times Basic amount is disregarded. The amount of the supplementary pension depends on the number of pension-earning years and the yearly pension points. A full supplementary pension requires as a general rule 40 pension-earning years. In the case of less than 40 pension-earning years, the pension is reduced proportionally.

Pension points are computed for each calendar year by dividing the pensionable income by up to six times the Basic amount minus one Basic amount, with income between six and 12 times the Basic amount divided by 3. The maximum number of attainable pension credits for any one year is seven.

A full annual supplementary pension is 42 per cent (45 per cent of earnings before 1992) of the amount resulting from multiplying the current Basic amount by the average pension point figure for the person's twenty best income years (see example in box).

An example of calculating pension points and supplementary pension: A person earned NOK 300,000 in 2005. He or she has a membership period of 40 years. That year, the average B.a. was NOK 60,059. Pension points (P) = 300 000 – 60 059): 60 059= 4.00. If average pension points for the twenty best income years equal 4.00 as well, the supplementary pension works out at:

$$\frac{60\ 059 \times 4.00 \times 42 \times 40}{100 \times 40} = \text{NOK } 100\ 899$$

Persons with no, or only a small, supplementary pension, are entitled to a *special supplement* from the National Insurance Scheme. A full special supplement is payable if the membership period is at least 40 years. A supplementary pension is deducted from the special supplement. The basic pension + this special supplement give the *minimum pension* 15 000 euros for a single person and 27,500 euros for couples from 1.5.2007.[76]

The absolute and relative number of persons who are only entitled to the minimum pension has fallen gradually. Women are much more likely to subsist on a minimum pension than men. As Petersen and Åmark say, 'with the introduction of supplementary pensions, the male dominated labour market hierarchy was reproduced in the social insurance system' (2006:186).

Table 5.1 shows that while Norway has a higher pension age than most other countries, the basic old age pension is rather generous, despite requiring, like the other countries, 40 years of residence. All countries have also public earnings-related pensions. Norway does not have a public early retirement scheme like Denmark, but has a negotiated scheme, partly financed by the government (see table 5.1).

According to the classification suggested by Kangas et al. (2006), the Norwegian pension scheme can be regarded as *encompassing*: It guarantees basic security for its citizens and offers homogeneous earnings-related benefits on similar terms for most of the economically active. It is administered by the public authorities, and the main form of financing is through taxes and contributions. The present Norwegian scheme is based on the principle of *defined benefits*, while the new Swedish scheme of 1996 was based on the principle of *defined contributions*, which means that financial risk is transferred from the state to the individual worker. In the Swedish scheme benefits are now tied to past contributions (ibid.). The defined contribution approach gives better cost control than the principle of defined benefits (Palme, 2005). When it comes to *generosity* (net replacement rates), the Norwegian old age pension scheme is near the OECD average (OECD, 2006).

In addition to the public old age pension scheme, occupational pensions scheme are widespread: Most public employees are covered by a scheme that entitles them to a pension of 66 per cent of their end salary. Some private companies have a compensation rate of 70 per cent. Especially high-income earners thus receive a much higher old age pension than what is offered in the public pension scheme. Many high income earners have on top of their public and occupational pension an individual pension paid through tax deductable premiums.

---

76 www.nav.no/page?id=397, accessed 10.10.2007.

Table 5.1 Old age pensions in some European countries (January 2006)

	Norway	**Sweden**	**Denmark**	**Germany**	**France**	**Italy**	**United Kingdom**
Legal pension age	67 years	Flexible retirement age between 61 and 67 years	65 years	65 years	60 years (complementary scheme: 65 years)	65 years (men) 60 years (women)	65 years (men) 60 years (women)
Minimum pension	Yes 40 years of residence for full minimum pension	Yes 40 years of residence for Guarantee pension	Yes 40 years of residence for full pension	No	A remuneration equal to the amount of 200 hours of the minimum wage	40 years	Yes Contributions for 44 years (men) and 39 years (women)
Earnings-related pension	Yes, based on 20 best income years	Yes, 1) Earnings-related old age pension 2) A fully funded premium reserve system with individual accounts	Yes	Yes	Yes Full rate: Duration of the insurance period: 160 quarters (40 years)	Yes, based of years of insurance (max. 40 years) and earnings	Yes
Level of compensation (minimum (annually) in Euro	€ 13 500	€ 8 998	€ 7 779	No minimum pension	€ 6 760	€ 5 559 (insured after 1.1.96: No statutory minimum pension)	€ 6 240
Early retirement scheme	No, only a negotiated scheme, see below	No, The annually supplementary pension is permanently decreased by 0.5% of the old age pension per calendar month before the age of 65	No	Yes	Yes	Yes	No

Source: Mutual Information System on Social Protection in the EU Member States and the EEA (MISSOC) 2006.

Early retirement schemes

Industrial restructuring and company close-downs have resulted in many ad hoc early retirement schemes, both in the public and private sector. Such ad hoc early retirement payouts (gift pensions or lump sums) are footed by the companies or, in the case of the publicly owned enterprise, by the government. Examples are retrenchments in post, telecommunication, railways and road authorities. Redundant persons have either received remuneration from an ad hoc early retirement scheme or a so-called 'waiting wage', which is a form of severance pay.

In 1989, as part of a three-party agreement between business, labour and the government, a negotiated early retirement scheme (AFP) was introduced for everyone with at least ten years at work after the age of 50, and until the year that they took early retirement. The main argument for this scheme was to make it possible for manufacturing workers to retire early with dignity after years of toil, without having to end up on sick leave and in the end on disability pension. In practice, the scheme has been used as an early retirement scheme for all categories of employed. Annual income has to be above a certain level to receive AFP. It is estimated that around 70–80 per cent of all employed aged 62 are entitled to AFP. All employees in public sector (state and municipalities) are covered by this scheme.

The earliest pension age is 62. One is entitled to a full or partial pension (combine for example 60 per cent work and 40 per cent pension). By the end of 2004 retirement pensioners represented 18 per cent of population in the 62–67 age bracket, of whom the majority of these take out early retirement pension at the age of 62.[77] Three quarters of all persons receive a pension or benefit before the age of 67, and around 40 per cent of 60–66-year-olds are recipients of disability pension.[78]

A person on full early retirement pension who is also earning money from work will have their pension reduced by however much they are earning in excess of NOK 14,000 a year. The level of compensation in private sector varies for a single person, from 63 per cent of previous wage down to 40 per cent for those with highest wages (Engelstad, 2005). Old age pension from age 67 is not reduced if the worker has retired through AFP.

While the main path out of the labour market in most OECD countries is through early retirement schemes, sickness-related schemes, such as disability pension, account for the majority in Norway.[79]

---

77 St.prp. nr. 1 2005-2006 Arbeids- og sosialdepartementet budsjett 2006.
78 St.meld. nr. 2 2006-2007 *Revidert nasjonalbudsjett 2007*.
79 St.meld. nr. 9 2006-2007 *Arbeid, velferd, inkludering*.

Disability pension, rehabilitation allowance and benefits

Disability pension and rehabilitation allowance are meant to cover the living expenses of persons with reduced working capacity. *Basic* disability benefits are granted if the disability involves significant extra expenses (six benefit rates from 843 euros to 4225 euros per year). An *attendance* benefit is granted if the disabled person needs special attention or nursing (four benefit rates from 1407 euros to 9086 euros per year).

Disability pension

A person between 18 and 67, whose working capacity is permanently reduced by at least 50 per cent due to illness, injury or disability, is entitled to *disability benefit* for a limited time, or a disability *pension* if he or she has been a member of the national insurance scheme, i.e. resident in Norway for at least three years prior to incapacitation. A time limited disability benefit will be granted if it is deemed probable that the income capacity can be improved. This benefit is granted for one to four years, and shall be reassessed before the end of this period. The *time limited disability benefit* is calculated just like the rehabilitation allowance (see below). The full benefit is 66 per cent of the calculation basis. The highest monthly wage in the immediate pre-disability year forms the calculation basis, or the average of the three preceding years. The minimum annual benefit is 1.8 times the Basic amount. It is paid out five days a week or 260 days a year. A supplement of 3.38 euros per day is granted for each supported child. This benefit can be granted from one to four years.

The *disability pension* consists of a basic pension and a supplementary pension and/or special supplement (as for old-age pensions). Future insurance periods and future pension points up to and including the year of the persons sixty-sixth birthday are taken into account. Future pension points are assessed on the basis of the pre-disability income. Otherwise the basic pension and the supplementary pension are calculated as for old-age pensions. Insured persons born disabled or suffering disablement before reaching the age of 26 automatically gain 3.3 pension credits. In the case of partial disability, the pension is reduced proportionally.

Persons without or on a low supplementary pension are entitled to a special supplement from the National Insurance Scheme (see earlier presentation of the old age pension).

In 2005 vocational rehabilitation became a requirement prior to any a disability pension being granted. Permanent disability pension is only granted when improvements in work ability are not considered very likely.

A continuous increase in the number disability pensioners (from around 6 per cent of people aged 18–67 in 1980 to close to 11 per cent in 2005) has made the authorities worry.[80] Of new disability pensioners in 2005, 58.5 per cent were granted ordinary disability pension, 41.5 per cent a time limited disability benefit. As mentioned, 11 per cent of the working age population receives a disability pension, 13 per cent of women and 9 per cent of men. 40 per cent of the male and 48 per cent of the female population aged 65–66 are on disability pension.[81] The main diagnoses are diseases of the musculo-skeletal system (45 per cent) and mental diseases (17 per cent). Around 25 per cent of full disability pensioners have some paid work. The high proportion of female disability pensioners is a reflection of non-working women's eligibility for the basic disability pension. There has been a marked increase in the number of female disability pensioners. Spending on disability benefits and sickness benefits amount to 7 per cent of GDP in 2002, which is more than twice the OECD-28 average (OECD, 2002, 2).

In accordance with the IA Agreement (see chapter 3), steps are being taken to reactivate disability pensioners.

Rehabilitation allowance

A person under 67 may be entitled to rehabilitation allowance if he or she is resident in Norway and has been a member of the national pension scheme for three years immediately prior to claiming the benefit.

When the period of entitlement to daily cash benefits in case of sickness (see chapter 6) has expired, an insured person may be granted a rehabilitation allowance, if his or her working capacity is reduced by at least 50 per cent. It is required that he or she is in active treatment with a view to improving his/her working ability. Rehabilitation allowance is generally only granted for a period of 52 consecutive weeks. Exceptions can be made from this time constraint.

The calculation of rehabilitation allowance is based on previous earnings. The maximum benefit basis is six times the Basic amount. The benefit rate per year is 66 per cent of the calculation basis. A person with low, or no, income is guaranteed a minimal yearly benefit of 1.8 times the Basic amount. For persons born disabled or suffering disablement before reaching the age of 26, the minimum allowance is 2.4 times the Basic amount. [82] Recipients of rehabilitation allowance or time limited disability benefit have a right and a duty to help the Labour Market Service (NAV) devise an individual action plan for re-entry into the labour market. As from 2009, these time-limited allowances will be substituted by what is called 'clarification benefits' ('avklar-

---

80 St.meld. nr. 9 for 2006-2007 *Arbeid, velferd, inkludering*.
81 www.nav.no.accessed 10.10.2007.
82 (www.nav.no.accessed 10.10.2007.

ingspenger'. The level of compensation will be 66 per cent of previous earnings and maximum duration will be four years. Recipients of this new benefit will be entitled to get activity plans and will also be obliged to accept offers to take part in activity programs or training.[83]

From 1998 to 2003 there was a strong increase in number of recipients of rehabilitation allowance, but since then there has been a reduction mainly due a reduction of the maximum duration in 2004 to one year. NAV were also required then to consider vocational rehabilitation as soon as possible. By the end of 2004 there were 50,600 recipients of rehabilitation allowance, but the number has decreased since with the new time constraint. Less than a third of these recipients returns to paid work after the rehabilitation period.[84]

What can explain the development in the number of people on disability pensions?

In 2006, 500,000 man-labour year was lost from absence from work due to sickness, disability and rehabilitation. It is not easy to understand the increase in disability pension (and sick leave) awards, at a time with advances in public health and higher life expectancy, and when working conditions have not worsened (NOU 2007, 4). Is it due to expulsion (push-factors), attraction (pull-factors) or movement from work to something more attractive based on individual choice (jump-factors) (Solem and Øverbye,2004)? The disability pension has steadily become more generous, especially for low-income earners, making it more attractive to put in a claim. Since benefits can be regarded as paid leisure time, the cost of leisure for these low income earners declines. This, together with more private wealth, means that it is easier to maintain a decent standard of living on disability pension. Higher standards of living can be a motivating factor. Improvements in the private economy may mean that more people can afford to retire early. It is also more culturally acceptable to live on public support such as disability pension (Øverbye, 2006).

Perhaps doctors are more willing to diagnose mild and diffuse health problems (ibid), alternatively that hidden health problems have been detected such as for example mental illnesses.

Tightening of eligibility criteria over the years has made it more difficult to obtain disability pension (NOU 2007:4). Between 20 and 25 per cent of disability pension claims are rejected,[85] and there is no clear evidence of greater leniency. Yet claimants' lower education level, the higher probability of exit

---

83 According to interview with the minister of work and inclusion Bjarne Håkon Hansen in *Aftenposten* 13.11.2007.
84 St.prp. nr. 1 2005-2006 *Arbeids- og inkluderingsdepartementets budsjett for 2006.*
85 St.prp. nr. 1 2006-2007 *Arbeids- og inkluderingsdepartementets budsjett for 2007.*

from the labour market, especially in professions dominated by women such as auxiliary nursing, hairdressing and waitiressing (Fevang and Røed 2006). Immigrants from Pakistan, Turkey and Morocco who came to Norway in the 1970s, are strongly overrepresented in the disability pension tables mainly because they were hit harder than ethnic Norwegians by economic recessions (Bratsberg et al., 2006).

Nevertheless, more and more structural changes in the economy have made people redundant both in public and private sector. Especially older people have found it hard to find a new job, re-qualify or move. At least five per cent of the increase in disability pensions can be explained by such factors alone (St.meld. nr. 9 2006–2007 see also NOU 2007:4). Geographical variations in the proportion of disability pensioners indicate that lack of adequate jobs could be of importance.

The fact that more women become disability pensioners may be related to the reduced role of men in supporting their spouse. Social benefits offer an alternative to wage work. 'The social buffer' – having a partner and family – has been weakened by increasing divorce rates and family disintegration, making it more difficult for single parents to cope at both home and work. Economic help from the family has been supplanted by income from work *and* public support, such as the disability pension (Øverbye, 2007). Higher employment rates than most other European countries, may also increase the rate of disability pension awards. This is tied to the influx of women in the labour force (Solem and Øverbye, 2004).

It might also be culturally more acceptable for women to retreat into a 'sick role' (St.meld. nr. 9 2006–2007). The more people on disability pension, the less stigmatizing is it to live on 'welfare' (Blekasaune, 2005a). Employers may have used the disability pension scheme to justify close-downs and retrenchments. It turns out that the problems suffered by many disability pensioners started many years before the disability pension was granted, often with a spell of unemployment, or some manner of health or social problem. They may have a long record of sickness benefits, unemployment benefits, rehabilitation allowance or social assistance allowance. As mentioned, company retrenchments and restructuring of the public sector heightens the risk of employees filing for a disability pension (Fevang and Røed, 2005, 2006; Rikstrygdeverket 2006; Rege, Telle and Votruba, 2005).

Yet, most of the increase in the number of disability pensioners between 1990 and 2000, namely 55 per cent, is simply due to the fact that the working age population has become older (St.meld. nr. 9 for 2006–2007). And since 2001, demographic changes can explain even more – all of 89 per cent – of the increase in the number of disability pensioners (NOU 2007:4). So a high proportion of people on disability pension is the price to be paid for a high proportion of working elderly, not least elderly women (Øverbye, 2007).

A new disability pension scheme has been aired recently, to take over from the current one in 2010. It would raise the level of compensation to 66 per cent of the three best of the last five income years. An income at 6 x the basic amount – around 50,000 euros – would qualify for the maximum pension. A person would be eligible for disability pension with 33 per cent incapacity. The disability pension would be the same for married and single persons. It would also mean that single persons on low incomes – around 25,000 euros a year) – will experience a reduction in net compensation rates from today's 80 to 70 percent, while persons with higher incomes will get higher compensation rates (NOU 2007, 4).

In the mandatory occupation pension scheme (OTP) that was introduced in 2006, it is possible, in addition to the mandatory old age pension scheme, to insure employees against disability, making it possible to get a total (public and private) disability pension of 66 per cent of previous income.

Challenges of an elderly population: A new pension scheme

Despite the huge pension fund (see chapter 2), the government fears that The National Social Insurance scheme will not be economically sustainable in the long run, due to an ageing population and consequently higher expected pension and healthcare expenditures. In addition the ratio between elderly and people of working age goes up from 20 per 100 today to close to 40 per 100 in 2050 (St.meld. nr. 2 2005–2006). It has nevertheless to be kept in mind that *dependency ratio* (persons outside labour force as proportion to persons in the labour force) was higher in the 1970s than what is forecasted from 2035 and onwards (St.meld. nr. 6 for 2006–2007). Yet, future pensioners will have higher pension rights than the present ones (see chapter 10).

Fewer and fewer will be recipients of minimum pension only. One estimation indicates that future pension obligations on the National Insurance Scheme by end of 2006 was 463 billion euros, and increasing with 29 billion euros in 2006 alone. The present pension fund is not sufficient to cover future pension expenses,[86] and the future financial situation will depend heavily on the development in crude oil prices. Besides, there will be more *old* elderly: In 2050 it is estimated that between 80 000 and 160 000 persons will be 90 years or older, as compared with 27 000 in 2003 (Glad, 2003). These persons will represent a challenge for health care institutions. On the other hand, due to increased productivity, it is estimated that the gross domestic product (continental Norway) per capita will be doubled towards year 2050 (ibid.).

Such worries are also dominant within EU-union countries.[87] Fewer able-bodied people of working age have to support more and more elderly. This

---

86 Unless a crude oil price of US$ 75-100 a barrel is reached. (In fact, on 26.2.2008, the price for North sea-oil was for first time over 100 dollar a barrel.)
87 (www.eurospa.eu 16.2.2006.

will especially be the case in the Mediterranean countries as Italy and Spain (Glad, 2003). Such arguments are used to introduce measures that increase the actual pension age. Fewer people shall retire early. *The World Bank* has been a central actor in the discussing of pensions reform, see for example its 1994 publication 'Averting the Old Age Crisis', where it advocates a neo-liberal approach to the challenge.

The White paper by the pension commission (NOU 2004:1), proposed a voluntary pension age between 62 and 67 years, but where those who retire early will get a lower pension, about 25 per cent less per year than those who wait till they are 67 years old. The purpose is to maintain the sustainability of public finances, to strengthen the incentive to work and to establish a flexible relation to the demographic development.

The commission will also encourage people to combine pensions and paid work. In contrast to today's scheme, pension points will be earned throughout the whole working life (between 16 and 75 years). According to a compromise between all political parties, with the exception of the Progress Party, new pensioners will get a pension at the same level of compensation, namely 54 per cent of previous income if they have had earnings for 40 years, i.e. 1.35 per cent per year up to 7.1 times the basic amount. Unpaid caregivers for own children will earn pension points – annually 4.5 times the Basic amount – of maximum six years per child.

To stabilise expenditures people belonging to the same age cohort will have to work more years if life expectancy goes up. Alternatively they will have to reduce their annual pension. In the future pensions will be adjusted with the average annual wage increase minus 0.75 perentage points. This is in contrast to today's scheme which is adjusted according to the wage increase alone. The new pension system is to be financed jointly by employees and employers. It is still unclear at what time this new scheme will be implemented.

A person, who has worked for 43 years and had an annual income of 43,750 euros, will receive a pension of 25,400 euros from the age of 67, which is higher than in today's scheme 22,900 euros. If he or she retires at the age of 62 the pension is reduced to 18,800 euros. If he or she works until the age of 70 and has 43 years of earnings, the annual pension will be 31,000 euros. Maximum old age pension at the age of 67 will be 32,400 euros, and at 70, 39,500 euros. So in the new scheme it pays to work longer. Nor will be deductions in pensions (as from 62 years) even if the person is earning money, in contrast to today's scheme for pensioners between 67 (68) and 70. If the longevity of the age cohort rises, the annual pension will be reduced somewhat.

An earlier compromise between the former government (Bondevik II), the present parties in government was reached with the help of the major labour unions. Certain problems remain to be settled concerning the position of early retirement scheme under the new pension scheme. Some are afraid that low-income earners will lose out under the system. The problem is how to avoid a guaranteed minimum pension which makes it pay not to work. Also in the present scheme low-income earners risk ending up with the minimum pension – now called a guarantee pension – because the supplementary pension is lower than the special supplement (see earlier information about old age pension). According to the agreement, there needs to be more consistency between a person's earnings record and their pension awards. In other words, every year in paid work will count. The ambition is to set up a scheme that ensures persons with earnings always get more than the guaranteed minimum pension.[88] The old early retirement scheme will by 2025 be replaced by a new early retirement scheme, with eligibility at 62.

A revised *individual pension scheme* offered by private insurance companies will be launched in 2008. Premiums paid into the scheme below a ceiling of 1,875 euros will be tax deductable (St.meld. nr. 2 2006–2007).

Organised labour, however, wants to keep the present early retirement scheme, so the end result is still unclear. The debates over a new pension reform demonstrate the strong degree of institutional inertia. It is politically difficult to change welfare programmes. Pension schemes are long-term contracts between generations, so an economic crisis may be necessary to get the necessary public support for a pension reform. Pension reforms in Finland and Sweden have probably paved the way for the Norwegian reform. Also recommendations from OECD (recent publication in 2006) have been used in the political debate to illustrate the necessity of a reform.

The proposed changes cannot be regarded as systemic changes, but rather as structural adjustments (distinctions proposed by Schiller and Kuhnle, 2007).

---

88 With an annual income of 22,500 euros a person today will only get the minimum pension of 14,100 euros, while in the new scheme he or she will be entitled to 16,638 euros at the age of 67 (*Aftenposten* 22.3.2007).

Chapter 6

Health for all!
The Health care system: medical treatment and sickness benefits

Health services are vital for quality of life. They include the curative, rehabilitative and nursing/caring activities. An ageing population and expectations of longer lives in good health challenge a health system largely run and financed by the state. We examine in this chapter health policy, legislation and organization of health services at central and local level, the role of professional health workers, how services are financed, health statistics, priorities and challenges relating to health inequalities, medical-technological progress, patient rights and quality control/supervision. We shall look at sickness benefits, award criteria and entitlement and ask why the number of persons on such benefits has risen so much.

Historical background

As early as in sixteenth-century Europe, illness was regarded as a collective risk and a public responsibility. Main protagonists in the development of the health system were doctors, workers' organizations and voluntary health organizations. Driving forces were fear of epidemics and social unrest. It was therefore imperative for the ruling classes to improve the health situation of poor people. The first hospital in Norway was established as early as in 1277, but hospitals in most counties came later, in the eighteenth and early nineteenth century. After World War II,[89] health policy was linked with social policy. Public welfare and economic growth required better public health. The means were preventive medicine, a primary health service and health institutions. The responsibility for health institutions devolved to the county authorities in 1960, but due to problems of coordination and inefficiency, centralization brought these institutions under the wing of state in 2002. Norway and Iceland are the only Nordic countries were the state is responsi-

---

89 For a historical development of hospitals, see Haave 2006.

ble for the hospital sector (NOSOSCO 2007). The National Insurance Scheme provides a daily cash benefit for sickness and absence from work to care for a sick child. The present scheme was introduced in 1978.

Since the end of World War II relations between central and local government have undergone continuous evolution. In the 1970s, responsibility for health care services devolved increasingly on local government (see chapter 9). NGOs have also founded and run hospitals (see chapter 7). A process of decentralization has taken place, although the emergence of regional health authorities went in the opposite direction, towards greater centralization. Specialized care is handled by the regional hospitals. In order to reduce waiting lists, 24 private clinics and hospitals were allowed in 2005 to treat patients for (minor) problems on behalf of regional hospitals. Decentralization had led to problems of service coordination and accountability (WHO, 2000).

The medical market has been liberalised. In 2001, the retail market was liberalised; dispensaries could now be set up and owned by anybody, not just qualified pharmacists.

Health policy: Legislation, goals and priorities

All legal residents have an equal right to use the health services. This is a central feature of a universal welfare state. A Patient's Rights Act came into force in 2001. Its preamble states that 'the purpose is to contribute to secure the population equal access to health care of good quality', provided that the treatment is assumed to be beneficial and the costs are reasonable viewed in the light of the outcome (effectiveness). Access to health care should therefore be equal irrespective of social status, geographical locality and economic situation. The patient is to be treated as an equal party in the relationship with care providers.

This goal is to be fulfilled through publicly financed health services subject to control by the electorate. Although some private health institutions are allowed to operate, it is a widely held opinion that health care services should not be governed by the market and the need to profit. There are several exceptions, including the pharmaceutical sector, dental services[90] and general practitioners, the greater part of whose income derives from consultation fees, though they receive an annual grant from the state and refunds from the National Insurance Scheme.

---

90   80 per cent of all dental services were in 2004 produced in the private market (Statistics Norway, 2007: *Private og offentlige tannhelsetjeneser. Forbruk av private helsetjenester øker mest* (www.ssb.no/ssop/utg/2007/03/07).). Free and public dental service is only available for youth up to the age of 18. The same is the case for elderly, long-term sick, disabled, prison inmates and mentally retarded receiving nursing or care services. Youth between 19 and 20 years pay 25 per cent of actual expenses. For the rest of the population, the national insurance scheme refunds only a small part of the services done in private dental offices.

An example of a patient right is the right to treatment and to choose which hospital to attend. One may choose a hospital anywhere in the country rather than having to wait for treatment at the local hospital. Hospitals need to be more consumer-oriented in order to attract patients. Free choice of hospital also helps hospital capacity utilisation and reduces queues. According to the Patient's Rights Act one is also entitled to a second opinion and an individual treatment plan when coordinated care is needed. Participatory rights include informed consent to treatment, access to medical journals and information. All referrals from general practitioners to hospitals have to be considered by a specialist within 30 working days. The patient has the right to be given a deadline for treatment at the hospital of their choice. If it is exceeded, the patient may seek treatment at a private hospital or hospital abroad.

The regional health authority (see below) pays for treatment at another hospital. These measures were a response to the most urgent problem facing the health care system, the long queues for non-emergency treatment. A registration system for patients awaiting non-emergency treatment showed that in 1997 around 280,000 were waiting at any one time (WHO, 2000). Since 2002 there has been a minor reduction in waiting lists (Opedal and Stigen, 2005). Still, in 2005, waiting for necessary health treatment was on average 74 days for men and 68 days for women.[91] Patients who are not prioritised have to wait on average for 170 days for treatment, 30 days less than six years earlier.[92]

The act gives patients the right to complain to the county medical officer should their rights be violated. It also states that every county shall provide for an *ombudsman* for patients in the specialised health care system. The ombudsman shall speak on behalf of the patients and help protect their interests. He or she guides patients, informs them about their rights, and helps them to be fulfilled. In 2003 all hospitals were obliged to register various indicators of quality and which are published on a national website. Information on the quality of the services is readily available to the public, and comparisons can be made between hospitals.

These overall goals are operationalized in the so-called *Priority Setting Regulations* ('Prioriteringsforskriften'), which specify when a patient can claim priority for necessary health care. Making priorities means that some get treatment while others do not, and that some are given treatment before others (Botten, 2006). A condition for priority treatment is that the patient's chance of survival is in jeopardy or at least a significant reduction in life quality if health care is postponed. Patients expected to benefit from health care are also prioritised, provided that the costs are reasonable in proportion to the effect of the intervention. Three priority criteria are thus mentioned: gravity, benefit and cost (Bringedal, 2005). A national priority advisory board

---

91 Sosial- og helsedirektoratet 2006. *Utviklingstrekk i helse- og sosialsektoren.* Oslo
92 Jan Erik Askildsen, conference on Health Economics, Bergen 21st May 2007, cited *Aftenposten* 22.5.07.

for health care – established in 2000 – is charged with ensuring an effective and just distribution of health services.

Making priorities challenges ideals of equality. Should we, for example, set an upper age limit for some forms of treatment? The purpose of the *Priority Setting Regulations* is to make implicit prioritising –by medical personnel in their daily activities – explicit. At the macro level the main form of explicit prioritising includes budgeting for certain forms of treatment and care, and preparation of government instructions for the regional health authorities (Botten, 2006). A consequence of prioritising is the increased reliance on and growth of private health insurance facilities, which guarantees the insured treatment within a certain time limit. Such privatisation in the health sector favours those with economic resources (ibid.).

In June 2001, peopled gained the right to choose who their general practitioner should be (the Regular General Practitioner Scheme). The basic principle of this reform is that everybody can choose whether they want to participate in the system or not. Patients can switch GPs twice a year and also have the right to a second opinion from another general practitioner. The aim of the reform is to improve the quality of local medical service. It is expected that the accessibility of health care services is improved. The reform will hopefully contribute to continuity of care and a more personal patient–physician relationship. Each and every practitioner has to give priority to patients on their list.

Organization of the health care system

The system of health care provision is based on a decentralized model. The state is responsible for policy design and overall capacity and quality of health care through budgeting and legislation. The state is also responsible for hospital services through state ownership of regional health authorities (RHAs). The RHAs are separate legal entities owned by the central government. This reorganisation took place in 2002 inspired by New Public Management. Elected bodies replaced the old professional boards of directors and management. Under the regional health authorities, (81) somatic and psychiatric hospitals (and some hospital pharmacies), are organized as hospital trusts (helseforetak), 33 in total (Opedal and Stigen, 2005). Norway is divided into four health regions. The *Ministry of Health and Care* is still legally liable for health care. This national health system, run by the state and financed by taxation, differs from insurance-based health systems financed by premiums, which are quite common in many EU countries like Germany and France. Political control of the RHAs is through legislation, annual health plans and yearly budgets, but it is the board of each RHA that has responsibility for reaching national targets (and prioritising) consonant with legislation, health plans and budgets. Hospital doctors' evaluation of the hospital reform indicates that it has not resulted in better organization or improved medical quality, but that the productivity has improved (Aasland et al 2007). On the other hand, the experience of patients with somatic hospitals seems generally positive (Nasjonalt kunnskapssenter for helsetjenesten 2006).

In order to improve health services, the government initiates programmes. One such was the 1999–2008 *National Mental Health Programme*. It was designed to address mental health service deficiencies at all levels and insufficient preventive measures (Norwegian Ministry of Health and Care Services 2005). As a result, outpatient and inpatient treatment capacity has increased. The aim was also to decentralize the mental health service, offering treatment where the patient lives. Supervision at home following consultation was to be improved. Other aims included patient empowerment, information campaigns to raise public awareness of mental health issues, strengthening community based services and expanding specialised services for children and adolescents (Norwegian Ministry of Health and Care Services). Other examples are a five-year *National action plan against cancer*, presented in 1998, and the *National strategy for habilitation and rehabilitation 2008–2011*.

The municipalities are responsible for primary health care, both preventive and curative. Local authorities manage school health services, health centres, child health care, children's health visitors, midwives and physicians. They are responsible for diagnosis, treatment and rehabilitation, such as general medical treatment (including emergency services), physiotherapy and nursing. Institutional and domiciliary nursing is also a municipal responsibility (see chapter 9).

Outpatient treatment of somatic and mental diseases has increased dramatically, while the average time spent by a patient in hospital has fallen equally dramatically. Hospital bed capacity was halved over twenty years or so, as more and more patients receive outpatient treatment such as day surgery.

The county authorities are responsible for providing public dental services for children and adolescents (under 21 years of age), mentally handicapped adults and elderly, disabled and the chronically ill whether residents of an institution or living at home. As mentioned earlier, the rest of the population relies on private sector dentistry, with treatment paid by the patients (NOMESCO 2007).[93] Opticians are private sector businesses too, supplying spectacles and contact lenses.

Most of habilitation and rehabilitation institutions are private, but run in agreement with and financed by the Regional Health Authorities.

The Norwegian Board of Health is an independent professional body, which in collaboration with nineteen county medical officers is responsible for promoting quality and supervising legal safeguards of the Norwegian

---

93 A dental health reform is imminent. It addresses the tendency of financially disadvantaged patients to postpone dental treatment, and jeopardise their dental health.

health sector.[94] *The National Institute for Public health* conducts health research and advises the government.

Health expenditures and financing

The most expensive health services are in-patient curative care (24 per cent); out-patient curative care (19 per cent); and in-patient long-term nursing care (16 per cent) (see figure 6.1).

Figure 6.1

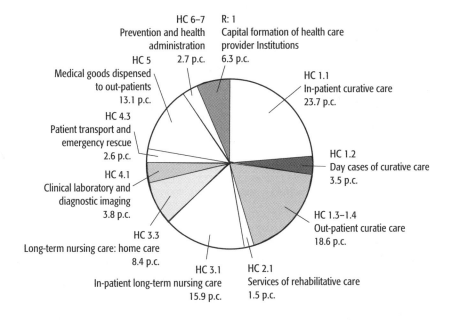

Health expenditures by function. 2006. Per cent

2007 © Statistics Norway: Health accounts 1997–2006. www.ssb.no/helseat_en/main.html. 30.4.07)

Around 14 per cent of in-patient hospital admissions for curative care are related to cardiovascular diseases.[95]

---

94 www.helsetilsynet.no/templates 20.04.2006.
95 Statistics Norway, 2007. *Pasientstatistikk 2006.*

Figure 6.2

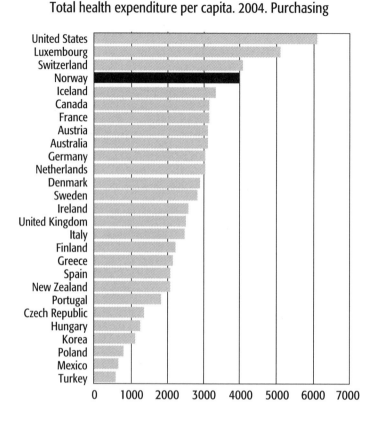

Source: OECD

Statistics Norway: Health accounts 1997–2006 (www.ssb.no/helseat_en/main.html. Accessed 30.4.07)

In 2003, health and care service spending was 10 per cent of GDP, but fell to 8.7 per cent in 2006.[96] Spending per capita in Norway is among the highest in the OECD countries. Only the United States, Luxembourg and Switzerland spend more on health (see figure 6.2). Most US citizens need private health insurance to cover costs. And it is costly: 13 per cent of the premium goes to administering the scheme, compared to only two per cent in the federal Medicare.[97]

Compared with other OECD countries Norway has a high number of

---

96 Statistics Norway 2007.
97 According to Paul Krugman and Robin Wells in *New York Review of Books* 23.3.2006.

health care professionals per capita.[98] Doctor/patient ratio was 280 per 100,000 population (369 per 100,000 in 2005[99]), which is high compared to other EU/EES-countries. The dentist ratio is also higher than EU average, (81 per 100,000).[100] There were 3.8 hospital beds per 1,000 population in 2002, well below the EU average. There were 16,263 hospital discharges in 2002 per 100,000 inhabitants. 12 per cent was hospitalised in 2003 (ibid.). If we take the United States as an example, however, it turns out that the correlation between spending and public health is pretty tenuous. A country's socioeconomic standing and, not least, the level of socioeconomic equality, are much better indicators (Castilla, 2004). As it was put in a white paper on 'Prescriptions for a Healthier Norway': 'Our own choices and the way we jointly organize and adapt society in a number of different areas play a far more important role' (Ministry of Health 2003, 5).

World Health Organization has Norway in third place on its health goal attainment barometer, and eleventh on efficiency of 191 countries. The barometer looks at health, patient satisfaction, methods of finance and total expenses.[101] In comparison with health care in the OECD, Norway and the UK scored highest on an index comprising private health expenditure as percentage of GDP, private hospital beds (percentage of total bed stock) and public health care system coverage (percentage of population) (Bambra, 2005:207). Another ranking based on patient rights and information, waiting lists and results, Norway was seventh of 29 European countries (*Dagens Medisin*, 2007). Satisfaction with the state of health services in Norway averages lower than several other European countries.[102] One explanation could be higher expectations among Norwegians given the country's prosperity.

The number of physicians and nurses rose by 80 and 60 per respectively 1990–2004.[103] In comparison with OECD, Norway has more health professionals per capita. Nevertheless, remote areas often find it difficult to attract health professionals. The nursing profession is dominated by women working part-time, and at times nursing shortages have been met by inviting guest workers from other countries to come and work in Norway. In the near future there will be lack of nursing auxiliaries.

Doctors are one of the leading gateways into the disability pension scheme by virtue of their diagnostic powers. Their expertise and collaboration with the pharmaceutical industry fuel the 'medicalization' of society. What used to

---

98 St.prp. nr. 1 2005-2006 *Helse- og omsorgsdepartementets budsjett 2006*.
99 NOMESCO, 2007. *Health Statistics in the Nordic Countries 2005*. Copenhagen (www.nom-nos.dk., accessed 16.10.2007.
100 European Commission. 2005. *Health in Europe*. Luxembourg: Eurostat.
101 St.meld. nr. 30 2000-2001. *Langtidsprogrammet 2001-2005*.
102 Mean scores on a scale from 0 to 10, with Norway at 5.71 Belgium 7.19, Luxembourg 7.06, Finland 6.89, Denmark 6.42 and France 5.76 (European Social Survey 2004/2005).
103 Sosial- og helsedirektoratet. 2006. *Utviklingstrekk i helse- og sosialsektoren*. Oslo.

pass as everyday problems are increasingly seen as illnesses in need of treatment. Since salaries represent 70 per cent of total health expenditure, recent wage increases, especially for doctors, make it difficult to run hospitals in a more cost-efficient manner.

The government pays most of the health care bill (47 per cent of public spending); counties or municipalities come next (33 per cent), with the social security fund making up the rear with 20 per cent in 2004.[104] The municipalities recoup spending from local taxes, block grants from the government and the National Insurance Scheme (fee-for-service financing in health care), which is financed by fees paid by employers and employees (see chapter 2). There is only a weak connection between individual health risks and costs. Only around 16 per cent of total expenses are directly paid by households in the form of out-of-pocket payments,[105] about the same proportion as the other Nordic countries.[106]

Health region operations are financed under a government block grant. A modified block grant system includes activity-based revenues, i.e. earmarked fee-per-patient scheme. The ratio of activity-based financing to block grants is about 40/60.

The per-case payment is based on the Diagnosis Group Specific costs system (DRG). Diagnosis Group Specific costs are calculated on the basis of national, historical data of average costs of treating patients within each diagnostic group. These costs form the basis of the pricing system. The government reimburses hospitals for patients treated in each diagnostic group. It has been a successful undertaking, overshooting government performance targets and shortening queues faster. An unfortunate corollary is hospitals' tendency to favour profitable patients at the expense of patients whose needs may well be greater.

In addition, the government earmarks annual budget items for investment in buildings and medical equipment. The regional health authorities are also entitled to borrow money from the state to finance investments, but interest on these loans has to be financed under the ordinary annual budgets.

Public spending on health accounts for an increasing share of *total* public spending, reaching 19 per cent in 2006.[107] End-user payment is supposed to reduce the demand for health services and medication. But since healthcare and medication are (almost) free to members of the National Insurance Scheme, the payment system is unlikely to make much difference. Patients pay a certain sum for treatment provided by their local GP, non-hospital con-

---

104 Statistics Norway, 2007. *Gir et inkluderende arbeidsliv økt sykefravær?*(www.ssb.no/magasinet/analyse/art-2007-03-13-01 html. 23.04.07).
105 St.prp. nr. 1 2005-2006 Helse- og omsorgssdepartementets budsjett 2006.
106 NOMESCO, 2007. *Health Statistics in the Nordic Countries 2005*. Copenhagen (www.nom-nos.dk., accessed 16.10.2007.
107 Statistics Norway 2007.

sultant, psychologist and physiotherapist, as well as laboratory tests and X-ray examinations. Finland and Sweden only charge for hospitalisation.[108]

User payment is an increasingly popular way of financing healthcare (St.prp. nr. 1 2006–2007), but can be expensive for people with chronic ailments. Steps have therefore been taken to ease the burden in particularly onerous cases (Bringedal, 2005). One example is the so-called 'free card', a way of sharing expenses between patients and the state. At a cut-off point set by parliament each year, the state pays the patient's healthcare expenses. In 2005, more than one million 'free cards' were issued.[109] In addition, many essential medicines are heavily subsidized under what is called the 'blue prescription' scheme. Cost of medicine for chronic conditions is also covered. Medical examinations during pregnancy and after birth are free of charge.

If consultant operates in private market, i.e. is not contracted to the local authorities, patients are required to pay the whole bill.

In order to avoid waiting for hospital treatment some individuals and companies as well as municipalities provide employees with a complementary health insurance. There are many private health care centres in urban areas as well. Membership gives access to specialist treatment outside public hospitals.

The state of public health

In 1900, life expectancy was 54 for men and 57 for women. In 1970, women lived longer in Norway than in any other OECD country, with male longevity in third place. By 2006, women could expect to live 82.7 years and men 78.1 years (see chapter 2). The increase in life expectancy is first and foremost due to higher standards of living, reduced poverty, improved housing, better nutrition and safer working environments, and also better health services.[110]

Despite steadily increasing life expectancy over the past 100 years, several countries are ahead of Norway. There is great *regional* variation in life expectancy. Infant mortality is among the lowest in the world. In 2004, 3.2 infants aged less than a year died per 1000 living newborn children (infant mortality rate).[111] Healthy Life Years Expectancy (HLYE), i.e. expected length of life spent in good health, was at birth 70.4 years for men and 73.6 years for women in 2002. This is among the highest in Europe.[112]

Three out of four adult Norwegians say that their health is good or very

---

108 NOMESCO, 2007. ibid.
109 St.prp. nr. 1 2006-2007 *Helse- og omsorgsdepartementets budsjett 2007*.
110 OECD finds a strong positive association between life expectancy at birth and GDP (R_=0,69) and between life expectancy at birth and health spending per capita (R_=0,57) (OECD 2005).
111 Statistics Norway 2005.
112 European Commission 2005 *Health in Europe*. Luxembourg: Eurostat.

good (self-perceived health). This figure is about the highest in Europe, though Ireland and Switzerland report even higher subjective health figures (see chapter 2). Around 5 per cent of Norwegians regard their subjective general health as bad or very bad, which is about the Nordic average.[113] 16 per cent of the Norwegian population suffered from a long-standing health problem or disability, which is the same as the EU-25 average.[114]

The *socio-economic* gap in health has widened in the past thirty years.[115] The leading cause of death for both men and women is cardiovascular diseases, followed by cancer, diseases of the respiratory organs and accident and injuries (home and leisure accidents, traffic accidents and suicide (15.8 per 100,000 inhabitants in 2005).[116] Although there has been a decline in cardiovascular diseases, the increase in incidence of Type II diabetes may reverse this trend. Around 15 per cent of the adult population suffers from mental illness, and about 10 per cent of them are regarded as seriously ill. Especially women suffer from depression and anxiety symptoms, while substance misuse is far more common among men. As many as 10–20 per cent of all children are afflicted by serious mental problems according to estimates. So far communicable diseases are less common in Norway than most other countries (Ministry of Health, 2003). One third of new disability pensioners suffer from musculoskeletal disorders, and every fifth from a psychiatric disorder (see chapter 5).

The main health risk factors in the Norwegian population are related to physical inactivity and unhealthy diets, resulting in overweight and obesity. 52 per cent of men and 36 per cent of women are overweight/obese according to the Level of Living survey of 2005.[117] Other health risks are high cholesterol levels and blood pressure, smoking (26 per cent are daily smokers), alcohol and drug consumption. High alcohol intake is associated with many accidents and violence. There are great social differences in health-related behaviour such as diet, smoking and exercise (Ministry of Health 2003).

Lifestyle diseases are proliferating in Norway too. Legislation is used to reduce risk of ill-health. Smoke-free public areas, including the total ban on smoking in the hospitality trade, help counter the harmful effects of tobacco (see latest amendment to the Act relating to prevention of the harmful effects of tobacco). Legislation is also intended to make it easier for people to choose healthier lifestyles. Other efforts to promote a healthier environment target car emissions, safer food and drinking water. By allying themselves with government bodies, non-governmental organizations (NGOs) can promote and

---

113 European Social Survey 2004, see also European Commission 2005.
114 Eurostat, 2007. *Living conditions in Europe. Data 2002-2005*, Luxembourg.
115 Folkehelseinstituttet. 2007. *Sosial ulikhet i helse. En faktarapport*. Rapport 2007:1. Oslo: Folkehelseinstituttet, St.meld. nr. 20 2006-2007: *Nasjonal strategi for å utjevne sosiale helseforskjeller.*
116 NOMESCO 2007.
117 NSD-nytt 1/2007

facilitate a healthy and active lifestyle. Since it turns out that loneliness and social isolation are strong determinants of poor life quality, NGOs can play an important role by offering meaningful activities and social contact.

The greatest challenges are connected with social inequalities in health that form a *gradient* throughout the population: life expectancy, mortality, incidence of various diseases and self-perceived health correlate with socio-economic groups defined by occupation, education or income, or a combination of the three. Also gender, geography, ethnicity and family status show marked differences in health. The higher one's socio-economic status, the better one's health.[118] It has even been suggested that social inequalities and social divisions in themselves cause illness. As income gaps widen, so does social distance between social strata, resulting in less solidarity and community spirit.[119]

Different theoretical approaches favour their own explanations of social inequality. Economics posits economic disparity, psychology looks at psychosocial factors like mental stress. Materialists find causes in people's physical surroundings and environment, behaviourists in behaviour like smoking, diet, drinking, physical activity etc. Others find causes in the health service and selection mechanisms (The Norwegian Directorate for Health and Social Affair 2006).

The government has launched an action plan to address social inequalities in health (ibid.). It will seek to narrow income differences, create equal opportunities for children, promote inclusion in the workplace, reduce social differences in nutrition, physical activity and smoking, ensure equal access to health services and promote social inclusion of marginalized persons (St.meld. nr. 20 2006–2007).

Absenteeism and sickness benefits

The *National Insurance Act* of 1997 provides for relatively generous sickness benefits compared to other OECD countries. Coverage is also generally greater since it is a public scheme. Most countries have waiting days and offer less than complete compensation of previous wage. In some countries the scheme is negotiated between business and labour. This is the case in Sweden where many employers set the level of compensation at 100 per cent (St.meld. nr. 1 2006–2007). It is also quite common in Norway for those earning more than six times the Basic amount (G) to receive full wage compensation from their employers. The public, bank and finance sectors and many white collar occupations do so, for instance. The maximal duration is, however, as long or longer as other European countries (Halvorsen, 1998),

---

118 St.meld. nr. 20 2006–2007 *Nasjonal strategi for å utjevne helseforskjeller.*
119 Folkehelseinstituttet. 2007. *Sosial ulikhet i helse. En faktarapport.* Rapport 2007:1. Oslo.

see table 6.1. And in most, the employer pays part or all (such as the Netherlands) of the sickness benefit.

Sickness benefits are given to employed persons rendered incapable of working and earning a livelihood by illness. To be entitled to sickness benefits an insured person must have an annual income of at least 0.5 basic points (see chapter 5). Employment should also have lasted at least 14 days. Regardless of the amount of lost income maximum benefits are six times the Basic amount, i.e. 50,000 euros from May 1 2007. Up to that limit the level of compensation is 100 per cent. For salaries over and above this threshold, percentage compensation declines incrementally.

It is paid from the first day of sickness for a period of 260 days. Daily sickness benefits are paid by the employer for the first 16 calendar days and thereafter by the National Insurance Scheme. Self-employed are entitled to sickness benefits corresponding to 65 per cent of earnings from the seventeenth day of sickness for a period of 248 days. A self-employed person may receive 100 per cent of previous income from the seventeenth day or first day of sickness by voluntarily paying a higher premium. Sickness benefits are paid out on the basis of a declaration filed by the insured person for the first three days (8 days if the employer has signed up for an IA-agreement, see chapter 3). If the person is still ill after this period, a medical certificate has to be obtained for payments to be continued. After a year on sickness benefit, the person can only enter upon a new sickness benefit period after a six month interval in good health. Alternatively, the sick person will be eligible to rehabilitation allowance (see chapter 3).

In addition, an insured employee who is absent from work to look after a sick child under the age of 12 is entitled to daily cash benefits for ten days per calendar year, fifteen if more than two children need caring for. There are more generous rules for single parents, for disabled and/or chronically sick children. Parents are also entitled to cash benefits should their offspring be hospitalised – up to 18 years of age for disabled or chronically sick children.

The extent of generosity of sickness benefit schemes has been measured through an Index. Among OECD countries Germany, Denmark, Italy and Sweden scored highest on this index, while Norway was on fifth place. This low ranking seems mainly to be due to a somewhat lower take-up rate in Norway (Bambra, 2005), since to be eligible one must have a work record (see above).

Over the last ten to fifteen years there has been an increase in absenteeism from work, especially for periods of more than 3 days, which increased for women from an average of ten days in 1994 to 17 days in 2002, and for men from seven to 11 days respectively. If one includes short-term absence from work, average days off sick was around 24 in 2003 (St.prp. nr. 1 for 2004–2005, Hauge 2005). After 2005 the absenteeism has stagnated, but it increased during the end of 2005.

Table 6.1 Sickness benefits among employees (2006)

	Norway	**Sweden**	**Denmark**	**Netherlands**	**Germany**	**United Kingdom**	**France**
Benefits paid from day	1st day	2nd day	1st day	1st day	1st day	4th day	4th day
Maximum duration	52 weeks (Up to 16 days paid by employer)	In principle no time limitation (14 days paid by employer)	52 weeks within 18 months (2 weeks to be paid by employer)	104 weeks (paid by employer)	78 weeks over a 3-year period	52 weeks (28 weeks paid by employer)	12 months period of 3 consecutive years
Level of compensation	100% of earnings (limit 6 x Basic amount)	80% of earnings (limit 7,5 x basic amount)	100%, Calculated on the basis of earnings (maximum € 447 per week)	70% up to a maximum of € 168	70% of earnings (but not exceeding 90% of net salary)	Fixed amount (24-26%)	50% of daily earnings

Source: Mutual Information System on Social Protection in the EU Member States and the EEA (MISSOC) 2006.

Many explanations for this increase have been suggested, including changes in general health, changes in the working environment, changes in attitudes towards sickness and changes in diagnostic practice among GPs. A deterioration of the work ethic has also been mooted (Røed 2006). None of these explanations has been substantiated empirically. The changing composition of the labour force could be a possible reason, as sections of the population with higher risks of absenteeism, for example women with pregnancy related illnesses, move into the labour market.[120] Another is the ageing of the workforce: sickness increases with age.

Absenteeism is also associated with labour market and business cycles. When unemployment rises, sick days decline, only to rise again when unemployment starts falling (Hauge, 2005). High unemployment makes employees fear for their jobs, and eschew anything likely to increase job insecurity like taking time off sick (Blekasaune, 2005b). Restructuring and redundancies, apart from their direct impact on the individuals concerned, will also result in increased absenteeism among the remaining workforce due to the stress of restructuring (St.meld. nr. 9 2006–2007).

When eligibility and sick note issuance criteria were tightened in 2004, it

---

120 Statistics Norway. 2006. *Labour Statistics 2006*, Oslo.

may have worked together with the IA Agreement (see chapter 3) to cause the stagnation in numbers on sickness benefit (Blekasaune and Pedersen, 2006).

In an international comparison, generosity of sickness benefits was found to be positively correlated with level of absenteeism in some but not all of the countries included in the study (Dyrstad and Ose, 2005).

Right-wing political parties would like to cut sickness benefit, but are up against an adamant left-wing opposition backed by the trade unions. To reduce sick leave, the centre–left government, business and labour came up with a plan entailing more frequent and detailed checkups and allowing employers to seek out private healthcare for sick employees. Besides it shall be possible to buy health treatment for employees on sick leave, so that they can get back to work earlier.

Efforts to reduce absenteeism do not seem to have a long-lasting effect. With an ageing workforce and increasingly stressful working environment, new ways of reducing absenteeism will have to be considered. Ongoing experiments with reduced working hours and sabbaticals for people in stressful professions such as nursing will show whether this is a sensible way forward.

Challenges

The health sector faces four challenges. First, high costs and budget deficits. Second, low capacity and long waiting lists. Third, imbalance between public and personal responsibility. And fourth, lack of health professionals, especially nurses.

Private health clinics and hospitals divert money and expertise away from the national health service. Very high salaries of doctors in both private and public sector make it difficult for the regional health authorities to compete and keep costs down. New technology and advances in diagnostics, transplant surgery and other treatment necessitates more staff, all factors that contribute to spiralling costs in health care. New technology can save many more lives (for example organ transplants), but is extremely costly. More than ever it is therefore necessary to ask how money should be spent, particularly as the medical needs of the baby boomers start proliferating. The public's high expectations of the health service cannot possibly be met with the resources available to the health service. The medical professions predominant role in health care policy making seems to be shattered while politics are of greater importance. Continuous reform of the financing, governing and management of the national health service has been the cause of this development (Haave, 2006). Yet the huge budget deficits of most hospitals are financed by loans, making it extremely difficult to balance future budgets without substantial cuts in treatment capacity.

There are regional variations in the average length of stay in hospitals. They are caused not only by regional variations in sickness, but by variations in nursing home and domiciliary care capacity. More than half of the patients in hospital are over 66. Even after treatment many of them have to stay in hospital, since they cannot get the necessary care at home. The result is hospital over-crowding and patients in the corridors. And as the population ages, more hospital beds will be needed. The substantial reduction in hospital beds during the 1990s (Haave, 2006) has to be reversed.

Waiting days for treatment even of serious diseases such as breast cancer and prostate cancer are still unacceptably long, i.e. around 80 median waiting days in 2004, while median waiting days for less serious illnesses, such a varicose veins, was around 180 days.[121] As mentioned earlier, the reduction in waiting days for prioritised treatments has not been significant since 2001 when the state assumed responsibility for the hospitals. One would have expected a more significant reduction in waiting days as a consequence of the hospital reform. There are greater disparities between health regions when it comes to dealing with the most critical patients (Askildsen et al., 2007).

Mental health care represents great challenges. The number of beds at psychiatric units fell rapidly after the reforms of the '70s, and more and more people with mental problems are living in the community. Local authorities have not kept pace with this development. Preventive measures are insufficient and specialised services inadequate. It turns out that inpatient stays are often too short, and monitoring after discharge lacking. A national mental health programme was introduced in 1999, but despite the added money diverted to the sector and its root-and-branch reorganisation, the problems remain. Psychiatric units are only able to handle around 20 per cent of people with mental health problems. There are long waiting lists for treatment by psychologists.

Many somatic and mental health problems can be prevented or reduced by early intervention, at least in theory. In practice, it seems difficult to find politically acceptable mechanisms of prevention and early intervention (Elvbakken, 2006). In the report *Prescriptions for a Healthier Norway* (Ministry of Health, 2003), the ministry outlined a broad strategy for a healthier Norway. Prevention is difficult because it's about what *may* happen, not what is happening (ibid. 5). The purpose of prevention is to increase years of healthy life in the population as a whole, and address health disparities between social classes, ethnic groups and the sexes. It's a strategy which places responsibility for our health and welfare more squarely on our own shoulders.

There is a need to address discrimination in health care delivery and reduce disparities in health. If regional authorities make different priorities, the same treatment will clearly not be available across the board. People in the low income and education brackets will again be the losers. The wealthy can always afford to pay for treatment at private hospitals abroad. We therefore risk higher social as well as regional disparities in health in the future. Anoth-

---

121 St.prp. nr. 1 for 2005-2006 *Helse- og omsorgsdepartementets budsjett 2006.*

er challenge is the increase in life-style diseases and medicalization of everyday problems. Prevention would be better than treatment here too.

Finally, we need to learn how to train health professionals and keep them in the medical profession, not least in connection with the rapid expansion of the health care sector at the local level (see chapter 9). According to a report by the Norwegian Directorate of Health and Social Affairs on ethical recruitment of health workers, the government will not be recruiting staff from developing countries (Sosial- og helsedirektoratet, 2007).

Chapter 7
The ineradicable poverty

In most modern welfare states there is a 'last safety net' for those unable to provide for themselves through work, cannot rely on help from the family and are not entitled to social benefits such as unemployment benefits, old age or disability pension. This 'last safety belt' has different names: *social contribution* (Sweden), *economic support* (UK), *minimum integration income* (France), and *social assistance* (Germany and Norway; in Norwegian *sosialhjelp*). Historically, these arrangements are a legacy of the nineteenth century poor relief system. National systems of social assistance vary in terms the role in the total welfare system, in terms of generosity, legal entitlements, and the relationship between economic support, counselling and the obligation to work. In Norway, the social assistance system has a residual role, as social assistance benefits constitute only 1 – 2 per cent of total social expenditure. In this chapter, we shall describe the history of social assistance against the backdrop of the struggle to alleviate widespread poverty.

From poor relief to social assistance

The first national poor laws in Norway were introduced in 1845, delegating responsibility for the welfare of persons unable to fend for themselves to local authorities. A municipal board appointed a poor relief committee to decide on a discretionary basis who and what kind of assistance people in need should receive. Benefits were kept to a minimum to avoid tempting people to live off poor relief handouts. The system embraced something similar to the *less eligibility principle* of the British poor relief system: even the lowest paid salaried job should be preferable to poor relief. The municipal law of 1837 established municipal autonomy and local democracy – despite its limited suffrage (cf. chapter 1). Local authorities could raise taxes locally to finance the new poor relief system. The idea was that the local community was best placed to control the behaviour of the poor, how they spent what they received, and, not least, their willingness to work (Terum, 1996). A new, slightly reformed, poor law was adopted in 1900, but the basic principles were not changed.

After World War II, the Joint Programme of the political parties promised a new set of social laws and the end of the poor relief system. In the years to come, the new old age pensions, child benefits, unemployment benefits, etc. helped many groups avoid recourse to poor relief, which remained in place, and was in fact a last resort for people without rights to welfare under the universal social security system that was the responsibility of the state.

It was not until 1964 that the Storting got rid of the old poor relief system. With the *Social Care Act* of 1964, politicians wanted to break with the old ideology and modernize the social assistance system. For the incapacitated, the focus shifted from handouts to counselling and rehabilitation. The principle of *family treatment* was introduced, and this meant that all members of a family should be counselled by the same person. It was an expression of the general climate of the 1960s, when many looked optimistically to the new social sciences and the potential effects of social counselling and treatment. People in need of social assistance should be helped to return to working life and provide for themselves. Cash benefits should be temporary and awarded on a discretionary basis, and only enough to secure the basic necessities of those in need. But the law exacerbated incompatibilities between the administration of cash benefits, counselling and rehabilitation. Despite the new ideological wrapping, in practice the new law was not much different from the old, except in two respects. Social assistance was no longer considered a loan, to be paid back when circumstances improved, and parents and adult children were no longer obliged to provide for one another (Terum, 1996).

From the late 1960s other important changes took place. Storting required municipalities to establish social welfare agencies. Investments were made in social work training, and during the 1970s there was a veritable influx of social workers into jobs at municipal social administrations where they managed social assistance benefits, counselling, child care and support and rehabilitation of alcoholics and drug addicts. During the 1980s, many local councils adopted new rules on cash benefits (sosialhjelp), leaving it to the social welfare agencies to handle claims. At the same time, the Ministry of Social Affairs issued guidelines advising local authorities and social welfare agencies how to interpret the law. Benefits should be sufficient to ensure 'a reasonable standard of living'. Then in 1980 the Ministry recommended the national social insurance scheme's minimum rate as a point of departure, but responsive nevertheless to individual means-testing.

The present system: The 1991 Social Services Act

The present law on social services came into force in 1993. It was not radically different from the previous law. Social assistance is still managed by local authorities, and social workers still combine counselling and cash handouts. However, the new law reflected the wider European trend towards *workfare*. *Workfare* conditioned the payment of social benefits on participation in work or activation programmes (see chapter 3).

The law states that:
- Those who are not able to provide for themselves through work or by claiming entitlement to economic benefits are entitled to economic support.
- The support should aim at making the person able to provide for him- or herself.
- The social welfare agency may also give economic support so that a person may supersede or adjust to difficult circumstances of life.
- The agency may impose conditions for giving economic support, for instance that the client should perform a piece of work as long as she receives social assistance.[122]

Table 7.1 Persons who receive social assistance or equivalent benefits[123] (2005). Per cent of the population and income tested programmes as a per cent of public social expenditure (2003)

	Norway	Sweden	Denmark	Germany	UK
Social assistance	3.2	2.9	3.2	3.6	3.5
Income-tested programmes in cash	8.8	4.7	7.2	6.5	21.9

Sources: Social assistance calculated on the basis of figures from Nordic Social-Statistical Committee (http://www.nom-nos.dk/nososco.htm, accessed October 10 2007), Statistics Norway, Statistics Sweden, Statistics Denmark and from Statistisches Bundesamt Deutschland, Office for National Statistics, UK. Income-tested programmes: OECD Social Expenditure database: An interpretative Guide. OECD 2007. Version February 2007

Table 7.1 should be interpreted with caution, as there are additional means-tested or targeted benefits in these countries. However, it does indicate residual role of social assistance and means-tested cash benefits in the social protection systems in the countries included here, as those who receive social assistance benefits constitute only a small per cent of the population. However,

---

122 Lov om sosiale tjenester, § 5-4.
123 The figure for Germany is from 2004 and includes those who received social assistance monthly and assistance to persons in difficult circumstances, whereas the figures from other countries refer to all those who received social assistance at least once a year. Besides, the German social assistance system was revised in 2005, when a large number of people on Arbeitslosenhilfe were included in the social assistance system.

means-tested cash programmes play clearly a more significant role in cash transfers in the UK than in the Nordic countries and in Germany.

Economic support is still given on a discretionary basis, though the Ministry of Work and Social Inclusion can recommend amounts for specific types of client. Such guidelines are not binding, and a 2006 survey of 108 local authorities found that a third of them offered less than the Ministry's recommended level.[124]

The Ministry's 2006 recommendations are specified in table 7.2.

Table 7.2 Recommended social assistance benefits to different kind of households 2006 – housing expenses excluded.

	NOK	Euro
Single person	4 270	527
Couple/cohabitants	7 100	876
Each child 0–5 year	1 630	201
Each child 6–10 year	2 160	267
Each child 11–17 year	2 720	336
Person in a shared household	3 350	414

In addition, entitlement to social assistance is coupled to housing support, within reasonable limits. This applies to other extraordinary expenses as well. Income from work and social benefits such as child benefits and cash support shall be deducted. The amounts shall cover food, clothes and shoes, household goods, TV licence, telephone expenses, subscription to a newspaper, leisure, transport, heating and recreational activities for children.

In a comparative perspective, it adds up to a more generous package than most other countries offer their citizens. In an analysis of social assistance in 18 OECD countries, Norwegian social assistance benefits at levels recommended by the Ministry of Labour and Social Inclusion are ranked at the top, and estimated to be twice as high as the UK's, 76 per cent higher than the level in Sweden, and 40 per cent higher than Denmark's (Nelson, 2007). Although these amounts are generous compared to the level of social assistance benefits in other European countries and the US, it is generally considered low given the cost of living, average wages and other social benefits in Norway. Besides, there is an asset test. This means that savings must be spent

---

124 Kommunal Rapport March 30 2006.

before social assistance is granted. If a person requires social assistance over the longer term, but the welfare authorities find them leading a lifestyle grossly out of proportion to their basic needs (owning and using a car for instance), they can require the person to cut down on consumption, find a new place to live, sell the car or other goods. Students are not entitled to social assistance, inasmuch as loans and grants are available from the *Norwegian State Educational Loan Fund* (see chapter 4). Finally, social assistance is available to refugees and asylum-seekers (see chapter 9).

Apart from its relative generosity in an international perspective, discretionary means-testing is a prominent feature of social assistance in Norway, along with the lack of binding national rules and poor opportunities of appeal. Whereas nations such as the UK and Germany have established national rules for the social assistance benefits, in Norway the law instructs social workers to assess the circumstances and needs of each client and adjust the type and quantity of assistance accordingly. The basic aim is to tailor assistance to the individual claimant's situation. Besides, means-testing is considered both efficient and inexpensive a way of assisting those who are in real need, in contrast to more widely applicable universal arrangements that may be more expensive to run for the authorities and the tax-payer.

However, the problems of means-testing are well known. It does not result in equal treatment. As research shows, municipal councils do not base social assistance rates on the cost of living in the local community nor on the claimant's circumstances (Terum, 2003). The amount of money which a client receives is more influenced by the local council's wider budget, by the extent to which local politicians support redistribution and by the social workers' subjective perceptions of the claimant's needs. Means-testing is often associated with high stigma, and with making social integration more difficult. Some are afraid the child welfare authorities will suspect them of child neglect if they file for social assistance. A third weakness is the low benefit take-up in the target groups. When means-testing is based on complicated criteria, unclear rules and a discretionary approach, clients will find it difficult to get to know and understand the system. Means-testing can create a poverty trap that locks people in a difficult situation. In Norway, if a claimant earns money – however little – it is deducted from his benefit. People on benefit have few incentives to improve their situation by working part time in low paid jobs. Studies indicate how long-term take-up of social assistance saps the capacity of recipients to lead an active and autonomous life. The higher the benefit, the better the quality of life of the recipients (Borgeraas, 2006). In response to these problems the Directorate of Health and Social Affairs advised the Ministry to consider adopting a system of minimum benefit rates.

As mentioned above, another characteristic of social assistance is the limited right of appeal. A person who thinks that she or he does not receive a reasonable amount of money is not entitled to appeal to the county governor to review the discretion of the social welfare agency, as is normal when it comes to a range of other decisions of the municipality. The county governor can only review a social assistance decision if it is 'clearly unreasonable'. The right to appeal is stronger in for instance Sweden.

Who are social assistance recipients?

In 2006, 2.6 per cent of the population – 122,000 persons – received social assistance once or several times. If we include spouses and children, around 5 per cent of the population received social assistance. The low figures illustrate the universal character of the social welfare system in Norway – and that an inability to earn a livelihood tends to be mitigated by general arrangements as old age pensions, invalidity pension, unemployment benefits, etc.

On average, clients received a monthly sum of NOK 7,079 (c. 885 euros) over a period extending to 5.3 months. Shorter periods dominate, however, with 21 per cent at only one month and 44 per cent between one and three months. Only a small percentage seems to be incapable of providing for themselves over the longer term. Of those who took up social assistance for ten months in 2004, 8.6 per cent had received economic support for ten months in 2003 or 2002 as well.[125]

Single men constitute the largest group of social assistance recipients. Most of them are in their thirties, but compared to the population, 20–24-year-olds are more likely to take up social assistance benefits. In this group, around eight per cent has taken up social assistance each year since 1998. Single parents would probably have accounted for a higher percentage had it not been for the special type of social benefit for this group – the *transitional allowance*, which is described in chapter 4.[126]

We note that people in employment take up social assistance only infrequently. This indicates that wage levels in Norway are sufficient to the needs of the wage-earner and their family. An employed person will probably only need social assistance during critical periods such as when one of two wage-earning spouses is struck down by illness, accident or loss of other social benefits. Unemployment is a common reason to claim social assistance. People without work experience are not entitled to unemployment benefits (particularly the young – see chapter 3), or unemployment benefit may not suffice to cover mortgage instalments or living expenses.

A large per cent of social assistance recipients are classified as 'not seeking work'. 37 per cent of recipients receive other social benefits – disability or rehabilitation benefit, unemployment benefit and transitional allowance.[127]

---

125 See Statistics Norway, http://www.ssb.no/emner/03/04/30/soshjelpk/, accessed August 17 2007).
126 Source: Calculated on the basis of figures in www.ssb.no/emner/03/04/30/soshjelpk/tab-2005-09-08-07, accessed March 15 2006.

For these groups social assistance supplements the other social benefits, which are their main source of income.

Only a small number of the elderly are on social assistance. Only 1.4 per cent of social assistance recipients are 67 or older, and only 0.2 per cent over 65 took up social assistance in 2006. The old age pension system, then, with its combination of universal minimum pension (see chapter 5) and income related supplementary pension, has almost eradicated poverty among the elderly in Norway.

Poverty

One of the main objectives of the social assistance system is to prevent poverty among people outside the labour market and without entitlement to other social benefits from the welfare state. This raises the question concerning the extent of poverty in Norway today, and the social assistance system's contribution to its eradication. The answers depend on how we define poverty. The literature on poverty offers several definitions. The most important are:
- Absolute poverty, which is defined as the lack of shelter, food and clothes.
- Relative poverty that most often is measured by income, most frequently as 50 or 60 per cent of the median income for the different types of households. Today, the European Union applies the 60 per cent income line.
- Poverty as relative deprivation. In his classic study on poverty in the UK Peter Townsend suggested that the poor should be defined as those who do not have the resources to the diet, activities and living conditions that else were common in the society in which they lived (Townsend, 1979).
- Consensual poverty. Joanna Mack and Stewart Lansley have in another key study (Mack and Lansley, 1985) argued that poverty should defined as not having what the majority deems necessary.

This is not the place to discuss the problems and weaknesses of these definitions. Suffices to say there is no objective definition of poverty since all are based on normative conceptions. However, most researchers support a relative definition of poverty as the most fruitful for modern welfare economies because being disadvantaged is not only measured by lack of food, clothing or shelter, but by the absence of goods and amenities enjoyed by people in general. Of the definitions mentioned above, the relative income definition of poverty is simplest and most suitable for comparative research, with 50 or 60 per cent of a country's median income serving as a poverty line.

In the 1970s, it was generally assumed that poverty had been eradicated entirely in Norway. During the 1980s, studies adopting a relative conception

---

127 Respectively 11, 9, 5 and 3 per cent of all recipients.

of poverty suggested a prevalence as high as 5–6 per cent (Stjernø, 1985), something the authorities had great difficulties in accepting. However, when the EU started to finance more research of this type, and Norway came out better than most other countries in Europe, resistance faded away. In the 1990s inequality and poverty became an issue of public concern (Seim, 2006). In 1994, activists founded what they named *The Poor House* in Oslo, giving the poor a public face and the media an opportunity to meet and write about them. The 1997 general election had poverty as an issue, and in the next one, in 2001, poverty was the *main* issue. Catching up with opinion, the conservative coalition prepared a white paper on poverty which was published in 2003 (St. meld. nr. 6 2002–2003). After 70 years, poverty was again an object of study in a government document. Before we delve into strategies discussed for combating poverty, let us take a look at what current research says about poverty in Norway today.

In the following we use the EU-sanctioned 60 per cent of median income as the poverty line.

Table 7.3 Poverty in selected European countries in 2004. Household income less than 60 per cent of equivalised median income. In per cent[128]

	Before social transfers	After social transfers	Poverty reducing effect
Norway	36	11	−15
Sweden	30	11	−19
Denmark	31	11	−20
Germany	24	16	−8
France	26	14	−12
UK	29	18	−11
Italy	23	19	−4
EU (25) average	26	16	−10

Source: Eurostat (2007).

---

[128] A median income is defined as the value that divides the population in two equal parts – meaning that as many persons have a lower and a higher income. Equivalised means that different types of households are compared according to the number of persons in the household by the means of a scale. In the EU scale the first adult person counts as 1, other adults above 16 years as 0.5, and each child under 16 years as 0.3.

Table 7.3 serves to illustrate four theses on poverty in Norway and Scandinavia. First, if there was no welfare state, the market would create approximately the same rate of poverty in Scandinavia as the other European countries – in Sweden and Denmark actually a little more. Second, poverty after social transfers is significantly lower in Scandinavia than in most other European countries – particularly compared to the UK and Southern European countries where the poverty rate is around 20 per cent. Third, this means that social transfers in the Scandinavian – particularly the Swedish and Danish – welfare states evidently reduce poverty more than in the other countries. Fourth, despite the universal welfare state in Scandinavia, there is still a group of around 11 per cent living on or below this definition's poverty line. However, on a 50 per cent median income level, poverty in Norway sinks to 5 – 6 per cent, widening significantly the difference between Norway and most countries on the continent. This is mainly due to the fact that persons on the basic old age pension are included in the 60 per cent definition, but not the 50 per cent one. Generally, the benefits under the national insurance scheme such as basic pension, disability and survivor benefits are much more effective at reducing poverty than social assistance.

Table 7.4 Feeling about present household income nowadays. In per cent

	Living comfortably	**Coping**	**Difficult**	**Very difficult**
Norway	55	36	7	2
Sweden	59	33	7	2
Denmark	68	27	4	1
Germany	24	58	14	5
France	29	54	15	2
UK	41	43	13	3
Spain	33	50	14	3

Source: ESS 2004/2005 (weighted).

As Table 7.4 shows, Scandinavians – particularly Danes – are more likely to express a sense of economic security. Whereas 50–70 per cent live comfortably on their present income in Scandinavia, a third at most would agree with this statement on the Continent, and 40 per cent of UK citizens. There are no big differences on variables like 'very difficult to cope', but whereas 20 per cent of Germans and 15 – 20 per cent of other nationalities find it difficult or very difficult to cope on current income, only 9 per cent say so in Norway and Sweden – and only 5 per cent in Denmark. Economic hardship is clearly less prevalent in Scandinavia than in other parts of Western Europe.

Who is poor in Norway today? That partly depends on the chosen poverty line. But whether it is 60 or 50 per cent, some tendencies seem to stand out (table 7.5).

Table 7.5 Poor in different groups in Norway in 2003 and 2006 (the whole population). Per cent

	Poverty line 50 per cent of equivalised median income	**Poverty line 60 per cent of equivalised median income**
The whole population	4.8	9.7
Single persons less than 35 years	20	30
Single breadwinners with children	6	15
Old age pensioners	6	15
Persons on disability pension	5	12
Persons on old age minimum pension living alone	27	69
Long term unemployed	19	33
Long term sick	7	16
Immigrants from Third World countries	24	35
Refugees	23	36
Social assistance recipients	26	43

Source: Statistics Norway (http://www.ssb.no.emner/05/01/inntind/tab-2005-10-14.12.html, accessed March 16 2006) and www.ssb.no/emner/056/01/iffor/tab,accessed, March 3 2008. EU-scale.

Irrespective of definition, the poor appear to be overrepresented in these groups compared to the total population. In other words, one is more likely to find poverty among immigrants from Third World countries, refugees, persons on basic old age pensions who live alone (mostly women), young persons living alone, and long term unemployed. One reason for the prevalence of poverty among immigrants and refugees is the generally poor level of integration in the labour market and chance of having a paid job. If we concentrate on poverty line at 60 per cent, a high proportion of people on the basic old age pension living in single households must be considered poor, with some overrepresentation of single breadwinners with children and long term sick.

An important characteristic of modern poverty in Norway is its transience for the majority of the poor. Only 2.2 per cent of the population were poor throughout the five-year period 1996–99 and only 1.5 per cent in the ten years between 1986 and 1995 (on the 50 per cent median income definition). About 50 per cent of the poor in one year will not be poor the year after. However, many of these will remain in the lower income brackets (Andersen et al. 2003), and will continue to live with scarcity and economic problems.

The ability of social assistance to reduce poverty is illustrated by the low prevalence of poverty among social assistance recipients – 26 per cent at a 50 per cent level and 43 per cent at 60 per cent of median income (Hatland and Bradshaw, 2006; Hatland and Pedersen, 2006). With the poverty line at 50 per cent, no more than a 1/3 of the poor took up social assistance in 2000 and social assistance only cuts the rate of poverty from 4.7 to 3.9 per cent. While a 60 per cent definition would have some affect on the figures, the conclusion would probably be the same: social security and taxation are much more effective in reducing poverty than social assistance. With the present social security system, support for families such as child benefit and cash support is more effective in reducing poverty than social assistance (Andersen, et al. 2003).

Shame and stigma

Why do we observe such a weak relationship between being poor and receiving social assistance? What alternatives to social assistance are available to the poor? Some people are unaware of their chances of getting social assistance. Some prefer to live in scarcity than to ask for help from the state. They may be proud and prefer to retain a measure of independence by buying inexpensive food, foregoing consumer goods and not taking part in social activities. They may fear the stigma attached to social assistance, and a cause of shame and embarrassment for themselves and their family. Some get help from their family, others borrow money or work in the black economy, have recourse to criminality or prostitution. We know about these choices, apart from the stigma often associated with social assistance.

Historically, stigma and shame were part and parcel of poor relief. Generally, people looked down on the poor, a habit that survived into our own time with the modern social assistance system. Even today, as many as two-thirds of the population would dislike or dislike strongly others knowing that they needed social assistance from the social welfare agency. 61 per cent would be reluctant to file for social assistance, 22 per cent would find it inconceivable, and only 14 per cent say it would be okay (Hatland and Pedersen, 2006). Thus, social assistance continues to inspire a sense of shame and stigma, stopping many people from contacting the social welfare agency when in need.

Government strategy against poverty

The non-socialist government's report on poverty (St. meld. nr. 6 2002–2003) declared that nobody should have to live in poverty. But poverty was narrowly defined as below 50 per cent of the median income over a three-year period. The government invited voluntary organizations and social researchers to join in a brainstorming session on ways of eradicating poverty and promised to set up a report system on poverty. Further expansion of universal social security was not an option. Instead, means-testing and tailor-made services would be necessary to identify and establish contact with the poor. The main focus will be on efforts to ease participation of the poor in the labour market. Resources would be forthcoming for employment programmes with training for one thousand long-term social assistance claimants. The government report said nothing about tackling unemployment among people in poor physical or mental health, nor did propose raising social assistance for people unable to provide for themselves for whom other benefits are out of reach. Indeed, the government actually cut benefits for the unemployed and disabled, hoping to create an incentive to get back to work.

As mentioned above, the government pledged money to training for work programmes for 1,000 long-term social assistance claimants as part of its plan to reduce poverty. A research-based evaluation of the programme was unable to establish concrete gains from the programme. Of the 1,000 claimants, only 23 per cent had succeeded in getting an ordinary job after the programme, and it was impossible to say whether this was because of the programme or would have happened anyway. Many more were still on social assistance, drawing a disability pension, involved in rehabilitation or other training for work programmes (Lødemel and Johannessen, 2005). The problems facing this evaluation are common to studies in other countries: whether such programmes affect success in the ordinary job market is hard to pin down. For some clients with mental health problems, a Finnish study found, compulsory participation in such programmes may even exacerbate their condition (Mamberg-Heimonen, 2005).

At the end of the electoral period, the government could not document significant effects of its declared struggle against poverty. The poverty rate had not decreased, something the opposition blamed the government for in the 2005 election campaign. In its programme, the new red-green majority government of DNA, SV and Sp promised to address social inequality and eradicate poverty. It would reinforce public safety nets and facilitate a return to work for the unemployed. It presented a plan to eradicate poverty with these key elements:

- A determined public policy should aim at activating and including the poor in the labour market so that the poor could provide for themselves through income from work.
- A right to a welfare contract. Those who enter the contract with the intention to take part in training, employment, treatment shall receive more than social assistance benefits.
- Social assistance and housing benefit rates, particularly for families with children, will rise.
- Additional benefits for children will be made available through the social security programme.
- Patient fees will remain low for certain low-income groups.
- Labour, social security, and social assistance agencies will be merged (NAV).

The red-green government staved off calls to overhaul the social assistance system. While labour and social security agencies were integrated into one government agency, social assistance will be in the care of local authorities, not the state, contrary to what many social researchers have long been urging. The Ministry of Social Affairs recommended a modest 5 per cent rise in benefit payments in 2007, but with no further increase envisioned for 2008.

The red-green government seems wedded to participation in the labour market as its primary poverty-alleviation mechanism. In principle this seems to be wise move, but one must not forget the modern labour market's inability to absorb the poor in large numbers – people who in addition to poverty are often afflicted with physical and mental health problems, low skills and a record of instability. Efforts to encourage wider labour market participation coupled with the government's unwillingness to increase social security benefits may prove counterproductive to its poverty reduction plans.

Besides, the recent performance of the Norwegian economy and relative character of the definition of poverty (50 or 60 per cent of median income) don't make it easier to reduce the number of poor. In periods of strong economic growth, when more people have income from the capital market, economic inequalities tend to grow. And as wages rise, the gap between the well-to-do and low-income groups outside or on the margins of the labour market widens too. Thus, from 2004 to 2005, poverty (defined as 50 per cent of median income) increased from 6.1 to 6.2 per cent – and from 11.0 to 11.4 per cent with the 60 per cent poverty line (Bjørnestad, 2007; SSB, 2007). It remains to be seen if the red-green government can reverse this – or eradicate poverty as it has promised.

How should we explain the paradox of the public outcry over poverty in a country with one of the lowest poverty rates in Europe? One explanation could be sought in the prolonged period of economic health in Norway since the late 1990s. In this period, oil revenue ensure buyant economic growth, a healthy budget and foreign trade balance (see chapter 2). The government is stockpiling huge funds abroad. But the public find it hard to accept that 5 to 10 per cent of the population ostensibly live in conditions of poverty. At the same time, the way Norwegian politics is orchestrated nowadays makes poverty alleviation something of a political contest. On the centre-right, the Christian People's Party (KrF) considers social suffering and poverty a key issue, and the KrF Prime Minister was strongly personally engaged in this issue. On the centre left, the Socialist Left Party (SV) has been a strong defender of equality and against privileges. In this way, a competition between the two political camps was established.

Conclusion, challenges and dilemmas

The Norwegian social assistance system is still marked by the old poor relief system. It is administered by local authorities rather than by national laws and guidelines, compared to other Scandinavian and European countries at least. Benefits are in theory assigned on a discretionary basis, though in practice, welfare officials rely on municipal rules. In the UK and Germany, social assistance tends to be regulated by national laws and guidelines, and there is a wider right of appeal etc. The only point on which Norwegian social assistance can be said to improve on these countries is generosity. Against a background of sustained public criticism of the lack of legal safeguards and benefit levels and calls from the Ombudsman to take action the Minister of Employment and Inclusion acknowledged the need for a revision and possible overhaul of the system.[129]

This reluctance on the part of government to modernize social assistance, centralize its management and increase benefit rates is caused by a particular historical legacy and a dilemma intrinsic to the employment-oriented Norwegian welfare state. Ideologically, work – and looking for work – is supposed to be more beneficial and profitable than not working. Benefits cannot therefore be allowed to act as a disincentive, especially to low income sectors, to look for work.

Compared to many other European countries, social assistance recipients constitute only a tiny minority of social benefit claimants all told. The fact that Norway has not as many poor as most other nations is due to the combined effect of high labour market participation rates and the universal character of the social security system. Eradicating all poverty in Norway is confronted with many challenges. As the poor are such a heterogeneous and fragmented group, it is very difficult to find a strategy that works equally well

---

[129] See http://www.regjeringen.no/nb/dep/aid/pressesenter/pressemeldinger/2007/93.html?id=477629, accessed at August 17 2007.

for all of them. Some have problems only with finding employment, others are severely handicapped by somatic and mental health problems – including anxiety, social phobias, alcohol and drug abuse, etc. And there are the young with no labour market experience and little education; immigrants who face discrimination in the labour market; lone parents; single elderly women with expensive mortgages or rental accommodation and minimum old age pension. These groups have nothing in common apart from economic scarcity.

The government's poverty eradication strategy is caught in a dilemma: If they raise benefit payments, people may prefer to stay out of work. But if they don't, they face criticism for lack of generosity. An anti-poverty strategy which aims to make work pay runs the risk of making people who can't work even poorer. As owning stocks and shares has become quite popular, capital income has become widespread and made the income gap wider, this could increase the numbers facing relative poverty as described above. This happened in Denmark, where poverty rose by almost 50 per cent during the period of strong growth from 1995 to 2004 (LO 2007). Were the same thing to happen in Norway, it would represent a significant embarrassment to the present red-green government and may come to haunt it at the next general election in 2009.

A system of guaranteed minimum income (GMI) would probably do more to limit poverty than the present social assistance system. However, only SV and the Liberal Party (V) have so far demonstrated an interest in discussing a guaranteed minimum income. There are several reasons why the other political parties do not support a more fundamental reform of social assistance. As firm believers in the work ethic, the labour movement and Labour Party fear the consequences of over-generous social assistance benefits or GMI. They could erode the work ethic, lead to reduced participation in the labour market and harm the future financing of the welfare state – an attitude shared by most of the other parties. Besides, the Conservative party is opposed to a further expansion of universal benefits, and argues for benefits and services to be 'tailor-made' to fit the claimant's circumstances. The Progress Party is sceptical to social assistance claimants many of whom, it suspects, do not want to work and prefer living on government handouts. Finally, most of the parties – and the Ministry of Finance – think that a reform of social assistance would be too costly and increase public expenditure too much.

Chapter 8
Civil society: Trust and participation

The term *civil society* refers to that part of society that is separate from the market and the state, where people interact outside the market and the state. Civil society is social movements, voluntary organizations, self-help groups and primary relationships such as the family, neighbours and friends. *Social movements* bring people together in pursuit of a political or ideological objective. Common movements are the trade union movement, the missionary movement, temperance movement, women's movement, anti-globalization movement. Most often social movements are fronted by voluntary organizations, but the difference between a social movement and voluntary organization is not very clear. A *voluntary organization* can be a private, i.e. non-governmental, affair – though it may receive support from the government. Membership or participation is not compulsory, it is self-governing and does not work for or distribute profits to managers, stockholders, etc (Salamon, Sokolowski et al. 2003). In most voluntary organizations in Norway, members pay an annual fee, and elect representatives who elect the leadership of the organization at a general assembly. Examples are the *Red Cross* and the *Norwegian Association for the Blind*. As its name indicates, a *self-help group* is founded on the belief that people with similar problems can help each other. Self-help groups exist for people with mental health problems, drug and alcohol abuse, pathological gambling, etc.

Here we understand *civil society* to include all these phenomena. However, several other concepts are in use which means more or less the same thing – third sector, voluntary sector, and non-profit sector. Civil society is an essential part of any society, but the structure of civil society and the relationship between civil society and the state on the one hand and the market on the other varies quite a lot from one country to another. This chapter describes how civil society works in the field of welfare in Norway. We focus mainly on organizations and their work, but mention social movements and self-help groups whenever necessary.

Solidarity and trust

In some nations, the family or the extended family is considered the basic social unit. Loyalty is what binds social groups related by blood or marriage together. Loyalty is an obligation of mutual assistance, helping one another find work, business deals, positions of authority. Trust is not necessarily extended to outsiders, some of whom may be treated with hostility even.

Although this might describe the case in Norway as well, Norwegian society displays high levels of trust in people outside the family. Historically, non-related people have collaborated and assisted each other. In the nineteenth century, peasant solidarity found expression in a cooperative movement. It protected members from the hazards of life and market economy. Craftsmen's guilds organized schools and funeral funds for members (Christiansen, 1997). Neighbours sometimes helped each other out with food and money at difficult times, such as a death in the household. The Norwegian historian Knut Kjeldstadli has called the pre-working class solidarity of the nineteenth century 'the community of commoners' (*almuesamhold*) (Kjeldstadli, 1997). This sense of community was structured exchange of favours, services and help. The Norwegian concept of *dugnad* refers to a social activity in which neighbours, members of a local community or group come together to work for a common purpose or assist one of their members. The latter might entail rebuilding someone's house after a fire, painting a house, repairing a bridge, etc. In the late nineteenth and the first part of the twentieth century the labour movement developed an ideology of solidarity across sectional and geographical boundaries. Besides, a successful struggle for social reforms and the gradual development of the welfare state gave people a positive experience of the state (see chapter 1). All these factors created the basis for trust – both in other people (horizontal trust) and in the authorities and the state (vertical trust) (Halvorsen, 2007).

Also today, there is a relative strong normative ideology compared to many other countries that citizens should help each others, as is illustrated in table 8.1.

Second to the Greeks, Norwegians, together with the French are more often of the opinion that one should help others than citizens of most other European nations. Although the gap to the British and Germans is not very large, we shall see below that this attitude is combined with a higher level of trust and a higher prevalence of voluntary work.

Table 8.1 Persons who agree that citizens should spend at least some of their free time helping others. Per cent

Denmark	61
Sweden	68
Norway	79
Netherlands	54
UK	71
Germany	75
France	79
Greece	84

Source: ESS 2004/2005.

Table 8.2 Persons who agree that 'most people can be trusted (10) or you can't be too careful.' (1). Mean score 1 – 10

Denmark	7.0
Norway	6.8
Sweden	6.3
UK	5.4
Germany	4.7
France	4.4
Spain	5.1

Source: ESS 2004/2005 (weighted).

When asked to indicate a point along an axis extending from 'most people can be trusted' to 'you cannot be too careful', only Danes are more likely than Norwegians to indicate willingness to trust others. On an index from 1 (no trust) to 10 (complete trust) Norwegians score 6.8 whereas the British score 5.4 and Germans 4.7, and the French even lower. Trust is generally higher in social democratic welfare regimes than in liberal and conservative ones (Halvorsen, 2007). Several factors may explain the high levels of trust in Scandinavia. The Scandinavian countries are small and historically homogeneous, ethnically (until recently), linguistically, and religiously. Egalitarianism and positive experiences with collaboration and consensus-orientation may have contributed in the same direction. Low unemployment and poverty rates in modern times have prevented misery and kept crime within limits and reduced the need to be suspicious about the motives of others.

The historical heritage: The social movements

It is hard to understand Norwegian history and politics without understanding the special role of the social movements. In the nineteenth century, four social movements emerged in Norway. In the south and the west, there were oppositional groups founded on Pietism – ascetic Protestantism – allied with missionary zeal. The movement was critical of the established church's clergy and lifestyle of the urban middle class in the capital. From the same regions, a nationalist movement emerged, with an ambition to (re)create a Norwegian language. 'New Norwegian' (*Nynorsk*), as they called it, built on local dialects, in opposition to the Dano-Norwegian language, spoken in the cities by the upper classes and authorities. A temperance movement campaigned against the scourge of alcohol that caused so much misery among working people. The Pietistic, New Norwegian, and temperance movements distilled popular sentiment into a 'counter-culture', as a foil to that of the urban bourgeoisie.

In the 1840s, an embryonic labour movement could be observed as well. By the end of the century workers and intellectuals were joining forces to install trade unions. Sports clubs, choirs and brass bands proliferated (Wollebæk et al., 2000), taking hold of social and democratic currents in Norwegian society and mobilized around social, cultural and political issues. They formed the bedrock of the new voluntary organizations that developed into training grounds for broad political participation of farmers and workers before Parliamentary democracy was fully developed in 1884. These social movements also served to consolidate the sense of reciprocal trust among people (cf. table 8.2).

Voluntary organizations before the welfare state

Voluntary organizations played an important role as purveyors of social welfare in Europe before the welfare state came into being. In the UK liberalism became a hegemonic ideology in the eighteenth century. Voluntary social activities were given a prominent role and the well-to-do were expected to help the needy and support various forms of benevolence. In Germany, Catholics established welfareorganizations and Catholic social teaching influenced the development of the welfare state. While the state had a social responsibility, it should not be allowed to interfere with voluntary organisations and their work, though governmental support was welcomed. This *subsidiarity principle* became a key characteristic of the German welfare state and gave voluntary organizations a privileged position in organizing social and health care.

In Norway, things proceeded differently. As mentioned in chapter 1, the Lutheran Reformation resulted in the state confiscating Church property, crippling the Church's ability to help the sick and poor on a wider scale. Besides, there was not sufficient personal wealth to finance a large benevolent sector.

Nationwide voluntary organizations were established from the mid nineteenth century. The first national voluntary organizations were offshoots of the social movements of the 1840s. Humanitarian organizations multiplied between 1890 and 1940. Among these were organizations for women, such as the *Norwegian Women's Health Organization* (1906) and *National Council for Norwegian Women* (1904). They were also informed by the new women's movement, and acquired rapidly an important role in the field of health and social issues (Wollebæk, Selle et al., 2000).

Some organizations such as the *Red Cross* and the *National Council for Women* established hospitals and institutions for the treatment of alcoholism and for the mentally disabled. When the Labour Party came into power, some of the work in the voluntary sector was transferred to the state and its agencies. And as the voluntary organizations were generally happy to forgo the responsibility there was not much of a political conflict between the government and voluntary sector over their respective territories (Kuhnle, 1990). Unlike the situation in the UK and Germany, these organizations did not see themselves as an alternative to the state and government or in opposition to them, but as partners and collaborators (Sivesind, Lorentzen et al. 2002).

After 1945, a range of social political special interest organizations was established to serve people with physical disabilities – e.g. the blind, the deaf, the handicapped, etc. (Seip 1981). By the 1970s, the self-help movement was beginning to flourish. These various groups saw themselves primarily as advocates of social justice, spearheading campaigns for greater local and central government involvement and resources, sufficient to lead an independent life despite their handicap.

The voluntary sector in the modern welfare state

Thus, the voluntary organizations contributed to the expansion of the welfare state, and the expansion of health and social services was channelled into the public sector. The Labour Party, now in power, was not interested in a partnership with the voluntary sector in health and social policy. Nor did the voluntary organizations push in that direction. On the contrary, they wanted the state to meet social needs and establish health and social services – rather than calling for more money to the voluntary sector to fund expansion. So while Germany for instance gave voluntary organizations the resources to develop social services, putting the principle of subsidiarity into practice in other words, and liberalism in the UK assigned an important role to the voluntary sector, social democratic ideology had no room for the concept of voluntary organization. However, voluntary organizations continued to run a few hospitals and many social institutions and were junior partners to the government. They were included in government plans, regulated in law and largely subsidized or financed by the government.

From the 1960s and onwards, the voluntary sector began changing. The old social movements had lost much of their appeal and found it increasingly difficult to attract new members. The voluntary organizations that had grown out of these movements were similarly affected. Increasing prosperity and expansion of the welfare state reduced the need for voluntary humanitarian services. At the same time, a range of new voluntary organizations were evolving in new fields. They engaged with issues related to culture and leisure such as sport, choirs and other hobbies (Sivesind, Lorentzen et al., 2002). Organizations whose activities focused on social problems and political campaigning turned inwards to concentrate on their own members (Selle, 1999).

When in the late 1970s and the early 1980s the political and ideological climate changed in Europe, and the neo-liberalism of Margaret Thatcher in the UK and Ronald Reagan in the US became influential, attention turned to alternatives to public responsibility. In this perspective, the voluntary sector was seen as an obvious alternative to continued welfare state expansion. After the 1981 election, a non-socialist government headed by a Conservative prime minister took office in Norway. The new government appointed a committee to review the role of the voluntary organizations. The ensuing report *Voluntary Organizations* (*Frivillige organisasjoner.* NOU 1988:17) described the voluntary sector, but did not result in significant reforms or new support to the voluntary organizations. On paper, then, while the government seemed to accept the voluntary sector as a partner in social and health policy matters, it made no real difference to the sector's role in the welfare state. So reality changed considerably less than ideology.

In 1991 the Storting approved an experiment with *volunteer bureaus* in some municipalities, set up to liaise between the community and voluntary organizations. It would put potential volunteers in touch with organizations in need of staff, and persons in need of help with the appropriate charity or volunteer. The bureaus had a manager and were expected generate voluntary work that at least equalled the value of the resources provided by the government. At the end of the experiment, results were so good, the volunteer bureaus were put on a permanent footing. The next decade saw bureaus spring up in 200 municipalities (out of 420). Today, they generate the equivalent of 600–700 full-time jobs, but only a fraction of the voluntary sector's total input in Norway (Kloster et al., 2003). The bureaus are run by a variety of bodies, such as humanitarian organizations, parish councils, women's and pensioners' organizations, local authorities, etc. They have no common or clearly defined ideology, though the sense of doing something for the local community is important to most of the staff and volunteers.

In 1996, the government published a white paper *On the state's relationship to voluntary organizations* (St. meld. 27 1996–1997). In it they reviewed several reasons why the government should support the voluntary sector: First, local participation and activity are important. Second, voluntary organizations are important as a partner to the authorities in many ways. They run crisis centres, are engaged in alcohol and drug abuse work and so on. Third, the voluntary sector can often run schemes and institutions more cheaply and efficiently than the public sector. The white paper instanced nursing homes and alcohol and drug abuse institutions (Kloster, Lidén et al., 2003).

Since the 1980s, the role and function of voluntary welfare organizations have changed. Many national organizations are now less concerned with what their local branches get up to, preferring to attend to their own activities and relations with central authorities. At the same time, community activity groups and organisations have appeared. Membership of religious and women's organizations has fallen, the once broad social (and political) movements are no longer as broad, and in their place we have organizations for particular health and social problems (Sivesind, Lorentzen et al. 2002). While cultural, sporting and leisure pursuits are more prominent, humanitarian voluntary activities for people in need are declining.

The scope and tasks of voluntary organizations

Today, voluntary organizations play an insignificant role in providing economic security for people in need. Instead, pensions, unemployment benefits and social assistance provide the main channels of government cash transfers and wealth redistribution. The role of the voluntary sector today is mainly in the fields of:
- Advocacy: Organizations campaign and lobby on behalf of special interest groups and/or members and their particular needs (cf. chapter 1).
- Solidarity: They bring members together in different forms of social activity.
- They own and run health and social institutions that deliver social and health services consonant with the regulatory and financial framework set by the government.

Some organizations specialise in one or two of these fields, others manage them all, though the balance varies. Voluntary organizations in Norway have 5.8 million members, meaning that every person aged 16–85 is a member of 1.7 organizations. Sport and culture account for the majority, though social and humanitarian organizations are second largest group with one million members (Wollebæk, Selle et al. 2000).

Unfortunately, statistics on non-state health institutions do not tell us anything about their ownership arrangements, whether for instance they are owned by a voluntary organization, trust, private person or firm. However, in the area of hospital ownership overall, these arrangements are virtually negligible, accounting for less than 2 per cent of all hospital man-labour-years. In contrast, nearly half of the child welfare institution sector is under this kind of ownership.[130] Further, voluntary organizations predominate only in the field of alcohol and drug dependence, where almost two thirds of beds are in institutions owned by voluntary organizations, trusts, private persons or firms. This is more than Sweden, but much less than Germany.

Tables 8.3 and 8.4 illustrate where the voluntary sector in Norway differs from other European states and the US. First, Norwegians are more likely to do volunteer work and be members of voluntary organizations than people elsewhere. Whereas 52 per cent say that they did some voluntary work last year in Norway, it was 30 per cent in the UK and 10 per cent in Germany. Voluntary work for social and humanitarian organizations in Norway equals work performed for special interest organizations for the sick and disabled and large humanitarian organizations such as *Norwegian Women's Health Organization*, *National Council for Norwegian Women* and *Red Cross* (Wollebæk, Selle et al., 2000).

Table 8.3 Paid staff and volunteers as a percentage of all employed and of the adult population

	Norway	Germany	UK	Italy	US	Japan	South Africa
Volunteers. Per cent of the adult population	52	10	30	4	22	0.5	9
Volunteers. Per cent of the economically active population	4.4	2.3	3.6	1.5	3.6	1.0	1.6
Paid staff. Per cent of the economically active population	2.7	3.5	4.8	2.3	6.3	3.2	1.8

Source: Johns Hopkins Comparative Nonprofit Sector Project.[131]

---

130 According to Statistics Norway – see http://www.ssb.no/emner/03/02/speshelsesom/tab-2007-06-20-03.html, http://www.ssb.no/emner/03/03/10/barneverni/, and http://www.ssb.no/emner/03/02/speshelserus/tab-2007-06-20-01.html, accessed at November 7 2007.

131 Data to the Johns Hopkins Comparative Nonprofit Sector Project were collected at different points of time in the period 1995 - 1998. Collection methods differed slightly from country to country, and the data should be view with some caution. See http://www.jhu.edu/%7Ecnp/.

Second, persons employed by the voluntary organizations in the UK and Germany constitute a much larger per cent of all employed than in Norway, even though the rate is not high in either country. Third, in Norway the voluntary health and services employ a lower percentage of those employed by voluntary organizations than in countries such as Germany and Italy, where Catholicism has influenced social policy – whereas those employed in voluntary cultural organizations (including sports) constitute a larger share (table 8.4).

Table 8.4 The workforce of voluntary organizations by sector. Percentage

	Norway	Germany	UK	Italy	US	Japan	South-Africa
Health and Social services	20	49	24	44	56.3	50.6	15.5
Culture	41	20	28	24	9.0	5.5	17.6
Education	11	8	25	15	18.5	18.5	5.5
Development/International	7	6	15	4	4.3	3.5	17.9

Source: Johns Hopkins Comparative Nonprofit Sector Project. All sectors not included.

In Norway, most volunteers worked for cultural organisations, whereas volunteer labour in the health and social service sector accounted for around half of the total workforce of these organizations in the US, Japan, Germany and Italy.

Previous analyses have demonstrated that the higher participation in voluntary social organizations in Norway is part of a general pattern of organizational participation in the Scandinavian countries. Data from the *European Value Study* show that Norwegians and other Scandinavians are members of professional organizations, trade unions, political parties, solidarity organizations to a greater extent than citizens of other European nations (Stjernø, 1995). It is a legacy perhaps of the important historical role of social movements in Norway (cf. above and chapter 1). The social movements – particularly the labour movement – managed to get the state to accept responsibility for social security, and health and social service delivery. Voluntarily organizations have a more expressive function as platforms for religious, cultural, artistic, social and recreational interests and sentiments (Salamon et al., 2003).

Why do people take part in voluntary organizations? Comparative studies suggest that motives in Norway are not very different from motives in other countries. However, Norwegians are more likely to mention contribution to the local community and less frequently personal satisfaction. Religious motives seem to be less important here than in the UK and Germany (Stjernø 1995). As a recent study shows, members of social and humanitarians organizations are more likely to mention the wish to help others and influence decision making as reasons for participation than members of other voluntary organizations (Wollebæk et al., 2000).

Self-help groups

Self-help groups constitute another part of civil society. A self-help group tends to pursue a common problem, e.g., an illness. By coming together regularly they seek to change the way they relate to their problem and environment, mainly without professional input and without a profit motive. The basic principles of self-help groups are participation on equal terms and reciprocity. Self-help groups provide a space for face-to-face contact. Members come together and agree on the activities of the group. Sometimes they develop into a voluntary organization. It was estimated in the 1990s that there were 2,500 self-help groups with 25,000 members. Single persons, women, people with higher education, persons who are not well integrated in the labour market and with a high incidence of health problems were overrepresented in self-help groups (Hjemdal et al., 1998). This pattern is similar to those reported by research on self-help groups in other European countries (Stjernø, 1995).

Self-help groups address any number of concerns and problems – alcohol abuse, grief, physical and mental health, disability, parenthood and family issues, eating problems, etc. Whereas women are more often to be found in most types of self help groups, men predominate in alcohol abuse groups. Members of self-help groups most often see personal development and change as the most important objective of the group. Besides, growth and improving one's social relations are also mentioned. Almost none mention politics or society as their group's raison d'être.

The self-help groups in Norway do not seem to be very autonomous. 50 per cent are affiliated to a national charity, such as Alcoholics Anonymous or Anxiety Circle, two of largest national networks of self-help groups. 25 per cent are affiliated with a public institution. Most self-help groups have no contact with other self-help groups (Hjemdal et al., 1998), nor do they seem to play a very important role in Norwegian civil society, although group members generally appreciate the opportunity for contact with others in a similar situation.

Challenges

Today, civil society, voluntary organization and social network attract considerable attention both for social and economic theorists and observers of the welfare state. Theorists like Amitai Etzioni, James Coleman and Robert Putnam have made *social capital* the object of their analyses – that is networks, trust and norms that further reciprocity and cohesion and economic and social well-being in society and are convertible into social and political influence. Participation in voluntary organizations may be an indicator of social capital and conducive to increased health, social security and democracy. In 2001, the OECD published a report on social capital where the relationship between economic growth and group membership was discussed. Although it concluded that the evidence was so far inconclusive, there was strong interest in civil society (OECD, 2001). A Norwegian report found, somewhat hesitantly, a positive correlation between voluntary activity and social capital. Particularly young people's voluntary activity seems to strengthen trust in others. However, the authors warn, young people's interest in volunteering is on the wane, and therefore a cause for concern (Wollebæk et al., 2000).

The role of voluntary organizations in contemporary society can be grasped in several ways. One way is to see them as pressure groups that seek to articulate the interests of their members in a pluralistic society – a channel of influence in addition to the ballot box. Although this may be a fruitful approach to some organizations, especially health-related ones, it is not adequate as a general perspective. Another is corporatism: – to see them as corporatist partners with the government – as institutions that have been co-opted by and merged with public bureaucracy. As was mentioned above, in Norway voluntary organizations have sought to offer an alternative to public institutions, but accepted the expansion of the welfare state as a public responsibility and their own work incorporated in public plans and regulated by law. It is a perspective suited possibly to organizations that run health and social institutions.

Voluntary work and the voluntary sector face challenges in most developed nations. The dissolution of the great narratives and traditional ideologies grounded in religion and socialism undermines the foundations of voluntary organizations through which the social movements in a sense perpetuated themselves. Urbanization, secularization and consumerism have reduced the missionary, temperance and language movements to shadows of their former selves – in short, cultural opposition to the establishment in Norway, the 'counter-culture', has lost most of its bloom and efficacy. The labour movement is still an important factor in society, but aside from the trade unions, it does not spawn much voluntary activity. As traditional places of socialization such as the workplace, the family and the local community lose their efficacy, it could undermine people's motivation to volunteer. Individualization and other radical cultural changes affect participation in social movements and voluntary organizations. Voluntary organizations used to be affiliated to social movements with a distinct ideology. Today, membership is shrinking; the young are not as interested as their elders once were. Organizations of the late twentieth century are more often devoted to leisure, cultural and environmental pursuits. In what Anthony Giddens has called *reflexive modernity*, the individual is more preoccupied with creating a personal identity and realizing objectives and projects (Giddens, 1991). Many voluntary organizations must either remake their identity or lose members to more interesting pastimes.

Voluntary organizations in the health and social sector face the same challenges as the public sector. The introduction of quasi-market mechanisms in the public sector and emergence of what has been termed a 'contract culture' induces rivalry for contracts to deliver home help, manage nursing homes, alcohol and drug abuse clinics, etc. Voluntary organizations face largely the same problems as other sectors – calls for better cost control, efficiency, quality control (Kramer, 2004). It could transform the voluntary organization altogether, turning it into copy of a public institution or private company with the same pressures to beat the competition and deliver efficiently. At the same time, they have to meet government requirements, satisfy the public and clients, and work within laws and regulations. They must bureaucratize to meet government requirements on predictability and accountancy, and professionalize their staff to meet demands for quality of services. That there is a lack of hard evidence substantiating the impact of different types of formal ownership – private, voluntary, public – on performance is therefore not surprising (Kramer, 2004).

The challenge for these organizations is to combine service delivery with being a vibrant part of civil society – promoting membership democracy, voluntary activity and social participation. The danger lies in an evolution which threatens to wipe out the differences that matter between civil society, the market and the state.

Key researchers on voluntary organizations argue that it has become increasingly difficult to make out a specific 'voluntary' or 'third' sector in contrast to the public sector when it comes to delivery of social services in the welfare state (Evers and Laville, 2004). Instead of clearly defined sectors there is a new welfare mix of hybrid organizations. Public and voluntary service providers are both essentially part market and part state, reflecting the New Public Management ideology, with its focus on professionalism, bureaucratic control, tendering, incentives and quasi market mechanisms.

There is still a civil society with families, social networks, voluntary organizations and voluntary work. But it is increasingly difficult to see where it ends and the state and the market begin. This is particularly the case for the voluntary organizations discussed here – the health and social work charities. They have long been absorbed by public social policy and the public welfare system, and now they are increasingly party to quasi-market relationships.

Chapter 9
The municipal social service state

Most countries in Western Europe practise a three-tier system of government, i.e., national, county or regional, and municipal or local government. There are, however, great variations in the role and functions of municipalities and the county and regional authorities (Chandler, 1993). Historically, local democracy and municipal autonomy have been mainstays of Norwegian politics and administration. Norway was one of the first European countries to provide for local self-government through an act of Parliament back in 1837 (Larsen and Offerdal 2000). Although it was self-government only in a restricted sense, local councils were dependent on the state delegating powers to them, the idea of local democracy and municipal autonomy has proved remarkably resilient.

Most of today's welfare and social security schemes originated as local community initiatives. By 1882, local governments were allowed levy tax on income. After World War II, the state took action to ensure equal access to and uniform quality of the national services (Jensen, 2005). The social-democratic government now used municipalities and counties as welfare policy tools, clipping the wings of local autonomy quite severely in the process. Many responsibilities were transferred to higher levels of government, including hospital, child care, alcohol and drug abuse services.

Today, the number of municipalities is 433, each with an average population of 10,500. Municipalities with less than 10,000 inhabitants are home to 74 per cent of the population. Municipalities in some European countries, such as for instance France, are smaller, consisting of a few thousands inhabitants, while others, such as England and Sweden, have gone further in merging municipalities into greater units than in Norway. But calls to improve administrative viability by amalgamating municipalities is a regular topic in Norway as well.

The counties play a more modest role in governance. Besides, whereas Sweden and Denmark have made the regional level more important, there has yet been no regional reform in Norway, although this too is regularly deliberated in government and Parliament. The 19 counties nestle politically and administratively between the state and the municipalities. There are elections to the municipal councils every fourth year.

This chapter presents the main health and social services in the municipalities and how they are financed. The main areas of service delivery are the elderly and disabled, children, drug and alcohol abuse, asylum seekers and immigrants. Social assistance is also a municipal responsibility, but was described in chapter 7.

The welfare municipality

The 1992 *Local Government Act* represented a modification of the ideology of local democracy, in avoiding talk of local self-government and highlighting local government as an aspect of national policy. It confirmed what many had already observed – that local government had become part of the welfare state. This Act, with amendments in 2005, regulates the autonomy and the activities of the municipalities. The purpose of the Act 'is to make provision for functional democracy in local government and for efficient and effective management of the common local government interest within the framework of the national community and with a view to sustainable development' (§ 1).

In 1994 responsibility for social service organisation and delivery passed to local councils, though the various relevant acts remained in place, such as the Social Services Act, Municipal Health Services Act and Child Welfare Act.

The preamble to the *Social Services Act* states that its purpose is to:
- Promote economic and social security, to improve levels of living for the unfortunate being in a difficult situation.
- Contribute to increased equity and equality of status and prevent social problems.
- Contribute in giving each individual the possibility to live independently and to have an active and meaningful life together with others.

The *Municipal Health Services Act* requires local health services to promote public health and welfare, good social and environmental conditions and seek to prevent and treat illness, injury or defect. The health services shall provide information and encourage the public to take an interest in what people can do together and individually to promote personal well-being and the health of the community (§1-2).

The municipalities are in charge of day care, primary schools, primary health (preventive and curative), social services, social assistance, integration of asylum seekers and refugees, planning, housing, water, sewage and renovation, local roads and culture. County authorities are responsible for secondary schools and dental services among other things. The state operates social security, job centres and hospitals. In Denmark, unlike the Nordics generally, social benefits are administered largely by county and local authorities.

Financing

Local councils spent 14 per cent of GDP in 2001. Local councils employ 16 per cent of the labour force (Jensen 2005). Local councils rely mostly on income tax as their main source of income (see chapter 2). Municipalities are also entitled to levy property tax. The government provides block grants and earmarked transfers for specified purposes and reimburses local government outlays. The public pay for municipal services such as water, sanitation, healthcare, day care, etc. Charges vary widely among municipalities. For example, if your income is between two and three times the Basic amount (33,400– 49,500 euros) and you need help at home, you can be charged anything between 18.75 euros in one area and 262 in the next. Oslo charges people with household income below 15,700 2.50 euros per hour, rising to 24.75 if you earn more than 31,500 euros (according to the new rates which came into force 1. January 2007).[132]

Care for the elderly and disabled

The *Municipal Health Services Act* requires local authorities to provide 'necessary health assistance' to all members of the community, but within existing resources in terms of economy, personnel and equipment. In practice, health staff decide what kind of intervention is appropriate. Surveys indicate that the great majority (85 per cent) of the elderly in nursing homes are satisfied with the services.

The government wants as many elderly and disabled people to live in their own homes for as long as possible. To this end, local councils are encouraged to provide practical help and nursing care in people's homes for as long as possible. This includes medical and practical help with the cleaning, and with eating, bathing, physiotherapy etc. While more people avoid ending up in retirement or nursing homes, capacity is not keeping pace with demand, caused by the ageing baby boom generation. The government provides special funds to councils as an incentive to do more for the elderly. But in practice, thanks to efforts to provide all care home residents with their own room, many local councils are short of nursing home beds.

Some councils, like Oslo, outsource domiciliary care to private companies. The user decides whether to opt for public or private care delivery. The idea is that by separating *payment* from *provision* and introducing *customer choice*,

---

132 *Aftenposten* 12.7.07.

services will be cheaper and more effective. It's a model adopted by around 10 per cent of the Norwegian municipalities; the Swedes, though, use it in about 80 per cent of theirs (Szebehely, 2005).

Annually, local municipal nursing and care benefit 204,000 people, of whom 20 per cent are in institutions. 93 per cent of the elderly in institutions have their own bedroom. The number of residents *under* the age of 67 has been growing responsibility for physical and mental disability fell to local authorities. At the same time, there is a rise in the *over-80s*. Elderly care home residents have a variety of problems ranging across dementia, strokes, mental conditions and heart and lung diseases. 36 per cent of people aged 80 and above were helped at home in 2005, as in 1995. Around 50 per cent of all users were above 80 years old.[133]

Practical care sometimes falls short. Staff changes affect *continuity* of the relationship between the carer and the client. Carers have too much to do and too little time to do it in. And lack of flexibility makes it difficult to accommodate care provision to the needs of client (Rønning, 2004). Carers' schedules are tighter and performance is monitored more closely, both of which serve to detract from quality of care (Szebehely, 2005, 397). A recent study finds that some nursing homes were unable to adjust care to the needs of the residents. While 80 per cent of the beds were occupied by people suffering from dementia, little had been done to provide sheltered care and accommodation (Selbæk et al., 2006).

Capacity problems are causing long waiting lists in many areas. It is estimated that 25 per cent of the over-80s are in need of a nursing home place. There has in fact been a drop in the number of beds for the elderly in the last ten to fifteen years or so.[134] In fact, there is a current need for about 12.000 new beds. The number of nursing home beds started to grow recently, slowly, but retirement home beds fell sharply.[135] Assisted living is increasingly popular among senior citizens (called service housing or housing for care and services). In 2005, around 25,000 lived in assisted dwellings, a substantial increase over past figures.

Homes for the elderly and care homes (service homes) provide limited attention and care. Elderly living in their own home can avail themselves of day centres. Short-term stays in nursing homes (week-ends etc.) are offered to give the family a rest. Family carers appreciate the breaks facilitated by the local council. They might consider employing a professional family carer as well.

Provision of care to the elderly is equal across the board, irrespective of income, social status etc. In other words, it is universal. It is free of charge if the client has no income, and nursing home fees are balanced against income (i.e. pensions). The government requires patients to pay 85 per cent of their

---

133 St.prp. nr.1 2006-2007 *Helse- og omsorgsdepartementets budsjett for 2007.*
134 Sosial- og helsedirektoratet, 2006. *Utviklingstrekk i helse- og sosialsektoren.* Oslo.
135 St.prp. nr. 1 2006-2007 *Helse- og omsorgsdepartementets budsjett for 2007.*

annual income, though there's a cut-off point beyond which they get to keep excess income.

Another characteristic of Norway is the role of the public sector, particularly local authorities, in care delivery (Anttonen and Sipilä, 1995). 'Informal caring has been transformed from a private matter for families to a public matter for the state' (Anttonen 2005, 106). Most nursing homes are owned and run by local councils. Only 12 nursing homes are private for-profit establishments, 380 are private, not-for-profit establishments run by charities.[136] The market-inspired remodelling trend – New Public Management (NPM) – has not affected elderly care much. On the other hand, voluntary organisations are often contracted providers of welfare services in the care sector. Unpaid voluntary work, for example as friendly visitors and day centre staff, is frequently organised by a voluntary organisation (see chapter 8). These day centres help prevent the elderly from becoming over-dependent on others. They are mostly run by local authorities or at least partly financed by them. They offer various activities, meals, help with transport, and fulfil many social needs of the healthy elderly (Seland, 2007).

In 2002, spending on senior citizen represented 2 per cent of GDP; as for example compared with 2.8 per cent in Sweden, mainly due to the larger over-80 population (5.6 per cent in Sweden and 4.5 per cent in Norway).[137]

Municipal health care includes also child health care (health visitors, school health services), and primary health care (GPs, midwives and physiotherapists). Health centres offer ante- and postnatal check-ups, and vaccines according to the recommended immunization programmes (see also chapter 6).

More than 86,000 persons worked in the municipal nursing and care sector in 2004. The largest groups are auxiliary nurses (43,000) and nurses (25,000). Despite the strong increase in personnel numbers, there is trained shortage still of qualified personnel such as physicians, physiotherapists and nurses.

Public care means female employment and emancipation

Public nursing and elderly care have improved women's opportunity to work outside home and in the local community. To take one instance, a government senior citizen action plan which ran between 1999 and 2004 added 13,000 full-time jobs.[138] As we emphasized in chapter 4, this does not mean that informal care is of no importance. Families still provide 80 per cent of the care for aged, despite absence of legal obligations on adult children to

---

136 *Aftenposten* 25.4.06.
137 Sosial- og helsedirektoratet 2006. *Utviklingstrekk i helse- og sosialsektoren*. Oslo.
138 Sosial- og helsedirektoratet 2006. *Utviklingstrekk i helse- og sosialsektoren*. Oslo.

support their parents in old age. So the allegation that Norway, along with the other Nordic countries, has ignored the significance of informal care (Wolfe, 1989) is unfounded. That welfare state expansion has caused moral decline is out of step with reality. It was not true then, and is not true today.

Spousal care is the primary care alternative for older men, with adult children as option number two (Kröger, 2005). In any case, surveys of Norway show that older people prefer public care services rather than being dependent on the family – especially if their needs are intensive, highly personal and/or enduring (Daatland 1990). A 20-year follow-up study by Romøren (2001) of informal and formal care among a local population of 79+ year-olds, found that in 99 per cent of the cases, at least one informal carer was actively involved (family member, neighbour or friend); 73 per cent were admitted to a nursing home; 68 per cent used home nursing and 48 per cent home help.

Mental health, disability and substance abuse services

In cooperation with regional psychiatric centres, local authorities are required to compile personal care plans for psychiatric patients. The problem so far has been that local councils have lacked the capacity to meet service requirements placed on them by the largely mismanaged deinstitutionalization of psychiatry and mental health care in the '90s. In hindsight one can say that it was a disservice to these patients. Before the reform, the mentally disabled were cared for in large institutions that were run by the county authorities. The reform (deinstitutionalization and decentralization) of 1991, transferred these duties to the municipalities. The aim was to move patients out of the institutions and into accommodation in the community where they could lead more independent lives, but under supervision (and control) of trained personnel.

The municipalities were obliged to procure suitable dwellings and the requisite medical and practical help to secure *inclusion* of these vulnerable persons. Local authorities were also constrained to consult with clients on service organisation and delivery. The greatest challenge in this area is respect of civil rights, not least in connection with coercive measures. The Norwegian Board of Health Supervision encourages practitioners to try all other means before resorting to coercion in treatment.

Municipalities are responsible for treatment and rehabilitation of substance abusers outside institutions. An example is maintenance treatment of heroin addiction (LAR: *Legemiddelassistert rehabilitering*). There are long waiting lists to this rehabilitation programme. Low threshold health services – including dental treatment – are established in several municipalities. Several of the social and health services for substance abusers have evolved in cooperation with voluntary organisations. The challenge is to rehabilitate and integrate earlier substance abusers into the local community.

Municipal housing policy

Historically, the government made housing policy (Ulfrstad, 2007). World War II resulted in a huge housing shortage. A state housing bank was established, offering cheap mortgages to people and cooperatives for homes, albeit of a modest standard. The bank is still active, but centred more towards helping especially vulnerable groups in the housing market. Interests on loans are tax deductible, which means that purchase of a dwelling is heavily subsidized i Norway (ibid.).

The Social Services Act constrains municipalities to procure decent accommodation for the disadvantaged. Priority has been given to people with psychiatric conditions, mental disabilities and substance abuse problems. The 'ordinary' homeless are entitled to temporary accommodation.

There are far too few dwellings for the mentally ill (Innst. nr. 150 for 2006–2007). Homeless people have complex problems, needing not only decent housing but other social services, such as substance abuse care. Another challenge is making accommodation accessible for people with a disability. Municipal flats for rent are mainly found in the cities. The number is small, and there are always waiting lists. In addition, they are small and of low standard. Given the shortage of cheap rental accommodation, shelters or hostels in the big cities, around 5,300 people are regarded as homeless (Sosial- og helsedirektoratet 2006).

State and municipal housing benefits are designed to help people pay the rent. It shall compensate for insufficient benefits or other incomes when housing costs are high (Ulfrstad, 2007). Most of these people are single parents or single pensioners.[139]

Child Protection

The 1952 *Child Welfare Services Act* requires local authorities to protect children at risk of negligence or abuse, to intervene and help families with children with behavioural difficulties. The municipal child welfare authorities primarily help families that are unable to give their children a good upbringing. They are obliged to investigate all reports of neglect. In 2004, 21,300 inspections took place, but only half of them warranted further response.[140] Each

---

139 NOSOSCO 2007. *Social protection in the Nordic countries 2005*. Copenhagen, p, 297–298.

county has a specialist committee whose authority is needed to remove a child from the custody of its family. Adoption is one route, though placement in a foster home are the more typical response. Children above the age of seven – and even younger children if they are considered able to form their own opinion – shall be informed and their views heard before selection of a foster home. Foster care is used with or without the biological parents' consent. Older children can be placed in special welfare institutions, but never as a permanent arrangement. Family based solutions are preferred. The Act also places emphasis on protection of the private sphere.

Day care

These institutions are of great importance insofar as they allow families (and especially women) to combine work and caring for the children. Affordable childcare and wider full-time and part-time job opportunities have reduced the number of non-economically active women considerably over the last 10–20 years. The high number of women who want work, but are unwilling to sacrifice motherhood (Esping-Andersen, 2001) is a distinctive feature of Norway's social landscape. With universal childcare, care is often *defamilized* (Rauch, 2007).

The 2005 *Day Care Act* regulates municipal child care. The government would like to see a day care place for every child in the country, and therefore offers municipal grants and subsidies to speed up provision. In 2006 a day care framework plan established guidelines for day care centre management.

By the end of 2006, 80 per cent of children aged 1–5 were in kindergartens, and 62 per cent of the 1–2-year-olds, lowest of all age-groups. Still, thousands of children are on waiting lists for a kindergarten place (full-day or flexi-day). The highest fee is 291 euros per child with a full-day place (St.prp. nr. 1 2007–2008). There is a political ambition to reduce maximum user payment to 219 euros per month per child, although the government has declared that full coverage (to be reached in 2008 or 2009) at present is more important than reducing the price.

52.7 per cent of day care facilities are privately owned, the rest by the authorities (municipality, county or state).[141] There are also child minders in families, working under municipal supervision.

Most municipalities run after-school activities for schoolchildren (aged 6–10).

---

140 St. prp. nr. 1 2005-2006 Barne- og familiedepartementets budsjett for 2006.
141 St. prp. nr. 1 2005-2006 (a) Barne- og familiedepartementets budsjett for 2006.

Table 9.1 Children enrolled in day-care institutions and municipal family day care in 2004 (per cent of the age group)

	Norway	Sweden	Denmark
1 – 2 years	54	67	85
3 – 5 years	91	95	95

Source: NOSOSCO 2007. Social protection in the Nordic countries 2005. Copenhagen: NOSOSCO.

Today, Norway has almost caught up with her neighbours in terms of day care for children aged three to five, but is lagging behind in the under threes (see table 9.1). Most parents prefer day care to the alternatives, and there a few public services rated as highly by the public (Ellingsæter and Gulbrandsen, 2005).

Nevertheless, according to data from 2002–2003, the Norwegian childcare scheme is less universal than would have been expected of a country with a Scandinavian social service model (ibid.). As mentioned, Norway is now catching up with the other Scandinavian countries, so hopefully by the end of 2008 this will no longer hold true.

Introduction of newly arrived immigrants

The Act on an introduction programme and Norwegian language training for newly arrived immigrants (*the Introduction Act*) required municipalities as of September 1 2004 to have in place an introduction programme for all immigrants aged 18–55 in need of basic qualifications. The form of this introductory programme is outlined in the Act. Its purpose is to give immigrants basic skills in Norwegian, basic knowledge about the Norwegian society and prepare them for participation in the labour market. The duration of the programme is up to two years. All participants in the programme are to have an individual plan based on their actual needs for training. Participants in the programme receive an introductory benefit. This introductory benefit is not paid out if the immigrant does not follow the programme. Municipalities are paid by the government a supplement for each immigrant during a five years period.

User involvement and complaints

Health and social legislation gives the user certain rights to professional help. This legislation is the result of the 'independent living' movement and greater emphasis on empowerment and democracy in modern societies. User involvement is stressed as an important right. For instance, a disabled person can hire and direct the work of a personal assistant (BPA: *Brukerstyrt personlig assistanse*) financed by the central and local government for practical help in the home (in 2005: 810 users in 229 municipalities and 14 city districts). Evaluations of this scheme indicate that it has resulted in higher self-determination and quality of life (St.prp. nr. 1 for 2005–2006, 233).

A person with protracted needs for multiple services has a right to a personal care plan. It strengthens the person's self-determination and ensures help is given according to his or her actual needs. Such plans are especially relevant for the physically and mentally disabled and substance abusers.

Complaints about the quality or lack of services are filed with the county governor's office or county office of the Norwegian Board of Health (a county medical officer), who are mandated to review and overrule local decisions. In order to improve user involvement the ombudsman for patients (see chapter 6) will as from 2008 also involve municipal health and social services.[142]

Conclusion and challenges

Municipalities are confronted with three challenges related to their role as service providers: the dilemma between decentralization and equality; the mismatch between resources and capacity one the one hand and growing demand for services because of demographic change; and, related to this, the issue of universalism.

The first challenge concerns the provision of social services as essentially a central and local government partnership. The state requires municipalities to provide certain public health and social services. The authorities enjoy considerably leeway to implement and organize services as they wish, though the state sees to it that certain minimum standards are met. Different priorities and discretionary decisions of practitioners often result in local authorities providing different services for clients with the same needs. Problems of coordination between political and administrative levels (state and municipalities) call for new ways of organising both services and payments of social benefits.

Municipal welfare policy needs to address two opposing priorities: One the one hand there is the welfare state's emphasis on equality and on the other the

---

142 Ot.prp. nr. 23 for 2007-2008 *Om lov om endringer i pasientrettighetsloven og psykisk helsevernloven.*

goal of decentralization of authority from the state to municipalities. Decentralization produces inequality in services and benefits because municipalities have unequal resources and priorities. A state-run system of supervision and appeals is in place to offset unfair treatment. The Norwegian Board of Health, both nationally and via its county representatives, is responsible for ensuring correct procedures, and the county governors oversee municipal social services. But state supervision is not sufficient to prevent wide differences between municipalities in terms of the volume and quality of services and level of fees. The government seeks to solve the problems by enacting legislation and issuing instructions, providing economic support, guidance and supervision, as well as require certain qualification of health practitioners.

The dilemma of decentralization is at times handled by having the state run services in the municipalities, for example job centres or welfare offices. It was in response to the lack of coordination with municipal welfare authorities that the NAV reform was introduced (see chapter 3). At present, municipalities have few incentives to keep people in the labour force. In fact, in order to save money on social assistance, it may pay to grant clients a state financed disability pension.

Denmark has solved this dilemma by giving the municipalities administrative and economic responsibility for rehabilitation and activation measures, disability pension as well as social assistance allowance. Only 35 per cent of the disability pension (førtidspension) is refunded by the state. This gives municipalities a strong economic incentive to activate the disabled in various ways and prevent the number of disability pensioners growing. In Norway, social assistance benefits is paid in whole by the municipality, while the government foots the whole bill for disability pension. In Denmark both share both, via a differentiated refund scheme, making it economically profitable for municipalities to take active measures instead of paying cash benefits. This may explain why Norway has had a dramatic increase in the number of disability pensioners, whereas Denmark has not, in the 1990s at least (Øverbye 2004). The large number of small municipalities in Norway, with few local jobs available, may, however, make it difficult to emulate the Danish solution without negative side effects.

Another challenge is related to the ageing population. The number of 67 year-olds and older will have increased more than twofold between 2000 and 2050 (Innst. nr. 150 for 2006–2007), especially the 80–89 age bracket towards 2020. The elderly of tomorrow will have higher expectations of services. This means for example that more doctors will have to be transferred from hospital work (today there is one doctor for every second patient) to nursing home work (today: one doctor per 180 patients) (Aalborg 2007). The government believes that user involvement and individual adjustment of services will be necessary (St.meld. nr. 25 2005–2006). It might be difficult to finance these services without a substantial increase in taxes or patient fees.

In addition, a future shortage of qualified personnel will make it difficult to meet a demand for higher quality services for an increasing number of persons. A solution could be to let those with the means pay (fully or partly) for services rendered – often by private providers. There is a fear that equality of care will become difficult if not impossible. There are already significant problems of coordination between primary health care authorities and practitioners, nursing homes and hospitals.

Finally, the combination of increasing demand for health and social services, the need for more resources and the political difficulties of raising taxes will probably fuel doubts as to the usefulness of 'universalism' and 'equality' as ideological premises of the health and social services in Norway. A comparative study of social services for the elderly and day care for children, service guarantees, admission tests and user fees concludes that of the Nordic countries only Denmark has a universal system of social services. Norway falls short on service intensity to the elderly (only providing 2.3 hours per week), and neither Norway nor Sweden have a higher overall universalism than, for example, the Netherlands or, partly, France (Rauch, 2007). It might well be that the increasing number of middle-class and well-to-do elderly in the years to come will place higher demands on social services than municipalities can afford. This could easily find expression in calls for more widely differentiated services, for higher fees and/or more private sector involvement in the personal service sector.

The red-green government has announced a 'care plan 2015' and has promised to inject an additional 10,000 person-years into municipal care services by the end of 2009 (St.meld. nr. 25 2005–2006). The qualifications of personnel, quality of the services, and the economy of municipalities will be improved. The government is not in favour of further commercialisation of health and social services, but wants to encourage civil society and individuals to take greater responsibility for personal care. It remains to be seen if this is sufficient to reverse the downfall of 'universalism' (see chapter 10) as the bedrock of social service delivery in the decades to come.

Chapter 10
Prospects and challenges

We started this book by drawing attention to the fact that all welfare states are characterized by a mixture of different 'providing systems' – the labour market, the family, the state's public transfers and services, and the voluntary sector. Compared to the welfare state in other industrially developed nations, the Norwegian welfare state is similar to those of the neighbouring Nordic countries in its mix of provisions. Employment and participation in the labour market are emphasized. Women and the elderly are more likely to have a job outside the home, particularly when compared with many countries on the Continent (Germany, the Netherlands, the Mediterranean). The family is of course still important, but less central as a providing unit than it is in most European countries. Women often are more independent because they are employed, and perceived more often as independent individuals by the rest of the family. The state takes on more social responsibility, both in the cash transfer area and social and health service delivery, often at the local level, compared to Anglo-Saxon and most the Continental countries. High taxes finance welfare and redistribute wealth. Finally, the voluntary sector, relatively speaking, has a more insignificant role in delivering social and health services. The result of this mix is a lower incidence of poverty than in most other European countries.

But it also combines with a competitive economy to provide a relative flexible labour market, influential but collaborative trade unions, a business-friendly climate for entrepreneurship with less red tape than in many other industrially developed countries. [143] Norway and the other Nordic countries constitute an alternative to the American model with its strong labour market flexibility, weak trade unions, low social security, wide inequality, and high incidence of poverty.

---

143 According to a World Bank report, Norway ranks high on an index of 'business-friendliness' with not many bureaucratic rules for establishing business, rapid processing of permissions, simple ways of registering property, paying taxes, etc. Bjørnestad, S. (2007). Verdensbanken: Flott å drive business i Norge. *Aftenposten*. Oslo.

However, lines are blurring, and there are no clear dividing lines between the Nordic countries as a whole and the rest of Europe. In some respects, some European countries are more like the Nordic countries, and the Nordics are not alike in all respects. As mentioned in chapter 9, day care coverage in France is higher than Norway's, and the Netherlands has a level of services for the elderly which outshines that of Sweden (Rauch, 2007). Besides, Norwegian dental services are below those of many other countries.

Although there are basic similarities between the welfare states of Norway, Sweden and Denmark, we have already noted certain differences. For instance, the Norwegian welfare state is often more frugal than either Denmark or Sweden on unemployment benefits, old age pensions and dental care. One exception is the sickness benefit (cf. chapter 6). Norway has until recently lagged behind Denmark and Sweden in terms of day care for children.

A social democratic welfare state?

The Nordic welfare states are most often characterized as *social democratic welfare states* (Esping-Andersen, 1990; Huber and Stephens, 2001). Prominent academic scholars such as Walter Korpi (1983), Gösta Esping-Andersen, and others (Esping-Andersen, 1990; Huber, 2001) have argued for a 'power-resource' mobilization thesis – referring to a working class mobilized for welfare reforms through the labour unions and the social democratic parties. However, although social democratic parties have been influential in all of the Nordic countries, the role of social democracy has differed. Whereas the social democratic party has been clearly hegemonic in Sweden, the social democratic parties in Denmark, and even more in Finland, have had to share government with other parties, particularly in the political centre. Norway is closer to Sweden than Denmark and Finland in this respect, as social democracy enjoyed government power until 1965. However, after that, governments have alternated between the Labour Party and centre right. Leading Norwegian scholars on comparative social policy argue that most important reforms enjoyed broad political consensus (Kildal and Kuhnle, 2005). The historian Peter Baldwin (1990) maintains that the universal character of this welfare state is mostly due to the interests of the peasants and the middle class to be part of a system that was financed by taxes.

These are valid arguments by and large. Certainly, key features of the welfare state were established in a period when the Labour Party – DNA – achieved hegemony and was more or less permanently in office. Financing social benefits by taxes was Labour's policy to begin with, but soon accepted by other parties. On the other hand, universalism (see below) – or better: extending benefits to new groups – was often first advocated by other parties before Labour came round to the idea. Certainly, the geographical periphery and centre parties made labour market policy less centralized and industry less concentrated than in Sweden. As mentioned in chapter 4, under the influence particularly of the Christian People's Party Norway lagged far behind in day care provision. Nor was there any social democratic 'master plan' or clear vision of a universal welfare state among Labour leaders (Øverbye, 2002). They were pragmatic politicians concerned with piecemeal reforms and willing to compromise with other parties.

At the end of the day, whether *social democratic welfare state* is useful or not depends on whether one considers it appropriate in the post-social democratic age, when governments alternate between centre-right and centre-left coalitions, and the definition of social democratic politics and ideology is not very clear.

Is *universal* more adequate as an adjective for the Norwegian welfare state? 'Universal' and 'universalism' are conceptually unclear and often invested with different meanings (Øverbye, 2002; Kildal og Kuhnle, 2005). One common definition is that universalism refers to the degree of coverage of a social benefit or service. Thus, a benefit to which all residents in a country are entitled might be said to be universal. Universalism can also refer to a welfare system in which categorical or 'objective' criteria decides who are entitled to a benefit, and where discretion plays an insignificant role in cash transfers. Finally, it can signify a low degree of user fees in the delivering of health social services or the absence of gatekeepers and their discretionary power. The welfare state in Norway is universal if we want it to mean coverage of non-discretionary social benefits based on residency. In that sense, universalism is more universal in Norway than in either Anglo-Saxon or Continental welfare states. This applies primarily to the basic old age pension and child benefits. However, supplementary and invalidity pensions, along with the unemployment benefit are conditional on past wage work, a requirement of most other welfare regimes as well. In the health services, every resident is entitled to medical assistance, and the system is fairly universal, even if doctors act as gatekeepers and fees are charged. Contrary to this, day care, practical help and nursing at home can hardly be called universal, because of waiting lists and the proliferation of patient/client charges. Thus, compared to other welfare states, there is more universalism in Norway, but calling the welfare state 'universal' should only be done while keeping these reservations in mind.

Modern welfare states are today generally confronted with more or less the same challenges: Nation-states face global economic competition as national and transnational companies are free to move operations across borders. At the same time, the type of government policy available to the electorate is narrower as a result of international treaties and membership of global and regional organizations. Globalization undermines in that sense the autonomy of the nation-state, which historically was a precondition for the development of the welfare state. Immigration results in a more heterogeneous society and may weaken public perceptions of a shared destiny and social risks, while raising the issue of rights and duties anew. Ageing populations make governments worry about the sustainability of public pension schemes and financing of health and social services. These changes are accompanied by evolving cultural and ideological values and preferences among people. Finally, they change the balance of power between the political parties and may give rise to new political constellations and government office.

To what extent will these changes – globalization, immigration, cultural and political – affect the Norwegian welfare state in the years to come?

Globalization

The years after 1985 have witnessed increased movement of capital across national boundaries. At present, the liberalization of competition in services and agriculture is on the agenda of many international organizations including WTO. In politics, international and global actors have become more important, such as the EU, the World Bank, International Monetary Fund (IMF), ILO, WTO, GATS (General Agreement on Trade in Services) – whose policies are often opposed by new trans-national networks and voluntary organizations with roots in civil society such as ATTAC, World Social Forum, International Confederation of Free Trade Unions, World Council of Churches, etc. Increasingly, economic, political and cultural activities are regulated by international conventions, laws, and courts of justice such as the European Court of Human Rights.

Here we shall primarily concentrate on the possible effects of the economic globalization on the welfare state. In principle, liberalization of capital, trade and services could affect the welfare state in industrially developed nations in various ways. Increased mobility of capital could disempower the trade unions, reducing their bargaining power in export industries. It could make it harder or impossible for nation-states to have a substantially higher level of taxation of business and profits than neighbouring or competing countries, harming the potential for redistribution. Increased competition from low-cost countries could threaten competitiveness and jobs. It could result in social dumping – i.e. nations competing for investments by reducing social protection. Increased labour migration could result in an underclass of low-skilled and low-paid workers. Finally, the flow of capital makes capital income more important, and as capital is already unequally distributed, the result could be to widen inequalities further.

How does Norway fare in this picture? *It does exceptionally well.* First, Norway has always had an open economy; foreign trade has always been important, and Norway's competitiveness is strong. Although behind the other Nordic countries, Norway is high on the World Economic Forum's global competitiveness index, as it is on international business-friendliness and transparency/no corruption indices (table 10.1).

Table 10.1 Indices on competitiveness, business-friendliness and transparency

	Global competitiveness	Business-friendliness	Transparency index
Switzerland	1	16	7
Finland	2	13	1
Sweden	3	14	6
Denmark	4	5	4
Singapore	5	1	5
US	6	3	20
Japan	7	12	17
Germany	8	20	16
Netherlands	9	21	9
UK	10	6	11
Hong Kong	11	4	15
Norway	12	11	8

Sources: World Economic Forum index on competitiveness; World Bank's index on business-friendliness; Transparency International's Corruption Perceptions Index.[144]

Although wages are high, productivity is high too – on a par with other OECD nations and above the US (St. meld. nr. 8 2004 – 2005). This is mainly due to a highly qualified workforce, which furthers innovation and mobility. Besides, the egalitarian wage structure lowers the relative price of qualifications. Universal social benefits have protected workers against adverse consequences of industrial and workplace restructuring, and made trade unions less antagonistic towards closing or downsizing of workplaces which are not profitable.

Second, oil provides a protective buffer. The government's Oil Fund and Pension Fund was worth NOK 2000 billion – 261 billion euros in 2007, with the Ministry of Finance – which generally is cautious – foreseeing growth into the NOK 3500 billion region by 2012 (St. meld. nr. 1 Nasjonalbudsjettet 2008). As mentioned in chapter 2, Norway has no foreign debts and there is a huge surplus on the annual government budgets.

Third, China's strong economic growth of late has only positive effects on the Norwegian economy. Chinese textile and consumer goods exports are no

---

144 See http://www.weforum.org/en/initiatives/gcp/Global%20Competitiveness%20Report/PastReports/index.htm; http://www.doingbusiness.org/economyrankings/; http://www.infoplease.com/ipa/A0781359.html - accessed October 29 2007.

threat to industries or jobs in Norway, they were wiped out by foreign competition many decades ago. Instead, import of cheap consumer goods keeps inflation low and increases purchasing power. At the same time, Chinese demand is boosting prices of profits from petroleum, raw materials from important sectors of the Norwegian economy.

Thus, the effects of globalization, often perceived as threats to welfare, do not threaten Norway or its welfare system. On the contrary, Norway's financial health is excellent. Employment is not threatened – on the contrary. According to a report by Statistics Norway, the number of people in jobs is increasing, and unemployment is at an all time low, 2.7 per cent in 2007. The average wages is rising by 5 per cent each year, and private consumption will increase by 17 per cent from 2006 to 2010 (SSB, 2007 b). The British scholar Will Hutton describes the Nordic combination of high labour market participation rate, strong productivity, and high social spending as a win-win economy (Hutton, 2007).

In the present period of globalization Norway has the best economic starting point to maintain and develop the welfare state. This situation benefits the already strong popular support of the welfare state. People are even prepared to pay more tax to preserve or expand social benefits and services, as has been documented by surveys and research. The oil money bolsters popular opinion in this respect. The work intensive universal welfare state which protects the unemployed against the danger of marginalization and poverty and other hazards of modern life makes people less wary of restructuring or downsizing. Of course, workers worry if a company is facing closure, but the concern is not usually translated into a struggle against poverty and misery. Finally, compared to countries where welfare state financing is based on the insurance principle – where employees and employers contribute to a social security fund – tax financing is advantageous because it lowers the cost of labour, and dissuades employers from sacking, rather than keeping people or transferring jobs to low wage countries where social legislation is largely lacking.

This does not mean the Norwegian welfare state will not be affected by globalization. As a contracting party to the European Economic Area Agreement (EEA), Norway is part of European single market. Since the enlargement of the EU in 2004 an increasing number of workers and craftsmen from the new member states have been seeking work in Norway. In 2005, 37,000 works permits were granted and in 2006 almost 57,000 (UDI, 2007). 70 per cent of these permits were granted to Poles. Because they are often employed on low wages and contracts in Norwegian terms, they may squeeze Norwegian workers and artisans out of the market. Trade unions are therefore worried about social dumping – that Norwegian employers shall be tempted to demand reductions in wages and social benefits for Norwegian workers. As mentioned in chapter 2, the government gave a commission[145] authority to decide

---

145 The commission consists of one representative from the employees, one from the employers and three 'neutral' members.

whether a national collective agreement between trade unions and employers' associations within a defined area should be made binding on all workers within the same field. This happened in the construction industry, where there are many foreign workers. The extremely favourable labour market situation and demand for labour has protected Norwegian workers against the negative effects of workers flowing in from EU countries. Besides, it benefits the macro-economy by curbing inflation. Another possible effect of EEA membership, and something EU critics fear in particular, is that EU directive on services will make it impossible for national authorities to control working conditions, and result in liberalization and privatization of health and social services.

Globalization affects the distribution of income and traditional strong emphasis on equality in Norwegian society. Although Norway has less income inequality than most OECD countries (Förster and d'Ercole, 2005), income differences are increasing, mainly due to the very strong growth of capital income. Capital income rose from 29 per cent of all income in 2000 to 36 per cent in 2006, and the 10 per cent richest got 94 per cent of the capital income (Christensen et al., 2007). In 2005, dividends rose by more than 50 per cent, and the upper income brackets – the upper decile – enjoyed 30 per cent income growth in real terms, while the lowest decile had to make do with 1 per cent (SSB, 2005). On the other hand, the total income of shareholders fluctuates from year to year according to the business cycle and tax rules. From 2005 to 2006, income differences between high and low earners was somewhat reduced again (see also chapter 2). However, as Norwegians increasingly reach a level of affluence, the purchasing power in the upper classes may create a market for more private medical and social services.

Both The Labour Party and the Conservatives are strong supporters of Norwegian membership of the EU, but do not want a new referendum until the polls suggest that a stable majority is in favour. As long as The Labour Party wants to share government with SV and Sp, both of which are against membership, a new referendum is out of the question. Anyway, whereas other EU countries have had to cut pensions and welfare to keep within exceeding EU's 3 per cent of GDP constraint, this would not be an issue for Norway, as Norway has a large surplus and there are no prospects of deficits as far as we can see. As an analysis of the effect of the EU on Danish social policy has demonstrated (Kvist and Saari, 2007), the weak ambitions of EU to harmonize social policy and soft coordinating mechanism (the open method of coordination) do not constitute a short term threat to welfare arrangements in the Nordic countries either. On the other hand, the long term effects of the EU directive on services and the continuous liberalization of the labour markets are still to be seen, and much will depend on the ruling of the EU Court of Justice. So far it has tended to rule in favour of EU's basic principles of free move of goods and services and not to protect national labour law.

A multi-cultural society

The Norwegian welfare state came about in a society that was more homogeneous than most European countries. Class differences were not as pronounced and Protestantism was the dominant religion. If we except the small Sami minority in the north, it was an ethnically homogeneous population. Its uniformity and the reciprocal trust that it inspired may have been important as premises for the universal and solidaristic welfare state (Baldwin, 1997). In a study on social expenditure and ethnical diversity in 56 countries Alesina and Glaeser (2004) found that the more ethnic diversity the smaller the GDP per capita is spent on welfare. They argue that great ethnic diversity is one of the most important reasons why a welfare state that redistributes large resources never developed in the US. This diversity constituted a hindrance for the development of solidaristic and collective politics because the majority saw the welfare state as an institution that redistributes from 'us' to 'them'. If this is right, the development of a multicultural society with many ethnic minorities may constitute a challenge to the welfare state.

Persons from other European countries such as Sweden, Germany and the Netherlands have for centuries come to Norway to find employment or start businesses, but immigration from Third World countries only started in the late 1960s (Tjelmeland and Brochmann, 2003). In the years 1968 – 1970 a few hundred Pakistanis, Moroccans and Turks came to seek work, generating calls to limit immigration. When 600 Pakistanis left Germany only to turn up in Oslo in 1971, the authorities clamped down on immigration. Foreigners from Third World countries had to produce a work permit before they left their home country. In 1975, Parliament halted immigration altogether. It was a temporary measure to start with, but became permanent. The main argument was that time was needed to organise proper housing, schooling and social facilities for immigrants. Putting its case in several white papers the government argued that Norwegian society was too small and patterns of habitation and employment made it difficult for the dominant culture to absorb and integrate people from others (Bø, 2004).

These new restrictions reduced the numbers of immigrants seeking work, and from the 1980s, immigrants were mainly refugees and asylum seekers. As a UN member, Norway is bound by treaty to accept a number of refugees (700–1,500 a year). Asylum criteria are restrictive as well, and it is a long and complicated process. In 1996, Norway entered into an agreement with the EU countries and joined the so-called Schengen group. It entailed an obligation to integrate EU rules on immigration and border control.

Compared to European countries in general, Norwegian immigration policy is very tight indeed. Only a small number of immigrants are allowed in. Having said that, equality and diversity are accepted, and integration is seen as the reciprocal adjustment of the majority to the minority and vice versa. Universal welfare arrangements are combined with positive discrimination in matters such as language training to speed up integration. It differs from both the British and the French way of viewing immigration. In the UK, the hegemonic liberal tradition implies accepting inequality and diversity and letting immigrants maintain and cultivate their own culture, with the authorities supporting immigrant organizations and activities. Immigrants, as other citizens, are expected to provide for themselves and welfare arrangements are reserved for groups at risk. The traditional French republican model is founded on equality. Everybody living on French territory is accepted as a citizen and treated nominally in the same way; there are no special welfare arrangements for minorities. The differences between these models have never been particularly sharp, and in recent years they have tended to blur even more.

Table 10.2 Immigration into selected countries 2001 in 1000, proportion born abroad and of non-citizens in different countries. Per cent

	Immigrants in 2001 (1000)	Per cent born abroad	Per cent non-citizens
Germany	685.3	12.5	-
France	141.0	10.0	5.6
UK	373.3	8.3	-
Sweden	44.1	12.0	5.3
Denmark	25.2	6.8	5.0
Norway	25.4	7.3	4.3

Source: Dumont and Lemâitre (2005).

In 2005, there were 365,000 immigrants in Norway, i.e., first-generation immigrants of non-Norwegian origin or persons born in Norway but whose parents were both born abroad.[146] Immigrants constitute 8 per cent of the population (20 per cent of the capital, Oslo). As we see in table 10.2, although the definition is slightly different, the percentage born abroad but living in Norway is low compared to Sweden and many European countries. Among the countries included here, only Denmark's population of non-Danish-born citizens is smaller. Non-citizens make up 4.3 per cent of the population, which is somewhat less than Sweden and Denmark, but compared to the proportion of immigrants, there are relatively more non-citizens than in neighbouring countries.

The largest groups of Third World immigrants are the Pakistani, the Vietnamese, the Iraqi, the Iranians, the Turks, and persons from Sri Lanka. Dif-

---

146 According to Bureau of Statistics – see http://www.ssb.no/emner/02/01/10/innvbef/, accessed at March 27 2006).

ferent African nations are represented with some tens of thousands, and there is a small number from South and Latin America.

Whereas Sweden requires five years' residence before granting citizenship, Norway requires seven years (and Denmark nine years). Unlike Sweden, Finland, the US and some other countries, Norway and Denmark do not allow dual citizenship. Applicants must demonstrate adequate knowledge of the Norwegian language or complete a 300-hour language course. In 2006, the government introduced a voluntary ceremony and loyalty oath for immigrants granted Norwegian citizenship.

A report co-financed by the EU gives Norway eighth place among 28 European countries on immigrant integration indices. They include measures against discrimination, rules for family reunification, citizenship, residence permit, political participation, and access to the labour market. Norway scores high on immigrants' political participation, but low as for active anti-discrimination policy and rules for admitting citizenship. Sweden is first with high scores on most indicators; Denmark does poorly – number 21 of the 28 countries (British Council 2007).

As Table 10.3 shows, attitudes to immigration are not very unlike attitudes elsewhere in Europe, though the Swedes stand out as somewhat more positive to immigration than other European nationalities – included Norwegians, whereas the Danes are more sceptical to immigration in certain respects that other Europeans.

Table 10.3 Attitudes to immigration. Mean score 1–10 (10=completely agree; 1= completely disagree) and persons who agrees that there should be a law against discrimination in the workplace (per cent)

	Culture enriched by immigrants	**Immigrants make country a better place to live in**	**Immigrants take out more than they contribute**
Germany	6.2	4.8	5,1
France	5.2	4.5	4,8
UK	5.1	4.6	5,3
Italy	5.3	4.5	4,4
Sweden	7.1	6.2	6,3
Denmark	5.8	5.5	6,8
Norway	5.8	4.8	6,5

Source: ESS 2002. On the last issue respondents were asked whether a law against ethnic discrimination in workplace would be good/bad for the country with 1 'extremely bad' and 10 'extremely good'. The percentage here are those who rated 7–10 and thus agreeing that such a law would be good for the country.

The aspect of immigration which people like best is cultural enrichment. Here, the mean score varies from 5 to 6 for most of the countries included, with Norwegians scoring 5.8, which is lower than Sweden and Germany, but higher than the UK, France and Italy. Norwegians follow the Germans, French and British in disagreeing with the statement that immigrants make their country a better place to live in. Although scepticism has declined in recent years, a substantial minority – 45 per cent – still find that 'immigrants are a source of insecurity in society'. On the other hand, 69 per cent are of the opinion that immigrants make a useful effort in the working life.[147]

From a welfare state perspective it may be more important that people in the relatively generous Scandinavian welfare states tend agree more with the statement that 'immigrants take out more than they contribute' than people in less generous welfare states such as Italy, France, Germany and the UK. A more detailed analysis (Hagen 1999; Halvorsen, 2007) demonstrates that Mediterranean countries are more positive to immigrants in this respect than either liberal and social democratic welfare regimes (Halvorsen, 2007). Danes are particularly liable to think that immigrants take out more than they contribute. These findings can be related to the fact that Mediterranean countries redistribute less to immigrants than welfare states in the north. Thus, perhaps these answers do not reflect differences in attitudes towards generosity, but the actual degree of redistribution in the different nations.

The Swedes – despite the large numbers of immigrants in Sweden – are more positive to immigrants than the Danes and the Norwegians, which seem to contradict Alesina and Glaeser's assertion that ethnic diversity in itself makes people less inclined to support the welfare state (see above). As Taylor-Gooby (2005) sees it, moreover, the empirical relationship between ethnical diversity and welfare expenditure per capita of GDP declines if we exclude the US from the analysis. This relationship is much weaker in other countries, and even disappears if we include the strength of social democratic or left-leaning parties in the analysis. Consequently, immigration may not affect the welfare state significantly at all if it does not reduce the political strength of the traditional parties of the labour movement. However, immigration has become the great issue for right-wing populist parties in many European countries – including the Progress Party in Norway. The Progress Party indeed competes with Labour for some working class votes, people sceptical to immigration, and on several occasions have beat Labour in polls taken after the 2005 election.

That Scandinavians are more prone to think that immigrants receive more than they contribute seems to support the assumption that increasing ethnic diversity may be a challenge to the generous and universal welfare state. Even if a majority of Norwegians disagree with the statement that 'most immigrants

---

147 Statistics Norway http://www.ssb.no/emner/00/01/30/innvhold/tab-2005-11-24-01.html, accessed March 29 2006

are abusing social benefits', a not negligible minority of 37 per cent feel that they do abuse the system. On the other hand, another report from Norway suggests that attitudes to collective welfare are not influenced by the number of immigrants in a municipality. Nor does a large immigrant population affect trust. Attitudes towards immigrants become more positive the more immigrants there are in a municipality. The authors interpret attitudes towards immigrants as a cultural product, and that more knowledge and contact will increase acceptance of immigrants. However, there is a certain tendency, however weak, for people to associate immigrants in a community with negative attitudes to redistribution (Bay et al., 2007). Another analysis of solidarity with immigrants in 28 European countries found higher solidarity among citizens in high spending welfare states, and that more immigrants makes people more solidaristic (Oorschot and Uunk, 2007). Although Norway was not included in the analysis, this seems to contradict the general assumption that ethnic multiculturalism undermines the welfare state.

As we emphasized in chapter 3, the Norwegian welfare state is founded on a strong work ethic where generous social benefits are expected to elicit readiness on the public's part to contribute to the common weal as wage earners in the labour market. Consequently, the challenge to universalism will probably grow if immigrants fail to find employment and take up disability pensions and social assistance – social benefits which are less accepted and more stigmatized than others. In 2005, immigrants were three times as likely to be unemployed than non-immigrants (see chapter 3). Unemployment is highest among immigrants from Africa (17 per cent – with Somali refugees topping the statistics) and Asia (11 per cent). High unemployment among immigrants is also due to the short time many immigrants have lived in Norway, but exacerbated by poor qualifications among different immigrant groups and employer discrimination. If efforts to integrate immigrants into the labour market fail, creating a non-working, poor underclass, this will probably pose a greater challenge to the universal welfare state than if they merge into society through employment, education and social mobility. Although immigrants today are overrepresented among the poor and unemployed, it is too early to draw any firm conclusions. If the prospects of finding a job remain favourable, it will probably benefit immigrants as well, although discrimination is harder to abolish.

The most burning issue connected to immigration is perhaps not the welfare state, but cultural issues which create conflicts about how to live together. In the 1970s, public policy focused on integration. Assimilation – whereby immigrants are expected to become like 'us' – was rejected. One should respect cultural differences and cultural identities of immigrants. During the '80s and '90s government documents show a shift in thinking towards reciprocity and duty to participate. In a late '80s white paper (St. meld. nr. 39 1987 – 1988), the government argued that immigrants, like Norwegians, must respect the laws and basic values of society. As 'basic values' were mentioned democracy, equal status for women and men, and the rights of children. Available options did not include the right to remain an outsider. One could not, for instance, expect to avoid learning the Norwegian language or acquire knowledge about the Norwegian society (Brochmann, 2002). As mentioned above, almost 50 per cent of all Norwegians think that immigrants should make an effort to be like ethnic Norwegians.

In addition to the rules of immigration, controversial issues today are those related to religion, female emancipation and the degree to which immigrants should respect 'Norwegian' customs and behaviour. According to Norwegian law, a husband is not entitled to beat his wife, and parents are not allowed to beat their children – irrespective of the behaviour of the children. Should parents decide with whom a daughter or son should marry? Should the veil be accepted at school? Should daughters be allowed the same freedom as sons? Should young persons be allowed to go back to the country of their parents to find a spouse or marry a cousin? Should one require imams to deliver their sermons in Norwegian? Should imams be educated in Norway? Such issues are at the centre of the debate. On most points the Progress Party has taken the most restrictive position and demanded that immigrants adjust to and accept 'Norwegian' behaviour, whereas the Socialist Left Party and the Liberal Party have demonstrated higher tolerance of immigration and immigrants.

The red-green government manifesto touches on these issues as well. The government will fight discrimination on ethnic, religious, and sexual grounds, it says. To further integration it will give minority language children free sessions in day care centres and more money to schools in areas with high ethnic concentrations. It will increase the number of immigrants employed in government institutions and workplaces, etc. On the other hand, immigrants must expect to participate actively in Norwegian society, support the laws and basic democratic basic values. The government promises to take steps to ensure that women belonging to ethnic minorities are regarded as autonomous persons with their own right to information, training in the Norwegian language, education and employment. The government will also expand the obligatory programme in the Norwegian language and social studies. Thus, an emphasis on integration is combined with the ambition to change some aspects of the culture of the immigrants. But what kind of cultural adjustments is it reasonable to demand of immigrants – and what kind of adjustments are reasonable to demand of the ethnic majority?

Two structural dilemmas

If globalization, immigration and the general economic situation pose no threat to the sustainability of the welfare state, two structural dilemmas confront any government and most political parties. The first is of a general character and to do with Norway's enormous oil wealth. The problem is that it can be used to stimulate personal consumption, pay for higher social benefits and improved social services, but only within certain limits. Excess spending will cause inflation and higher interest rates. Inflation exacerbates labour costs in export industries, reduces their competitive edge and may even threaten the survival of many industries (see chapter 2). In a worst case scenario, the industrial base could disintegrate. Know-how would evaporate, leaving Norway nothing to live on when oil and gas reserves run dry. Many people are unable to understand these simple economic truths. Instead of a penny pinching government they turn to the populist parties (cf. the Progress Party below).

The other dilemma is more closely associated with social policy and the dominance of work for welfare (cf. chapter 3). The government seeks to maximize the supply of labour by stimulating people to defer retirement, and to opt for a paid job rather than living off a disability benefit or social assistance. In the government's mind, generous social benefits and low pensionable age are likely to take some of the wind out the activation policy. Naturally, it creates tension within government, particularly as Labour wants to concentrate efforts on increasing labour force participation while the Socialist Left Party campaign for higher social benefits for the disadvantaged. As the dominant party, Labour has had the upper hand. People who are either unwilling or unable to work are therefore lagging behind, and the number of relative poor is set to increase – as it did in the last year of the centre-right government (cf. chapter 7) despite of its avowal to reduce poverty. If this concentration on getting benefit recipients, immigrants and other 'vulnerable' groups into work continues, the centre-left government may be forced on the moral and political defensive in the next election campaign.

A greying population

In most industrialized and post-industrial countries, the age profile of the population will change significantly in the decades to come, and this is the case in Norway as well. UN prognostications predict increasing numbers of senior citizens. In addition, financing the pensions, social and health services for these people will fall to a an ever diminishing workforce. As table 10.4 shows, while the over-65s only account for around 25 per cent of the population, by 2030 it will be more than 40 per cent, increasing to 50 or 60 per cent in 2050. Similar trends are predicted further afield, Japan for instance, though high-immigration countries such as the US are likely to do better at maintaining a young population.

Table 10.4 Persons aged 65+, 15–64 years and 80+. (Per cent of the whole population)

	2005		2030		2050	
	65+	80+	65+	80+	65+	80+
Norway	22.9	4.9	39.1	6.8	45.1	10.3
Sweden	27.1	5.6	46.0	9.0	54.5	12.2
Denmark	23.1	4.2	40.0	7.1	43.8	9.7
Germany	27.9	4.3	46.2	7.6	54.7	13.2
France	25.0	4.5	39.8	7.1	46.7	10.2
Italy	29.4	4.9	47.3	8.5	68.1	14.1
UK	24.3	4.5	40.4	9.0	47.3	10.8

Source: UNECE Statistical Unit (http://w3.unece.org/stat/scriptsdb/variables.asp, accessed March 24 2006).

These demographic prognoses mean the cost of pensions will increase (see chapter 5). And as life expectancy increases, there will be more people over 80, and, more of them living alone. Although better living conditions improve the health of the elderly, an increasing number will probably need help at home, a place in a nursing homes and/or medical attention. Not to mention the cost of medical progress, with new technologies and treatments, and calls for higher investments in the health system.

These demographic changes constitute a challenge to all European welfare states. The contingent of 65+-year-olds will double in many countries – also in Norway – from 20 to 25 per cent in 2005 to around 45 per cent in 2050. However, most other European countries are worse off than Norway. Whereas 45 per cent of the Norwegian population in 2050 will be at least 65, Sweden and Germany will have to cope with 55 per cent, and Italy as much as 68 per cent. (Italy has a particularly low fertility rate at present.) The demand for healthcare among octo- and nonagenarians will rise, as the group grows from less than 5 per cent in 2005 to 10–15 per cent of the population by 2050. And Norway is not particularly bad off in this respect either. Many OECD countries are looking to a doubling of retirees per worker will by 2050, though an OECD analysis characterized projections for Norway, Denmark and Sweden as 'moderate' compared to most OECD countries (OECD, 2006).

Table 10.5 shows likely future costs of the pension system.

Table 10.5 Projected number of pensioners and overall state pension outlays pensions in the National Social Insurance Scheme

	2001	2010	2020	2030	2040	2050
Pensioners (1000 persons)	915	1013	1224	1421	1589	1674
Costs of public pensions (billion NOK)	102	125	164	197	222	234
Pensions. Per cent of GDP (oil revenue excluded)	9,1	11,0	13,7	16,5	18,7	19,7

Source: NOU 2004:1. Including all persons on old age, disability, and survivor's pension.

According to these figures, the number of pensioners is set to rise from 915,000 in 2001 to 1.7 million by 2050, and the cost of public pensions more than double in the same period. Pension costs were 9.1 per cent of GDP in 2001, but will lay claim to almost 20 per cent by 2050.

Naturally, the likely effects of these demographic developments, not to mention the cost to the pension system, have attracted considerable debate. The predictions may be too gloomy, according to some observers. Increased immigration could increase productivity and create more private wealth, which in turn could serve as a lifeline for the National Insurance Scheme. According to others, in a globalized world there is a limit to how far demographic changes can be dealt with by higher taxes. A report by Statistics Norway notes the twofold increasing in the price of crude oil since the pension reform was presented (Reinertsen, 2007), and the financial reasons for the reform are less compelling in 2007 than some years ago.

There is one argument for pension reform that hasn't lost its force – the need to maximize the supply of labour. There are few incentives in present system to persuade older workers to postpone retirement – nothing, that is, that 'makes it pay to work'. So we are back to the significance of the work approach with its emphasis on increased employment and activation policy, a repeated theme of the book. But if the government makes it more attractive to defer retirement, the highly skilled in white collar jobs will probably take the bait, increasing inequality in old age.

Ideological and political challenges

If there is no serious threat to the welfare state from globalization, immigration, economic and demographic prospects, it remains to be seen whether ideological and political trends will present other challenges. Ideology and politics are of course almost inseparable from the economic and social developments described above.

Sociologists such as Ulrich Beck (Beck, 1992) and Anthony Giddens have developed theories of individualization in post-industrial capitalism. The market promotes individualism, Giddens argues (Giddens, 1991). The individual is disembedded from tradition, class, religion, and the family; Individual identities are no longer formed by socialization in these institutions, forcing the individual to ponder choices and identity and the different aspects of life. People must choose from a variety of life-styles, and the choice of lifestyle is increasingly important in the development of one's self-identity. Thus, we are living in an era of *reflexive modernity*. The core value is self-realization, and being 'true to oneself' weakens universal moral criteria. Giddens does not assert that increased individualism diminishes all forms of solidarity. He only claims that it changes the conditions of solidarity.

Although Giddens probably overstates his case, individualism seems to be flourishing and can come to affect the universal welfare state in different ways. It could result in a greater emphasis by the health and social services on personal choice (cf. chapter 4 as well). Stronger commitment to values of self-realization and autonomy may make people less inclined to make way for the sake of the common good. Decisions of that kind are no longer fashioned by a sense of working class collectivism, but contingent upon individual reflection. Solidarity itself becomes rarefied and unreliable (Stjernø, 2004).

These cultural changes go cheek by jowl with shifts in the ideology on which the Norwegian welfare state was founded. Individualism implies acceptance of more inequality. The meaning of equality has shifted, almost imperceptibly, from equality of outcome to equality of opportunity, and ideas of justice from equal terms to the matching of contribution to reward (obligations and rights, i.e. the principle of reciprocity) (Stjernø, 2008). The welfare state gives according to what it has received in the form of work or social insurance. These tendencies can be observed in most welfare states. Although Norwegians are still more likely to favour equality than citizens of most other European countries, the widening pay and wealth gaps (cf. above) are viewed with increasing indifference (Knudsen, 2004).

To such deep cultural and ideological changes we must add the political challenges posed by the ascent of neo-liberalism. The alliance between the industrial working class, rural land workers and small-holders, enriched later by allies from the middle classes on which the universal welfare state was built, exists no more. The industrial working class has been weakened numerically, ideologically and politically. The influence of class membership on voting has been weakened; social democracy no longer has sole claim to workers' loyalty, and the working class in Norway, as in Denmark, France and elsewhere, sets its light on a range of political parties. It is both an effect of neo-liberalistic thinking and a cause of its dissemination and influence.

There are two political parties on the right in Norway – the Conservatives and the Progress Party. None of them is an advocate of undiluted neo-liberalism, and both are less right wing than their compatriots in other countries. However, they do support market liberalism in economic policy and the use of markets and quasi market mechanisms and incentives in welfare policy, such as competition in the provision of social services, for instance. They want people to have a choice between private and public provision. And they are for tightening criteria for payment of unemployment benefit or disability pension, providing a stronger incentive to get back to work.

In the 2005 general election, the Progress Party (FrP) won enough seats in parliament to become leader of the opposition against the red-green alliance in office. Its strategy is a mix of neo-liberalism and state responsibility. In the FrP manifesto for 2005–2009, it denied that it was a government responsibility to reduce income differences created by the market. It recommends full labour market deregulation, with local bargaining replacing centralized settlements. In health and social policy, it would invite private sector operators to bid for contracts alongside public sector bodies. If people want more than the basic state pension they will need to invest in private insurance or collective arrangements in the labour market. And instead of funding day care, the party would spend more on child benefits. Although the manifesto is not a totally neo-liberalistic attack on the welfare state, the consequences of its policies would nevertheless be to transform it. It would result in individual responsibility rather than redistribution and in widening wage gaps. Female employment would decline because better child allowances would make it worthwhile to drop day care and stay at home with the children.

The Progress Party's success is partly due to this combination of liberalist economic policy, lower direct and indirect taxes, and wider private sector involvement in healthcare and social service delivery. Besides, its negative attitude towards immigration appeals to a segment of the electorate. Finally, and possible the most important point, it is the only party against applying macro-economic constraints to the management of the oil revenue, and the widespread disaffection with the government's guarded use of the oil money creates a favourable situation for the party.

The Conservative Party (H) has some of the same welfare policies as the Progress Party, but in a more diluted form. Like theirs, its manifesto favours greater labour market flexibility, and more choice for clients of the health and social services. It would cut sickness benefits and require people on benefit to do something in return – look for work, improve their qualifications, join labour market or workfare programmes. Although these are controversial issues, the Conservative Party is not anti-welfare per se, and except for such issues it seems to express what seems to be a consensus on Norwegian social policy.

Conclusion: No immediate danger, but are there clouds on the horizon?

We can safely conclude, then, that the Norwegian welfare state is not in any immediate danger. Optimistic prognoses concerning Norway's economy and situation in the job market, a more than healthy budget and trade balance paired with widespread public support for the welfare state are the main reasons for this favourable forecast. But Norway is part of the world economy, and not immune to global or regional recessions and instability. However, the oil fund nevertheless offers some protection against international stagnation or setbacks.

If there is a challenge, it is not economic, but political and ideological. While neo-liberalism was never the leading platform of a political party in Norway, the breadth of popular support for the Progress Party indicates a neo-liberalist mentality in parts of the public. And while the Progress Party and the Conservative Party are not likely achieve government power together at the elections in 2009, they may do. A right-wing coalition would not destroy the welfare state, but it would probably add momentum to a process of cutting back on some social benefits and speeding up the privatization of social services.

However, the most important challenges to the welfare state are probably the general cultural and ideological changes that we observe in the post-industrial, global information society. As traditional collectives crumble, and individualism flourishes, normative structures and values centred on justice, equality and freedom acquire new accentuations that differ from those of the era of classic social democracy. We are witness to an increasing acceptance of inequality, and equality of opportunity is overtaking redistribution as a key policy motive. Justice is more likely to be interpreted as receiving according to one's contribution. Freedom refers less frequently to the economic and material conditions without which choice doesn't exist, and more often to the freedom to choose in a market and between private and public services. These normative changes will probably affect what is seen as legitimate in the welfare state. As the pension reform exemplifies, benefits are linked more closely to contributions in the working life, and the redistributive mechanism of the pension system is taking back seat. Normative change will probably fuel a gradual transformation of the universal social democratic welfare state emulating the welfare states on the continent that were developed under the hegemony of Christian democracy. While it will not be the end of the welfare state, it will represent a transitional stage on the route towards the adoption of mainstream European social policy in Norway – though possibly with the exception of wider range of social services and higher social benefits than most other European countries.

List of boxes, figures and tables

Boxes

Calculation of old age pension in the National Insurance Scheme   77

Figures

Figure 2.1 Social expenditure 1980–2003 in per cent of GDP   33
Figure 2.2 Tax free transfers 2003   35
Figure 2.3 Life expectancy for males and females 1930–2006   36
Figure 3.1 Labour force participation rate 1973–2004   45
Figure 3.2 Female labour force participation rate 1973–2004   46
Figure 3.3 Unemployed, registered unemployed 1997–2007   47
Figure 6.1 Health expenditures by function   93
Figure 6.2 Total health expenditure per capita 2004   94

Tables

Table 1.1 Social reforms in Norway 1840–2005   18
Table 1.2 Main political parties, electoral support (per cent) and main electoral groups   19
Table 1.3 Parties in government 1945–2005. The party of the Prime Minister in bold   20
Table 2.1 Production and employment by sector in Norway 1960–2005   27
Table 2.2 Gross Domestic Product per capita (PPP US$) in selected countries 2005   29
Table 2.3 Life expectancy, Gini index, Gender-related development index, happiness, loneliness and subjective general health in selected countries (2002)   38
Table 3.1 Labour force participation and unemployment 1985–2005 (percentages)   44

Table 3.2 Employment rates 55–64 years for selected OECD countries (2005)	46
Table 3.3 Unemployment levels in selected countries (2005)	47
Table 3.4 Unemployment benefits in selected countries (1.1.2006)	55
Table 4.1 Family reforms in Norway 1892–2005	60
Table 4.2 Expenditure on families and children as percentages of GNP (2001), power purchasing parity (US$) and total social expenditure (2002)	63
Table 4.3 Fertility – births per woman in fertile age 2006	65
Table 4.4 Child benefits 2005	67
Table 4.5 Entitlements to maternal and paternal leave in 2005–2006	68
Table 4.6 Reconciliation of work and family life. Attitudes	70
Table 4.7 Persons who give unpaid help to a family member or relative outside the household – apart from – own children with child care, other care, housework or home maintenance	72
Table 5.1 Old age pensions in some European countries (January 2006)	79
Table 6.1 Sickness benefits among employees (2006)	101
Table 7.1 Persons who receive social assistance or equivalent benefits (2005)	107
Table 7.2 Recommended social assistance benefits to different kinds of household 2006	108
Table 7.3 Poverty in selected European countries in 2004	112
Table 7.4 Feeling about present household income nowadays	113
Table 7.5 Poor in different groups in Norway in 2003	114
Table 8.1 Persons who agree that citizens should spend at least some of their free time helping others	122
Table 8.2 Persons who agree that most people can be trusted	122
Table 8.3 Paid staff and volunteers as a percentage of all employed and of the adult population	127
Table 8.4 The workforce of voluntary organizations by sector	128
Table 9.1 Children enrolled in day-care institutions and municipal family day care in 2004	140
Table 10.1 Indexes on competitiveness, business-friendliness and transparency	148
Table 10.2 Immigration to selected countries 2001. Proportion born abroad and of non-citizens in different countries	152
Table 10.3 Attitudes to immigration	153
Table 10.4 Persons aged 65+, 15–64 and 80+	158
Table 10.5 Projected number of pensioners and overall state pension outlays in the National Social Insurance Scheme	159

References

Aalborg, Torbjørg, 2007. Dystre tall for framtidas eldre, kronikk, *Dagbladet* 26.3.
Aasland, Olav Gjerløw, Terje P. Hagen and Pål E. Martinussen. 2007. Sykehuslegenes syn på sykehusreformen. *Tidsskrift for den norske lægeforening* 17/2007: 2218–21.
Alesina, Alberto, and Edward L. Glaeser. 2004. *Fighting Poverty in the US and Europe*. Oxford: Oxford University Press.
Alstadsæter, Annette, Erik Fjærli and Aud Walseth. 2005. Skatter, avgifter og overføringer i Norge – noen hovedtrekk. In Statistics Norway. *Inntekt, skatt og overføringer 2005*. Oslo.
Andersen, Arne, et al. 2003. 'Økonomiske Konjunkturer og Fattigdom: En Studie Basert På Norske Inntektsdata, 1979–2000.' *Tidsskrift for velferdsforskning* 6, no. 2 (2003): 89–106.
Andersen, Arne Støttrup and Lars Gulbrandsen. 2006. Boligetablering. In *Bolig og levekår i Norge 2004. Nova Rapport 3*, ed. Lars Gulbrandsen. Oslo: NOVA.
Andersen, Jørgen Goul and Jan Bendix Jensen. 2002. Employment and unemployment in Europe: overview and new trends? In *Europe's New State of Welfare*, eds. Jørgen G. Andersen et al. Bristol: The Policy Press.
Andreassen, Jorun. 2003. *Må vi ta den jobben? – Aetats praktisering av mobilitetskravene i dagpengeregelverket*. FAFO-rapport 404. Oslo: Forskningsstiftelsen FAFO.
Anttonen, Anneli. 2005. Empowering Social Policy: The Role of Social Care Services in Modern Welfare States. In *Social Policy and Economic Development in the Nordic Countries*, ed. Olli Kangas and Joakim Palme. Basingstoke: Palgrave Macmillan.
Anttonen, Anneli and Jorma Sipilä. 1995. *Five regimes of social care services*, Paper prepared for the 8th Nordic Social Policy Research Seminar in Stockholm, February 9–11.
Arendt, Hannah. 1958. *The Human Condition*. Chicago: The University of Chicago Press.
Askildsen, Jan Erik, Tor Helge Holmås and Oddvar Kaarbøe. 2007. *Prioriteringspraksis før og etter sykehusreformen*. Notatserie i helseøkonomi nr. 5/07. Bergen: Program for Helseøkonomi i Bergen.
Baldwin, Peter. 1990. *The Politics of Social Solidarity*. New York: Cambridge University Press.
Baldwin, Peter. 1997. 'State and Citizenship in the Age of Globalisation.' In *Restructuring the Welfare State. Theory of Reform of Social Policy*, ed. Peter Koslowski and Andreas Føllesdal. London: Springer.

Bambra, Clare. 2005. Cash Versus Services: 'Worlds of Welfare' and the Decommodification of Cash Benefits and Health Care Services. *International Journal of Social Policy* 34 (2): 195–213.

Barstad, Anders and Ottar Hellevik. 2004. *På vei mot det gode samfunn?* Statistiske Analyser. Oslo: Statistics Norway.

Barth, Erling, Marianne Røed and Paul Schøne. 2005. Lønnsforskjeller mellom kvinner og menn i privat sektor: betydning av yrke og virksomhet. *Søkelys på arbeidsmarkedet*, no. 2: 211–216.

Bay, Ann-Helen, Ottar Hellevik and Tale Hellevik. 2007. Svekker innvandringen oppslutningen om velferdsstaten? *Tidsskrift for samfunnsforsking* 48, no. 3 (2007): 377–408.

Beck, Ulrich. 1992. *Risk Society. Towards a New Modernity.* London: Sage Publications.

Bjørnestad, Sigurd. 2007. Antall fattige øker. *Aftenposten* 2007, May 20.

Bjørnestad, Sigurd. 2007. Verdensbanken: Flott å drive business i Norge. *Aftenposten*, September 26.

Bjørnson, Øyvind.1990. På Klassekampens grunn (1900–1920). In *Arbeiderbevegelsens Historie i Norge* 2nd ed., ed. Arne Kokkvoll and Jacob Sverdrup,. Oslo: Tiden Norsk Forlag.

Blekasaune, Morten 2005a. Uførhet. In *De norske trygdene*, eds. Ann-Helen. Bay, Aksel Hatland, Tale Hellevik and Charlotte Koren. Oslo: Gyldendal Akademisk.

Blekasaune, Morten. 2005b. *Sykdom og sykefravær.* In *De norske trygdene. Framvekst, fordeling og forvaltning*, ed. Ann-Helén Bay et al. Oslo: Gyldendal Akademisk.

Blekasaune, Morten and Axel West Pedersen. 2006. Sykefravær: Innfallsporten til permanent trygding? In *Inkluderende arbeidsliv? Erfaringer og strategier*, ed. Torild Hammer and Einar Øverbye. Oslo: Gyldendal Akademisk.

Boarini, Romina, Asa Johansson and Marco Mira D'Ercole. 2006. *Alternative Measures of Well-Being*, Working Paper 33, Paris: OECD.

Borgeraas, Elling. 2006. Knapphetens økonomi. In *SIFO Oppdragsrapport 1*. Oslo: Statens Institutt for Forbruksforskning.

Bosma, Niels and Rebecca Harding. 2007. *Global Entrepreneurship Monitor. 2006 Results.* London: London School of Economics.

Botten, Grete. 2006. Prioriteringer i norsk helsetjeneste – er det mulig? In *Velferdspolitiske utfordringer*, ed. Nanna Kildal and Kari Tove Elvbakken. Bergen: Abstrakt forlag.

Brandth, Berit, Brita Bungum, and Elin Kvande. 2005. *Valgfrihetens tid. Omsorgspolitikk for barn møter det fleksible arbeidslivet.* Oslo: Gyldendal Akademisk.

Bratsberg, Bernt, Oddbjørn Raaum and Knut Røed. 2006. *The rise and fall of immigration employment*, Oslo: Frisch Centre, University of Oslo.

Bringedal, Berit. 2005. Egenandeler og prioriteringer i norsk helsetjeneste. *Tidsskrift for Velferdsforskning.* Vol. 8 (2): 100–110.

British Council. 'Migration Integration Policy Index.' (2007), http://www.integrationindex.eu/.

Brochmann, Grete. Velferdsstat, integrasjon og majoritetens legitimitet. In *Sand i maskineriet: Makt og demokrati i det flerkulturelle Norge*, ed. Grete Brochmann, Jon Rogstad and Tordis Borchgrevink, 9–55. Oslo: Gyldendal Akademisk, 2002.

Bø, Bente Puntervold. 2004. *Søkelys på den norske innvandringspolitikken: Etiske og rettslige dilemmaer*. Kristiansand: Høyskoleforlaget.

Castilla, Emilio J. 2004. Organizing Health Care. A Comparative Analysis of National Institutions and Inequality over Time. *International Sociology*, Vol. 19 (4): 403–435.

Christensen, Johan, Tone Fløtten and Jon M. Hippe. 2007. Rikdom i likhets-Norge. Kronikk, *Aftenposten* 24.8.

Christiansen, Niels Finn, and Pirjo Markkola. Introduction. In *The Nordic Model of Welfare. A Historical Reappraisal*, ed. Niels Finn Christiansen, Klaus Petersen, Nils Edling and Per Haave, 9–29. Copenhagen: Museum Tusculanum Press, 2006.

Christiansen, Nils Finn. 1997. Solidaritetens historie. *Dansk Sociologi*, no. 1 (1997): 9–18.

Daatland, Svein Olav. 1990. What are families for? On family solidarity and preference for help. *Ageing & Society* 10(1): 1–15.

Daatland, Svein Olav and Katharina Herlofson, 2004. *Familier, velferdsstat og aldring. Familiesolidaritet i et europeisk perspektiv*. NOVA Rapport 7/04. Oslo: Norsk Institutt for forskning om oppvekst, velferd og aldring.

Daatland, Svein Olav, and Ariela Lowenstein. 2005. Intergenerational Solidarity and the Family–Welfare State Balance. *European Journal of Aging*, no. 2 (2005): 174–82.

d'Addio, Anna Christina, and Marco Mira d'Ercole. 2005. Trends and Determinants of Fertility Rates in OECD Countries: The Role of Policies. In *OECD Social, Employment and Migration Working Papers*, ed. OECD, 1–63. Paris: OECD.

Dahl, Grete. Enslige forsørgere med overgangsstønad. Økonomisk situasjon etter avsluttet stønad. In *Notater*, ed. Statistics Norway, 1–72. Oslo: Statistics Norway, 2003.

Debes, Inge, 1939. Den nye sociallovgivning. *Socialt arbeid* 20.

Dumont, Jean-Christophe, and Georges Lemaître. 2005. *Counting Immigrants and Expatriates in OECD Countries: A New Perspective*. Paris: OECD.

Dyrstad, Jan Morten and Solveig Osborg Ose. 2005. Sykefravær, in *Det nye arbeidsmarkedet*, ed. Pål Schøne. Oslo: Norges forskningsråd/Arbeidslivsforskning.

Dølvik, Jon Erik and Arild Steen. 1996. Norwegian Labour Market Institutions and Regulations. In *Making Solidarity Work?* ed. Jon Erik Dølvik and Arild Steen. Oslo: Scandinavian University Press.

Dølvik, Jon Erik. 2007. Konklusjoner: Modernisering, konsolidering og nye utfordringer. In *Hamskifte – Den norske modellen i endring*, eds. Jon Erik Dølvik et al. Oslo: Gyldendal Akademisk.

ECON, 2006. *Egenandeler på sosiale tjenester*. R-2006-075, Oslo: ECON.

Edling, Nils, 2006: Limited universalism: Unemployment insurance in Northern Europe 1900–2000. In *The Nordic Model – A Historical Reappraisal*, ed. Niels Finn Christensen et al. Copenhagen: Museum Tusculanums Forlag.

Ellingsæter, Anne Lise. 2006. The Norwegian Childcare Regime and Its Paradoxes. In *Politicising Parenthood in Scandinavia Gender Relations in Welfare States*, ed. Anne Lise Ellingsæter and Arnlaug Leira. Bristol: Policy Press, 2006.

Ellingsæter, Anne Lise. 2003. Når familiepolitikk ikke virker. Om Kontantstøttereformen og mødres lønnsarbeid. *Tidsskrift for samfunnsforskning* 44, no. 4: 499–527.

Ellingsæter, Anne Lise, and Lars Gulbrandsen. 2007. Closing the Childcare Gap: The Interaction of Childcare Provisions and Mothers' Agency in Norway. *Journal of Social Policy* 36, no. 4: 649–69.

Elvbakken, Kari Tove. 2006. Regulering av helserisiki – ny forebyggingspolitikk i Norge? In *Velferdspolitiske utfordringer*, ed. Nanna Kildal and Kari Tove Elvbakken. Bergen: Abstrakt forlag.

Engelstad, Harald. 2005. *Pensjonsboka*. Oslo: Pensjonsboka Forlag.

Epland, Jon. 2004. Lavinntekt og inntektsfordeling. In Statistics Norway. *Økonomi og levekår for ulike grupper 2004*. Oslo: Statistics Norway.

Epland, Jon, and Mads Ivar Kirkeberg. 2007. Barn i familier med lavinntekt: Er effekten av kontantstøtten spist opp av redusert barnetrygd? http://www.ssb.no/vis/samfunnsspeilet/utg/200704/01/art-2007–09-20-01.html, visited October 8 2007.

Esping-Andersen, Gösta. 1985. *Politics against Markets. The Social Democratic Road to Power*. Princeton: Princeton University Press.

Esping-Andersen, Gösta. 1990. *The Three Worlds of Welfare Capitalism*. Cambridge: Polity Press.

Esping-Andersen, Gösta. 1996. After the Golden Age? Welfare State Dilemmas in a Global Economy. In *Welfare States in Transition*, ed. Gösta Esping Andersen. London: Sage.

Esping-Andersen, Gösta. 1999. *Social Foundations of Postindustrial Economies*. New York: Oxford University Press.

Esping-Andersen, Gösta. 2001. *Households, families and children*, Paper prepared for the RC19 Meetings. September. Oviedo.

Esser, Ingrid. 2005. *Why work? Comparative studies on Welfare Regimes and Individuals' Work Orientation*. PhD Dissertation. Stockholm: SOFI, Stockholm University.

Eurostat. 2007. *Living Conditions in Europe. Data 2002–2005*. Brussels: Eurostat.

Evers, Adalbert, and Jean-Louis Laville. 2004. Social Services by Social Enterprises: On the Possible Contributions of Hybrid Organizations and a Civil Society. In *The Third Sector in Europe*, ed. Adalbert Evers and Jean-Louis Laville, XI. Cheltenham: Elgar.

Fevang, Elisabeth and Knut Røed, 2005. *Omstillinger og nedbemanninger blant pleiere. En belastning for Folketrygden?* Oslo: Frischsenteret.

Fevang, Elisabeth and Knut Røed 2006. *Veier til uføretrygding i Norge*, Oslo: Frischsenteret.

Fleurbaey, March and Guillaume Gaulier 2007. *International Comparisons of Living Standards by Equivalent Incomes*, CEPEII working paper. Paris: CEPEII.

Furre, Berge. 1991. *Vårt Hundreår. Norsk Historie 1905–1990*. Oslo: Det Norske Samlaget.

Förster, Michael, and Marco Mira d'Ercole. 2005. *Income Distribution and Poverty in OECD Countries in the Second Half of the 1990s*. Vol. 1, Delsa/Elsa/Wd/Sem. Paris: OECD.

Geist, Claudia. 2005. The Welfare State and the Home: Regime Differences in the Domestic Division of Labour. *European Sociological Review* 21, no. 1 (2005): 23–41.

Giddens, Anthony. 1991. *Modernity and Self-Identity. Self and Society in Late Modern Age*. Cambridge: Polity Press.

Glad, Kristin 2003. Eldrebølgen slår lenger inn over Europa enn Norge. Statistics Norway: *Magasinet* (www.ssb.no/magasinet/norge_verden/art-2003-04-07-01.html 09.05.03).

Gullestad, Marianne. 2001. Imagined Sameness: Shifting Notions of 'Us' and 'Them' in Norway. In *Forestillinger om 'Den Andre'*, ed. Line Alice Ytrehus, 32–35. Kristiansand: Høyskoleforlaget.

Haave, Per. 2006. The hospital sector: A four-country comparison of organisational and political development. In *The Nordic Model of Welfare. A Historical Reappraisal*, eds. Niels Finn Christiansen et al.. Copenhagen: Musem Tusculaneum Press, University of Copenhagen.

Hagen, Roar. 1999. *Rasjonell Solidaritet*. Oslo: Universitetsforlaget.

Hall, P.A. and D.D. Gingerich, 2004. *Varieties of Capitalism and Institutional Complementarities in the Macroeconomy*: An Empirical Analysis. MPifG Discussion Paper 04/05. Cologne: Max Planck Institute for the Study of Societies.

Halvorsen, Knut. 2002. Unemployment and (un)employment policies in Norway: the case of an affluent, but oil-dependent eonomy: The paradox of plenty? *In Europe's new state of welfare*, eds. Jørgen Goul Andersen et al. Bristol: The Policy Press.

Halvorsen, Knut. 2004. *Når det ikke er bruk for deg – arbeidsløshet og levekår*. Oslo: Gyldendal Akademisk.

Halvorsen, Knut. 2005. Holdninger til arbeidsledige dagpengemottakere i Skandinavia (Attitudes towards unemployment benefit recipients in Scandinavia). *Søkelys på arbeidsmarkedet* 2005:22–19–28.

Halvorsen, Knut. 2007 Legitimacy of Welfare States in Transitions from Homogeneity to Multiculturality: A Matter of Trust. In *The Welfare State, Legitimacy and Social Justice*, ed. Benjamin Veghte and Steffen Mau, 239–60. Aldershot: Ashgate.

Hammer, Torild and Einar Øverbye. 2006. *Inkluderende arbeidsliv?* Oslo: Gyldendal Akademisk.

Hammer, Torild and Einar Øverbye. 2006. Strategier for et inkluderende arbeidsliv. In *Inkluderende arbeidsliv? Erfaringer og strategier*, ed. Torild Hammer and Einar Øverbye. Oslo: Gyldendal Akademisk.

Hardoy, Inés and Pål Schøne, 2007: *Lønnsforskjeller mellom kvinner og menn: Hvor mye betyr barn?*, ISF rapport 2007:003. Oslo: Institute of Social Research.

Hatland, Aksel. 1992. *Til dem som trenger det mest? Økonomisk behovsprøving i norsk sosialpolitikk*. Oslo: Universitetsforlaget.

Hatland, Aksel, 2005. Finansiering. In *De norske trygdene*, ed. Ann-Helen Bay, Aksel Hatland, Tale Hellevik and Charlotte Koren. Oslo: Gyldendal Akademisk.

Hatland, Aksel, and Jonathan Bradshaw. 2006. *Social Policy, Employment and Family Change in Comparative Perspective*, Globalization and Welfare. Cheltenham: Edward Elgar.

Hatland, Aksel, and Axel West Pedersen. 2006.Er sosialhjelpen et effektivt virkemiddel i fattigdomsbekjempelsen? *Tidsskrift for velferdsforskning* 9, no. 2 (2006): 58–72.

Hauge, Linda. 2005. Sykefraværet: Utvikling og årsaker. In *Arbeid, velferd og samfunn*. Oslo: Rikstrygdeverket.

Hellevik, Tale. 2005. Ungdom, etablering og ulike velferdsregimer. *Tidsskrift for ungdomsforskning*, no. 1 (2005): 89–110.

Hjemdal, Ole K., Sissel Seim, and Sigrun Nilsen. 1998. *Selvhjelp: Kunsten å løfte seg etter håret*. Oslo: Cappelen akademisk forlag.

Huber, Evelyn, and John D. Stephens. 2001. *Development and Crisis of the Welfare State. Parties and Policies in Global Markets*. Chicago: The University of Chicago Press.

Hult, C. and Stefan Svallfors. 2002. Production Regimes and Work Orientations: A Comparison of Six Western Countries. *European Sociological Review* 18(3): 315–331.

Hutton, Will. 2007. *The writing on the wall. China and the west in 21st Century*. London. Abacus.

Inst. nr. 150 for 2006–2007 *Innstilling fra helse- og omsorgskomiteen om framtidas omsorgsutfordringer (Mestring, muligheter og mening)*.

Jensen, Bjarne, 2005. *Kommune-Norge – velferd og finansiering*. Oslo: Kommuneforlaget.

Kangas, Olli, and Joakim Palme. 2005. Coming Late – Catching Up: The Formation of a 'Nordic Model'. In *Social Policy and Economic Development in the Nordic Countries*, eds. Olli Kangas and Joakim Palme, XX. Basingstoke: Palgrave Macmillan.

Kangas, Olli, Urban Lundberg and Niels Plough. 2006: *Three routes to a pension reform: Politics and institutions in reforming pensions in Denmark, Finland and Sweden*, Copenhagen: Danish National Institute for Social Research.

Kautto, Mikko. 2002. *Nordic Social Policy. Changing Welfare States*. Taylor & Francis e-Library ed. London New York: Routledge.

Kildal, Nanna, and Stein Kuhnle. 2005. The Nordic Welfare Model and the Idea of Universalism. In *Normative Foundations of the Welfare State. The Nordic Experience*, ed. Nanna Kildal and Stein Kuhnle. London: Routledge.

Kitterød, Randi Hege. 2002. Kvinner bruker mindre tid til husarbeid. *Samfunnsspeilet*, no. 4–5:23–31.

Kjeldstadli, Knut. 1997. Solidaritet og Individualitet. In *Historiens Kultur. Fortælling. Kritik. Metode*, ed. Ning de Coninck-Smith and Morten Thing. Copenhagen: Museum Tusculanums Forlag.

Kloster, Elisabeth, Hilde Lidén, and Håkon Lorentzen. 2003. *Frivillighetssentralen. Resultater, erfaringer, forandringer*. Rapport 2003:4. Oslo: Institutt for samfunnsforskning.

Knudsen, Jon P. Hva kan vi lære av andre? 2002 *Horisont*, no. 1: 38–40.

Knudsen, Knud. 2004. *Har det blitt mer eller mindre likhet?* NFR seminar October 10 2004 Velferd og valgfrihet. Oslo.

Knudsen, Knud and Kari Wærness. 2008. National context and spouses housework in 33 countries. *European Sociological Review* 24(1): 97–113.

Korpi, Walter. 1983. *The Democratic Class Struggle*. London: Routledge & K. Paul.

Kramer, Ralph. 2004. Alternative Paradigms for the Mixed Economy: Will the Sector Matter? In *The Third Sector in Europe*, ed. Adalbert Evers and Jean-Louis Laville, XI, 266 s. Cheltenham: Elgar.

Kröger, Teppo. 2005. Interplay between Formal and Informal Care for Older People: The State of the Nordic Research. In *Äldreomsorgsforskning i Norden. En Kunnskapsöversikt*. ed. Marta Szebehely. Copenhagen: Nordisk Ministerråd.

Kuhnle, Stein. 1978. 'The Beginnings of the Nordic Welfere State'. *Acte Seciologica Supplement*.

Kuhnle, Stein. 1985. The Growth of Social Insurance Programs in Scandinavia: Outside Influences and Internal Forces. In *The Development of Welfare States in Europe and America* ed. Peter Flora and Arnold J. Heidenheimer. New Brunswick, N.J.: Transaction Books.

Kuhnle, Stein. 2001. Velferdsstatens Idegrunnlag i Perspektiv. In Den Norske Velferdsstaten, ed. Aksel Hatland, Stein Kuhnle and Tor Inge Romøren, 262 p. Oslo: Gyldendal Akademisk.

Kuhnle, Stein. 2001. Norge i møte med Europa. In *Den norske velferdsstaten*, ed. Aksel Hatland et al. Oslo: Gyldendal Akademisk.

Kuhnle, Stein, and Per Selle. 1990. *Meeting Needs in a Welfare State: Relations between Government and Voluntary Organizations in Norway*, Los-Senter Særtrykk; 90/7. Bergen: LOS-senteret.

Kvist, Jon, and Juho Saari. 2007. *The Europeanisation of Social Protection*. Bristol: Policy Press.

Lappegård, Trude. 2007. Sosiologiske forklaringer på fruktbarhetsendringer i nyere tid. *Sosiologisk tidsskrift* 15, no. 55–71 (2007): 55–71.

Larson, Helge O. and Audun Offerdal. 2000. Political Implications of the New Norwegian local government act of 1992. In *Towards a new concept of self-government?* eds. Erik Amnå and Stig Martin. Bergen Fagbokforlaget.

Layard, Richard. 2005. *Happiness*. New York: The Penguin Press.

Leira, Arnlaug. 2006. Parenthood Change and Policy Reform in Scandinavia, 1970s–2000s. In *Politicising Parenthood in Scandinavia Gender Relations in Welfare States*, ed. Anne Lise Ellingsæter and Arnlaug Leira, IX, 286 s. Bristol: Policy Press.

Leira, Arnlaug. 2002. Working Parents and the Welfare State : Family Change and Policy Reform in Scandinavia. Cambridge: Cambridge University Press.

Lewis, Jane. 2001. The decline of the male breadwinner model: implications for work and care. Social Politics, 8(2): 152–169.

Lindert, Peter H. 2005. Välfärdsstatens expansion. Ekonomisk tilväxt och offentlig sektor under 200 år, Stockholm: SNS—förlag.

Lingsom, Susan. The Substitution Issue: Care Policies and Their Consequences for Family Care. Oslo: NOVA.

LO. 2007. Hvidbog om Ulikhet. Copenhagen: LO.

Lødemel, Ivar, and Asbjørn Johannessen. 2005. Tiltaksforsøket: Mot en inkluderende arbeidslinje? Sluttrapport fra evaluering av forsøk med kommunalt ansvar for aktive, arbeidsretta tiltak for langtidsmottakere av sosialhjelp 2000–2004. HiO-Rapport; 2005 Nr 1. Oslo: Høgskolen i Oslo Avdeling for økonomi- kommunal- og sosialfag.

Mack, Joanna, and Stewart Lansley. 1985. Poor Britain. London: Allen & Unwin.

Malmberg-Heimonen, Ira. 2005. Activation or Discourgement – the Effect of Enforced Participation on the Success of Job-Search Training. *European Journal of Social Work*. 8, no. 4 (2005): 451–67.

Midsundstad, Tove. 2005. Virksomhetenes sosiale ansvar. In Nytt arbeidsliv, ed. Hege Torp. Oslo: Gyldendal Akademisk.

Ministry of Health. 2003. Report No. 16 (2002–2003) to the Storting: Prescriptions for a Healthier Norway. A broad policy for public health. Oslo.

Mjøset, Lars. 2003. Den norske oljeøkonomiens integrasjon i verdensøkonomien. In *Det norske samfunn*, ed. Ivar Frønes and Lise Kjølsrud. Oslo: Gyldendal.

Mørk, Eiliv. 2006. *Aleneboendes levekår*, Statistiske Analyser, Oslo: Statistics Norway.

Nasjonalt kunnskapssenter for helsetjenesten. 2007. *Pasienters erfaringer med døgnenheter ved somatiske sykehus*, rapport nr. 1–2007. Oslo.

Nelson, Kenneth. 2007. Minimum Income Protection and European Integration: Trends and Levels of Minimum Benefits in Comparative Perspective 1990–2005. In ASA Annual Meeting. 'Is Another World Possible?' New York Swedish Institute for Social Research, Stockholm University.

Noack, Turid. 2003. Dagligdags og uutforsket. Samfunnsspeilet 1 (2003).

Noack, Turid. 2004. Familien i velferdsstaten: Fra støttespiller til trojansk hest? In *Velferdsstaten og familien: Utfordringer og dilemmaer*, ed. Arnlaug Leira and Anne Lise Ellingsæter, 39–66. Oslo: Gyldendal Akademisk.

Noack, Turid, and Ane Seierstad. 2003. *Heller jeg enn vi*. Statistisk Sentralbyrå, http://www.ssb.no/vis/samfunnsspeilet/utg/200303/03/art-2003-06-20-01.html.

NOMESCO, 2007. Health Statistics in the Nordic Countries 2005. Copenhagen.

NOMESCO, 2007. Social protection in the Nordic Countries. Copenhagen.

NOU 1994:1 *Modernisert folketrygd*.

NOU 2004:1 modernisert folketrygd.

NOU 2007:4 *Ny uførestønad og ny alderspensjon til uføre*.

OECD.2001 *The Well-Being of Nations : The Role of Human and Social Capital, Education and Skills*. Paris: OECD.

OECD. 2002. *Participative disability policies for the working-age population: Towards a coherent policy mix*. Draft OECD report 20th March. Paris: OECD.

OECD. 2005. *Health at a Glance:* OECD Indicators 2005. Paris.

OECD. 2005. *Social, Employment and Migration* Working Papers 25. Paris: OECD.

OECD. 2006. Live Longer, Work Longer, Paris: OECD.

OECD. 2007. *Agricultural Policies. Monitoring and Evaluation 2007*. Highlights. Paris: OECD.

Opedal, Ståle and Inger Marie Stigen. eds. 2005. *Helse-Norge i støpeskjeen*. Bergen: Fagbokforlaget.

Oorschot, Wim van, and Wilfred Uunk. 2007. Multi-Level Determinants of the Public's Informal Solidarity Towards Immigrants in European Welfare States. In *The Welfare State, Legitimacy and Social Justice*. Ed. Benjamin Veghte and Steffen Mau, 239–60. Aldershot: Ashgate.

Øverbye, Einar. 2002. *Deconstructing Universalism*. Preliminary Research Note. April 9 2002. Oslo: Oslo University College.

Øverbye, Einar, 2004. *Hva kan vi lære av Danmark? Sosialforvaltning i en desentralisert velferdsstat*. NOVA skriftserie 2/2004. Oslo: NOVA.

Øverbye, Einar, 2006. Hvorfor blir flere uførepensjonister? In *Velferdspolitiske utfordringer*, ed. Nanna Kildal and Kari Tove Elvbakken. Oslo: Abstrakt forlag.

Øverbye, Einar, 2007. *Full fart – og sol hele dagen*, Aftenposten, kronikk, 20/6.

Øverby, Einar, Signy Vabo and Knut Welde, 1986. Rescaling Social Welfare Polities in Norway. Vienna: European Centre for Social Welfare Policy and Research.

Palme, Joakim, 2005. Why the Scandinavian experience is relevant for the reform of ESM, Discussion paper, Stockholm: Institute for Future Studies.

Pedersen, Axel West. 2006.Trygd og inntektsfordeling. In *De norske trygdene*, ed. Ann-Helen Bay, Aksel Hatland, Tale Hellevik and Charlotte Koren. Oslo: Gyldendal Akademisk.

Pedersen, Siv Irene, Jon Epland and Tor Morten Normann, 2007. Sosiale indikatorer for personer 50–66 år. *Økonomi og levekår for ulike grupper*, 2006. Statistics Norway:, Reports 2007/8, Oslo: Statistics Norway.

Petersen, Klaus and Klas Åmark, 2006. Old age pensions in the Nordic countries, 1880–2000. In *The Nordic Model – A Historical Reappraisal*, ed. Niels Finn Christensen et al. Copenhagen: Museum Tusculanums Forlag.

Randøy, Trond and Ole Skalpe, 2007. *Lederlønnsutviklingen i Norge 1996–2005*, FoU-rapport 2/2007, Kristiansand: Senter for Internasjonal Økonomi og Skibsfart, Agderforskning.

Rauch, Dietmar. 2007. Is There Really a Scandinavian Social Service Model? A Comparison of Childcare and Elderly care in Six European Countries. *Acta Sociologica*. Vol 50(3): 249–269.

Reinertsen, Maria. 2007. På tide å forklare seg, statsminister. *Morgenbladet*, October 19–25 2007.

Rege, Mari, Kjetil Telle and Mark Votruba, 2005. *Social Interaction Effects in Disability Pension Participation. Evidence from Plant Downsizing.* Discussion Paper 496, Oslo: Statistics Norway.

Rege, Marit, Kjetil Telle and Mark Votruba. 2005. *The Effects of Plant Downsizing on Disability Pension Utilization.* Discussion Paper No. 435. Oslo: Statistics Norway.

Rikstrygdeverket, 2006. *Nedbemanning og sykefravær*, RTV-rapport 05/06. Oslo: RTV.

Risa, Alf Erling. 2006. Er sosial utjamning mulig i en meritokratisk velferdsstat? In *Velferdspoltiske utfordringer.* ed. Nanna Kildal and Kari Tove Elvbakken. Oslo: Abstrakt Forlag.

Rødseth, Asbjørn. 1998. Why Has Unemployment Been So low in Norway? In *Making Solidarity Work. The Norwegian Labour Market Model in Transition*, ed. Jon Erik Dølvik and Arild H. Steen. Oslo: Scandinavian University Press.

Røed, Knut, 2006. Veier ut av arbeidslivet – og tilbake igjen, Arbeids- og velferdsdirektoratet: *Arbeid, velferd og samfunn*, Oslo: Arbeids- og velferdsdirektoratet.

Røed, Knut. and Elisabeth Fevang. 2005. *Organisational Change, Absenteeism and Welfare Dependency.* Memo, Oslo: Økonomisk Institutt, Universitetet i Oslo.

Røed, Knut and Elisabeth Fevang 2006. *Veien til uføretrygd i Norge*. Reports 10/2006. Oslo: Frisch Centre, Universitetet i Oslo.

Romøren, Tor Inge. 2001. *Metusalems søsken. Forløp av funksjonstap, familieomsorg og tjenestebruk i høy alder.* Oslo: Universitetet i Oslo.

Rønning, Rolf. 2004. *Omsorg som vare*. Oslo: Gyldendal Akademisk.

Rønsen, Marit. 2005. Kontantstøttens langsiktige effekter på mødres og fedres arbeidstid. Oslo: Statistisk sentralbyrå.

Rønsen, Marit, and Kari Skrede. Nordic Fertility Patterns: Compatible with Gender Equality? In *Politicising Parenthood in Scandinavia Gender Relations in Welfare States*, ed. Anne Lise Ellingsæter and Arnlaug Leira, IX, 286 s. Bristol: Policy Press.

Salamon, Lester M., S. Wojciech Sokolowski, and Regina List. 2003. Global Civil Society. An Overview. In *The Johns Hopkins Comparative Nonprofit Sector Project*, 1–61. Baltimore: The Johns Hopkins University.

Schiller, Christof and Stein Kuhnle, 2007. 'Modell Tyskland' under ombygging: mot en stille systemendring? *Tidsskrift for velferdsforskning*, Vol. 10, No. 2:73–90.

Seim, Sissel. 2006. *Fattighuset som arena for kollektiv handling blant fattige. En Studie av initiativ, mobilisering og betydning av egenorganisering blant fattige.* Dissertation. Gothenburg: Gothenburg University.

Seip, Anne-Lise. 1981. *Om Velferdsstatens Framvekst*: Artikler. Oslo: Universitetsforlaget.

Seip, Anne-Lise. 1983. Omsorgsansvar og samfunn. Et Historisk tilbakeblikk. *Tidsskrift for samfunnsforsking* 24 (1983): 107–22.

Seland, Anne Cathrine. 2007. 35 000 for prisen av 3, kronikk, *Aftenposten* 18.3.

Selbæk, Geir, Øyvind Kirkevold and Knut Engedal, 2006. The prevalence of psychiatric symptoms and behavioural disturbances and the use of psychotropic drugs in Norwegian nursing homes', *International journal of geriatric psychiatry* in press (www.interscience.wiley.com).

Selle, Per. 1999. The Transformation of the Voluntary Sector in Norway. S. 144–66.

Sivesind, Karl Henrik, Håkon Lorentzen, Per Selle, and Dag Wollebæk. 2002. *The Voluntary Sector in Norway. Composition, Changes, and Causes.* Report 2002:2. Oslo: Institute for Social Research.

Skevik, Anne. 2004. The Development of Policies for Families with Children in Norway. In *Conference on Developing a normative framework for efficient and effective social security provisioning: an institutional perspective.* Cape Town: University of Cape Town.

Slagstad, Rune. 1998. *De Nasjonale Strateger.* Oslo: Pax Forlag.

Slagstad, Rune. 2001. *Rettens Ironi.* Oslo: Pax Forlag.

SSB 2005. *Inntektsstatistikk for Hushald 2005.* Oslo: Statistics Norway.

SSB 2007. Inntekt, skatt og overføringer. Oslo: Statistics Norway.

SSB 2007. *Inntektsstatistikk for Husholdninger* (Income Statistics of Households). Oslo: Statistics Norway.

SSB 2007b. *Økonomiske Analyser.* Oslo: Statistics Norway.

Stjernø, Steinar. 1985. *Den Moderne Fattigdommen Om Økonomisk Knapphet og Ydmykelse i 1980-Åra.* Oslo: Universitetsforlaget.

Stjernø, Steinar. 1995. Mellom Kirke Og Kapital. Tysk Velferdspolitikk Med Sideblikk Til Engelsk, Svensk Og Norsk. Oslo: Universitetsforlaget.

Stjernø, Steinar. 2004. Solidarity in Europe. The History of an Idea. Cambridge: Cambridge University Press.

Stjernø, Steinar. 2008. Social democratic values in the European welfare states. In *Culture and Welfare State. Values and Social Policy in a Comparative Perspective.* Ed. Wim van Oorschot, Michael Opielka and Birgit Pfau-Effinger. Cheltnham/UK: Edward Elgar.

Solem, Per Erik and Einar Øverbye. 2004. Norway: Still High Employment among older Workers. In *Ageing and the Transition to Retirement, ed.* T. Maltby et al.. Aldershot: Ashgate.

Sosial- og helsedirektoratet. 2006. *Utviklingstrekk i helse- og sosialsektoren.* Oslo.

Sosial- og helsedirektoratet. 2007. En solidarisk politick for rekruttering av helsepersonell. Rapport til Helse- og omsorgsdepartementet. Oslo: Shdir.

Statistics Norway. 2008a. *Inntektsstatistikk for husholdninger.* Oslo: SSB.

Statistics Norway. 2008b. *Levekår blant innvandrere 1996 og 2005/2006.* Oslo: SBB.

Stråth, Bo. 2001. Nordic Capitalism and Democratisation. In *The Democratic Challenge to Capitalism : Management and Democracy in the Nordic Countries*, ed. Haldor Byrkjeflot, Sissel Myklebust, Christine Myrvang and Francis Sejersted, 51–86. Bergen: Fagbokforlaget.

St.meld. nr. 8 2004_2005 *Perspektivmeldingen 2004 – utfordringer og valgmuligheter for norsk økonomi.*

St.meld. nr. 2 for 2005–2006 *Revidert nasjonalbudsjett 2006.*

St.meld. nr. 2 for 2006–2007 *Revidert nasjonalbudsjett 2007.*

St.meld. nr. 25 2005–2006. *Mestring, muligheter og mening.*

St.meld. nr. 6 2006–2007 *Om seniorpolitikk.*

St.meld. nr. 9 2006–2007 *Arbeid, velferd og inkludering.*

St.meld. nr. 20 2006–2007 *Nasjonal strategi for å utjevne helseforskjeller.*

St.prp. nr. 1 2004–2005 *Helse- og omsorgsdepartementets budsjett 2005.*

St.prp. nr. 1 2005–2006 *Helse- og omsorgsdepartementets budsjett for 2006.*

St.prp. nr. 1 2006–2007 *Helse- og omsorgsdepartementets budsjett for 2007.*

St.prp. nr. 1 2006–2007 *Arbeids- og inkluderingsdepartementet budsjett 2007.*

St.pr.p.nr. 1 2007–2008 *Kunnskapsdepartementets budsjett for 2008.*

Storsletten, Kjell, 2006. Kan planen svikte? *Aftenposten*, 2.6.

Svallfors, Stefan, Knut Halvorsen and Jørgen Goul Andersen. 2001. Work Orientations in Scandinavia: Employment Commitment and Organizational Commitment in Denmark, Norway and Sweden. *Acta Sociologica*, Vol. 44, No. 2, 2001:139–156.

Svennebye, Lars H. 2005. En internasjonal sammenlikning av lønnstakeres kjøpekraft. In *Äldreomsorgsforskning i Norden. En kunskapsöversikt*, ed. Szebehely, Marta. TemaNord 2005:508, Copenhagen: Nordisk ministerråd.

Svåsand, Lars, and Ingemar Wörlund. 2005. Partifremvekst og partioverlevelse: Fremskrittspartiet og Ny Demokrati. In *Partiernas Århundrade : Fempartimodellens Uppgång Och Fall i Norge och Sverige.* ed. Lars Svåsand and Marie Demker, Stockholm: Santérus.

Szhheheby, Marta ed. 2005. *Äldreomsorgsforskning i Norden. En kunskapsöversikt.* Tema Nord nr. 2005– 208, København: Nordisk Ministerråd.

Taylor-Gooby, Peter. 2005. *Ideas and Welfare State Reform in Western Europe.* New York: Palgrave Macmillan.

Teigen, Marit. 2006. *Det kjønnsdelte arbeidslivet. En kunnskapsoversikt*, ISF-rapport 2006/2. Oslo: Institute for Social Research.

Terum, Lars Inge. 1996. *Grenser for Sosialpolitisk Modernisering: Om Fattighjelp i Velferdsstaten.* Oslo: Universitetsforlaget.

Terum, Lars Inge. 2003. Portvakt i Velferdsstaten: Om Skjønn Og Beslutninger i Sosialt Arbeid. Oslo: Kommuneforlaget.

The Norwegian Directorat for Health and social Affairs. 2006. *Sosial ulikhet i helse som tema i helsekonsekvensutredninger.* Oslo.

Thoresen, Thor Olav, 2005. Utviklingen i skatteprogressivitet og politikkens innvirkning: inntektsskatten for personer 1992–2004. In Statistics Norway: *Inntekt, skatt og overføringer 2005.* Statistics Norway: Oslo.

Tingaard Svendsen, Gert and Gunnar Lind Haase Svendsen, 2006. *Social capital – en introduktion*, Copenhagen: Hans Reitzels Forlag.

Tjelmeland, Hallvard, and Grete Brochmann. 2003. I Globaliseringens Tid, 1940–2000. In *Norsk Innvandringshistorie*, Vol. 3, ed. Knut Kjeldstadli. Oslo: Pax Forlag.

Townsend, Peter. 1979. Poverty in the United Kingdom. *A Survey of Household Resources and Standards of Living*. Harmondsworth: Penguin.

UDI. 2007. *Eøs-Utvidelsen – Tillatelser Med Formål Arbeid 2006*. Oslo: UDI.

Ulfrstad, Lars-Marius. 2007. Boligpolitikken og velferdsstaten. In *Under tak – mellom vegger. Perspektiver på boligens betydning i velferdsstaten*, ed. Elisabeth Brodtkorp and Marianne Rugkåsa. Oslo: Gyldendal Akademisk.

UNDP, 2004. *Human Development Report 2004*. New York: United Nations Development Programme.

Vaage, Odd Frank. 2002. *Til alle døgnets tider. Tidsbruk 1971–2000*. Statistiske analyser 52. Oslo: Statistisk sentralbyrå.

World Bank. 1994. *Averting the old age cirsis*. Washington: World Bank.

Wærness, Kari, 1990. Informal and formal care in old age: what is wrong with the new ideology in Scandinavia today. In *Gender and Caring: Work and Welfare in Britain and Scandinavia*, ed. Clare Ungerson. London: Harvester Wheatsheaf.

Wollebæk, Dag, Per Selle, and Håkon Lorentzen. 2000. Frivillig Innsats. Bergen: Fagbokforlaget.

WHO. 2000. *Health Care Systems in Transition*. Norway. Geneva: WHO-Europe.

WHO-Europe. 2002. *Health Care Systems in Transition*. HiT summary. Norway. Copenhagen: WHO Regional Office for Europe.

Wolfe, Alan, 1989. *Whose Keeper? Social Science and Moral Obligation*. Berkeley: University of California Press.

Index

absenteeism 100–102
action plan, individual 82
activation 52
advocacy 126
ageing population 57, 85–88, 142
agricultural policy 17
allowance 54
anti-immigration 21
Arbeiderpartiet (DnA), see also *Labour Party* 11, 19
asylum criteria 151
asylum seekers 151
ATTAC 147
attendance benefit 81
attitudes 153

basic amount 53, 76–77
basic pension 19, 77
Beck, Ulrich 160
bed capacity 92
benefits 55
    child 15–16, 59, 66–67, 78, 81–82
    clarification 82
    disability 81
    introductory 140
    principle of defined 78
    unemployment 16, 19, 53–54
Beveridge, William 15
Bismarck, Otto von 10
block grants 96, 134
Brundtland, Gro Harlem 21, 61
Business–friendliness 147–148

capacity problems 135
capital income 150

care 135–137
carers 135
'cash for care' 23, 62–63, 66–67
Catholic social teaching 123
Catholic-conservative welfare states 73
centralization 16
centralized bargaining 49
Centre Party, see also *Farmers' Party* 17, 19
challenges 85, 102, 155
charities 11
children 15–16, 59, 66–67, 81–82, 127
    benefits 15–16, 59, 66–67, 81–82
    welfare institutions 127
Child Welfare Services Act 138
Christian democracy 162
Christian People's Party, see also *Kristelig Folkeparti* 19, 61, 118
Church the 12, 21
citizenship 153
civil society 120, 143
clarification benefits 82
class compromises 42
class structure 23
cohabitating couple 64
cohabitation 64
collective agreements 42, 150
collective bargaining 14
'community of commoners' 121
competitiveness 39, 42, 57
consensus 111, 145
consensus-orientation 123
conservatives 9, 12, 17, 150

Index

Conservative Party, see also *Høyre* 11, 16, 119, 161–162
continent 71
Continental Europe 20
corporatism 130
corruption 147
cost control 131
counter-culture 130
counties 132
Court of Justice, European 150
crime 39
crisis centres 126
customer choice 134
cuts 22–24, 116
cuts in social benefits and services 23

daddy quota 49, 68
day care 21, 61–62, 139–140
day care reform 62
Day Care Act 139
day centres 136
decentralization 89, 137, 141–142
defined benefits 78
deinstitutionalization 137
delivery systems 10, 24
demographic changes 84, 158
demographic prognoses 158
demography 64-66
dental services 89, 92
dependency ratio 85
disability benefits 81
disability pension 46, 74, 80–83, 142
   increase in 83
discrimination 153
diseases 98
diversity 152
divorce 59, 64
domestic work 69
domiciliary care 21
dual earner 59, 69
dualism 70
'dugnad' 121

early retirement 47, 76, 80, 87
Early Retirement Pension Scheme 76

earnings testing 75
earnings-related pension 76
economic growth 26, 30, 41
education 11–12, 50
education reform 11–12
Educational Loan Fund 109
EEA 149, 150
efficiency 131
egalitarian wage structure 148
egalitarianism 23, 122–123
egoism 72
election system 24
elementary school bill 11
employers' organization 14
employment commitment 41
empowerment 141
entrepreneurship 144
equal opportunities 33
equality 11, 33, 36, 65, 70, 91, 133, 141, 143, 160, 162
   gender 65, 70
   of opportunity 160
   of outcome 160
eradication strategy 119
ethnic minorities 21
ethnical diversity 151
Etzioni, Amitai 130
EU 147, 149–150
European Economic Area 149
European single market 149
expenditure 63, 93–94
   on families 63
export 26, 29
extension 121

family 35, 58–59, 61–66, 69–70, 72, 106, 121, 153
   allowance 35
   approach 69
   care 72
   expenditure on 63
   ideology 59
   male breadwinner- 69
   model 63
   policy 58–59, 61–63, 66, 70

policy models 69
policy, modern 59, 61, 66
reunification 153
structure 64–65
support theory 72
treatment 106
family-friendly social policy 61
farmers 24, 28, 123
Farmers' Party, see also *Centre Party* 14, 16
fascist party 15
fathers 62
female 22, 44–45, 56, 59, 61–62
female employment 22
female participation 59
feminist movement 61
fertility 56–57, 63–65
fertility rates 56–57, 63
financing 92, 134–136
Finland 16, 145. 152
first-generation 152
fiscal welfare 34
flexibility 144
'four freedoms' 25
free abortion 59, 61
free trade 25
freedom 23, 62–63, 162
freedom of choice 23, 62–63
Fremskrittspartiet (FrP) 19, 21, 161
French republican model 152
full employment 16, 26–27, 41, 50

GDP 29–30
per capita 29
gender 22, 59, 65, 69–70
emancipation 59, 69
equality 65, 70
ideology 22
perspective 22
-segregation 65
General Agreement on Trade in Service 147
generosity 63, 78, 109, 118
German occupation 15
German pension system 10

German welfare state 123
global competitiveness 29, 148
globalization 146–147, 149–150
goal attainment 95
government strategy 116
gradient 99

Haga, Aslaug 19
Halvorsen, Kristin 19
happiness 38–39
health 38, 89–99, 102–103, 133, 136, 143
and social services 133
care 91–92, 95–96, 102–103, 136, 143
care, mental 103
insurance 97
policy 89–91
primary 88, 92, 133
regions 91
Health Life Years Expectancy 97
hegemony 123
homelessness 138
homogeneity 23
hospitals 91–92
household work 44
housework 48
housing
benefits 138
policy 138
support 108
Høyre (H), see also *Conservative Party, conservatives* 11, 19–20
human development 36

IA Agreement 27, 51, 102
ideology 11, 22, 59, 123, 125
gender 22
neoliberal 22
illegitimate 59
ILO 147
IMF 147
immigrants 47, 114, 152, 155
immigration 21, 57, 146, 151, 153
anti- 21
policy 151

imports 29
income 30, 119, 150
   guaranteed minimum 119
income-related old age pension 19
individual
   action plan 82
   pension 78, 82
   pension scheme 87
   plan 140
   private pension 77
individualism 71, 160, 162
individualized rights 69
industrial accidents act 12
industrialization 10, 13, 25, 28
inequality 28, 36–37, 112, 116, 150, 152
infant mortality 97
inflation 157
informality 136
insurance principle 10, 12, 14–15, 33, 149
integration 156
International Confederation of Free Trade Unions 147
International Monetary Fund 147
Introduction Act 140
introduction support 52
introductory benefits 140
introductory programme 52

Jews 15
'Joint Programme' 15, 106
justice 21, 42, 160, 162

Keynesia 17, 22
Keynesian economic policy 22
Kristelig Folkeparti (KrF), see also *Christan People's Party* 19–20, 62, 118

labour force participation 43, 44–45, 56
labour market 17, 21, 42–43, 49, 62, 65, 144, 150
   participation 21, 62

policies 52
policy 17, 49
programmes 49
labour movement 123, 130
Labour Party 11, 14–17, 19–20, 22–23, 26, 61–62, 70, 124, 145, 150, 154, 157
labour, supply of 159
less eligibility principle 105
Liberal Party, see also *Venstre* 11–12, 14–16, 119
liberalism 123, 161
   market 161
liberalization 150
liberals 9, 17
life expectancy 36, 97
lifestyle 98
living standards 36
LO 14
Local Government Act 133
loneliness 38, 99
Lutheran Reformation 11, 21, 124
Lutheranism 11

market liberalism 161
marriage, rate of 59
maternal leave 49, 59, 61, 68
maternity grant 59
means-testing 12, 14, 109, 116
medicalization 95, 104
middle class 19, 123, 143, 145, 160
minimum pension 76, 78
mixed economy 26
motherhood 59
municipal 136, 141
municipal autonomy 105
Municipal Health Services Act 133–134
municipal law 105
municipalities 17, 92, 96, 106, 125, 132–134

narcissism 72
National Council for Norwegian Women 124, 127

National Health Programme 92
National Insurance Act, the 99
National Insurance Scheme 34, 74–75, 85, 96
NAV 52, 142
NAV reform 142
neo-liberal ideology 22
neo-liberalism 125, 160, 162
New Norwegian 123
New Public Management 91, 131, 136
New Public Management ideology 91, 131
non-governmental organizations 98
Norwegian Board of Health 137, 141–142
Norwegian Public Labour and Welfare Service (NAV) 52
Norwegian State Educational Loan Fund 71, 109
Norwegian Women's Health Organization 124, 127
Norwegians 153
not-for-profit 136
nursing 103, 134–136
 care 134
 homes 103, 134, 136
'nynorsk' 123

occupational injury insurance 75
occupational pensions 77–78
oil 22–23, 28, 30, 39, 118, 148, 157
 embargo 22
 prices 30, 39, 149
 production 28
 revenue 22–23
 wealth 157
Oil Fund and Pension Fund 148
old age homes 21
old age pension 12, 14–16, 74, 76–78
'ombudsman' 90, 141

paternal leave 62, 68–69
patient fees 117
Patient's Rights Act 89–90

'pay as you go' 76
peasants 11, 17, 121
pensions 19, 31, 34, 45–46, 74, 76–78, 80–83, 87, 142, 158
 age- 45, 76
 basic 19, 77
 disability 46, 74, 80–83, 142
 earnings-related 76
 income-related 19
 minimum 76, 78
 pension 78, 82
 pension scheme 87
 points 77
 scheme, individual 82
 supplementary 19
 system, future costs of 158
Pension Fund 31, 34
personal assistant 141
pietism 61, 123
political consensus 19, 24, 145
Poor House, the 112
poor laws 12, 105
poor relief system 105, 106
post-industrial capitalism 160
poverty 109, 111–118
 absolute 111
 as relative deprivation 111
 rate 116
 reduction plans 117
 relative 111
 trap 109
power-resource mobilization thesis 145
prevention 103
pre-working class 121
Priority Setting Regulations 90–91
private pension, individual 77
privatization 162
production 30
productivity 29, 39, 148
professionals 95
Progress Party, the, see also *Fremskrittspartiet* 19, 21, 154, 156, 161–162
proportional representation 24
protectionism 26

public consumption 29
purchasing power 29

qualification support 52
quality control 131
quasi-market mechanism 131
Quisling, Vidkun 15

Red Cross 124, 127
'red–green' government 23, 62, 117, 156
redundancies 101
reflexive modernity 131
refugees 114, 151
regional policy 17, 151
Regional Health Authorities 91–92
regional policy 17
rehabilitation 137, 142
rehabilitation allowance 74, 82, 100
residual role 105, 107
resistance movement 15
retirement homes 21
retirement, early 47, 76, 80, 87
retrenchments 84
revenue 118
right of appeal 109
risk factors 98
rural districts 16

Schengen group 151
School, primary 133
self-help groups 120, 129
self-help movements 124
self-reliance 41–42, 75
Senterpartiet (SP), see also *Farmer's Party, Centre Party* 19–20
service homes 135
shame 114–116
sickness benefits 16, 19, 99–100, 102
single breadwinners 114–115
single parents 66
social
 assistance 54–55, 105, 110–111, 142
 allowance 142
 recipients 110–111
 benefits 23, 74
 and services, cuts in 23
 buffer 84
 capital 130
 democracy 9, 12, 61, 122, 125
 democratic
  ideology 16–21, 145–147
  order 16–21
  parties 145
  welfare state 145–147
 distance 99
 dumping 43, 49
 expenditure 33–34, 51
 inclusion 99
 insurance 12, 20
 movements 120, 123, 128, 130
 problems 12, 21, 34, 125f, 133
 responsibility 51
 security net 50
 services 21, 23
 welfare agencies 106
 work training 106
 workers 107
Social Care Act 106
Social Services Act 55, 106–110, 133, 138
Socialist Left Party, see also *Sosialistisk venstreparti* 19, 118, 157
socio-economic gap 98
solidarity 15, 27, 99, 121–123, 126, 155
sosialhjelp 105
Sosialistisk Venstreparti (SV), see also *Socialist Left Party* 17, 19–20, 62, 118–119
state ownership 26
stigma 109, 115–116
student revolt 21, 59
subsidiary principle 123
subsidies 51, 97, 139
substance abusers 137
substitution theory 72
supplementary pension 19, 76–77

tax 30
tax financing 149
taxation 29, 31, 32
temperance movement 123
The Norwegian Boards of Health 92
Third World immigrants 152
time account 68
trade unions 42, 49, 149
Trades Union Congress 14
transitional allowance 66
transnational companies 146
transparency 147
transparency index 148
trust 17, 39, 121–123, 130

unemployment 16, 19, 43–44, 46, 48, 53–54, 75, 89, 101, 114, 135, 141, 143, 145–146, 155
   benefits 16, 19, 53–54
   hidden 47–48
   long term 46, 48, 114
universalism 16, 75, 89, 135, 141, 143, 145–146, 155
urbanization 28
user fees 32, 143
user involvement 142–144
user payment 96, 97

Venstre (V), see also *Liberal Party* 11, 20, 119
Vietnam War 22
vocational rehabilitation 51, 55–56, 81
voluntary
   health and services 128
   membership 12, 130
   organizations 11, 12, 19, 116, 120, 126, 128
   work 127, 130
volunteer bureaus 125
volunteers 127–128

wage 37, 49–50
   disparities 49
   gap 37
   subsidies 50
waiting list 90, 103
welfare
   contract 117
   fiscal 34
   institutions, child 127
   mix 131
   regimes 9, 122
   state 32–33, 37, 39, 41, 45, 73–74, 89, 123
   Catholic-conservative 73
   German 123
women 16, 21
work
   approach 42, 69, 75, 159
   ethic 11, 41, 52, 101, 119
   programmes 116
   test 53
'worker commission' 12
workfare 52, 55, 107
'work for all' 42
working age population 84
working class 24, 145, 160
Working Environment Act 42, 50
working hours 44, 48
working time 29
World Bank 147
World Council of Churches 147
World Economic Forum's competitiveness index 147
World Social Forum 147
World War II 15–16
WTO 147